DID GOD
KILL
JESUS?

Searching for Love in History's
Most Famous Execution

TONY JONES

HarperOne
An Imprint of HarperCollins*Publishers*

HarperOne

DID GOD KILL JESUS?: *Searching for Love in History's Most Famous Execution.* Copyright © 2015 by Anthony H. Jones. All rights reserved. Printed in the United States of America. No part of this book may be used or reproduced in any manner whatsoever without written permission except in the case of brief quotations embodied in critical articles and reviews. For information address HarperCollins Publishers, 195 Broadway, New York, NY 10007.

HarperCollins books may be purchased for educational, business, or sales promotional use. For information please e-mail the Special Markets Department at SPsales@harpercollins.com.

HarperCollins website: http://www.harpercollins.com

HarperCollins®, ®, and HarperOne™ are trademarks of HarperCollins Publishers.

FIRST EDITION

Library of Congress Cataloging-in-Publication Data

Jones, Tony.
   Did God kill Jesus? : searching for love in history's most famous execution / Tony Jones. — first edition.
      pages cm
   ISBN 978–0–06–229796–9
   1. Jesus Christ—Crucifixion. I. Title.
   BT453.J585 2015
   232.96—dc23   2015001468

15 16 17 18 19   RRD(H)   10 9 8 7 6 5 4 3 2 1

To Courtney, who saved me

*God was pleased to reconcile to himself all things,
whether on earth or in heaven, by making
peace through the blood of his cross.*

—St. Paul the Apostle

CONTENTS

FIVE: MINORITY OPINIONS

SIX: WHAT GOD EXPERIENCED ON THE CROSS

SEVEN: THE WAY OF THE CROSS

PART ONE

The Problem with the Cross

I

"As He Died, He Saw Your Face!"

I SAT IN a mountain lodge one weekend with two hundred junior high students. We'd embarked on three days of wholesome fun and getting jazzed on God.

I was twenty-four. A part-time youth pastor working my way through seminary, I'd taken a job at an evangelical church near campus. I had driven a vanload of students into the Southern California mountains for a winter weekend at the denomination's retreat center. We met up with busloads of kids converging from several churches in the region, and the air was laden with anticipation, no doubt driven as much by hormones as spiritual curiosity. Such is evangelical youth ministry.

On Friday, the highly touted and charismatic speaker for the weekend gave a talk in the evening chapel service that endeared him to all of the kids. He told funny stories about himself in middle school and how nerdy he was, and he set himself up as a credible authority on spiritual matters.

Then, on Saturday night, he brought the heat.

He told us a long, detailed story about a poor peasant woman in Russia who lived with her toddler daughter in a dismal, Soviet-era apartment. They had a horrible life, he told us, but at least they had each other.

Then, one night as they were sleeping, the shoddy Communist construction gave way during an earthquake, and the building collapsed on top of them. The mother was pinned beneath a huge piece of concrete. Miraculously, the young girl was unharmed, but they were both trapped in the rubble, with no way of escape.

A day passed, but no one came to their rescue. The little girl began to grow weak, and she complained to her mother that she was hungry and thirsty.

Another day passed, and the mother began lapsing in and out of consciousness. She knew that her young child would die of dehydration soon if she didn't do something.

On the third day, the mother realized that she was going to have to make a sacrifice for her daughter. So she reached out for a piece of broken glass, and she slashed open her palm and directed her daughter to drink her blood in order to survive.

The girl did as she was told, and she was rescued. The mother died.[1]

We were on the edge of our seats—what love the mother had to sacrifice herself for her daughter! Who doesn't want to be loved like that?

Now the speaker was worked up into a metaphorical lather, and his voice rose as he addressed the assembled eleven- and twelve-year-olds, turning the rhetorical corner from the Russian mother to Jesus. Jesus is like that Russian mother, he told us, and we are the helpless little girl. Jesus' blood on the cross saves us the same way that the daughter was saved.

Then the speaker explicated at length the ancient practice of execution by crucifixion. He went into excruciating detail about the pain of having spikes pounded through your wrists and ankles, about the enormous amount of blood, about the humiliation of hanging, naked, six feet in the air, and about how death comes slowly and agonizingly, not by blood loss, but by suffocation.

We heard about the extreme agony, even desperation, felt by a victim of crucifixion as he pulled himself up on the spikes in his arms and pushed himself up on the spikes in his legs to catch a breath until, completely exhausted, he couldn't rise anymore. Unable to inhale—coughing, choking, dying.

Now our speaker was screaming, sweating, spitting.

"That's how much Jesus loves you!" he cried.

"He died for you in the most horrible, gruesome manner that the Romans could imagine! And as he died, *he saw your face!* He whispered your name! Because *you* are a sinner, he had to die in *your* place!

"God *hated* you because of your sin! When he looked at you, all he saw was your sin!

"But Jesus stood between you and God, so now when God looks at you, he only sees Jesus.

"Tonight, you can accept what Jesus did for you and go to heaven instead of hell when you die. You can let Jesus stand between you and the terrifying, holy God.

"Tonight you have the chance to drink the blood from Jesus' hands to save yourself."

And the next part I remember verbatim. He concluded, "If tonight, for the first time, you've decided to accept what Jesus did for you, angels are celebrating in heaven; stay after chapel to pray with a counselor. If tonight you've decided to recommit your life to Jesus, angels are dancing and cheering; you should also stay after and talk to a counselor.

"And if you aren't ready to do either of those things, you are dismissed. There's popcorn and hot chocolate for you in the dining hall."

There are, of course, numerous problems with what happened that night, not least of which is using popcorn as a consolation prize for eternal life. The emotional manipulation of that talk—and the thousands of similar talks given to millions of kids over the past several decades of American youth ministry—is inexcusable. If the way that a person gets into heaven has to do with a spontaneous, fear-driven, adolescent decision, then the Christian faith is no more than a desperate sales pitch.

This speaker had the opportunity to woo kids into a life with God. He could have told about how God came to Earth to walk among us, about the amazing miracles that Jesus performed, healing the sick and raising the dead. He could have wowed us with the love of God. Instead he terrified us.

But what *really* troubled me about that night was the guilt. Jesus' blood was on *our* hands. According to this guy, these middle schoolers killed Jesus because they were "born into sin," and God hated them for it.

Let's think about this evangelist's message to those preteens: The God who created you, presumably out of love, now cannot stand so much as to look at you. You disgust God. And the only reason God doesn't explode in rage every time he sees you is because Jesus has stepped in between you two.[2] All God sees is Jesus, not you. We cower in fear behind Jesus, and God fumes with anger on the other side. What happened to the loving Russian mother who loves her daughter so much she sacrifices her own life? How did a story of a loving mom morph into a loving son who saves us from a wrathful heavenly Father?

Believe it or not, this is a fairly common framework for understanding what Jesus did on the cross. But it certainly does not fit cleanly with everything scripture tells us about God, Jesus, or the cross—such as how do we go from "God is love" and God sent his only Son for us because "God so loved the world" to God is so disgusted with us that he has to kill Jesus so that he can pretend to see only Jesus when dealing with us. Surely we have taken a wrong turn, because this story is supposed to be about love.

Not long ago, I was in the same position as that speaker, addressing a room of mostly middle schoolers and their parents. I'd been invited to speak to the confirmation class of a large Lutheran congregation, and the youth pastor said I should talk about the book that I was working on. That happened to be this book. So after some warm-up jokes, I asked the assembled crowd how many of them had ever been told, "Jesus died for your sins." As expected, every single person raised a hand.

"Alright," I said. "We're going to take a little test. I'd like each of you confirmands to turn to the adult who brought you and ask, 'How? How exactly does that work? Please explain to me how it works that the death of one man two thousand years ago takes care of all my sin.'"

The adults in the room groaned.

"One more thing," I added. "After they've answered you, you're going to give your adult a grade on their answer."

The groans doubled.

After a couple of minutes of discussion, I called the crowd back to order and asked some of the kids to shout out the grade they'd give their parent's answer. "C-minus," shouted one girl. "That's generous," her mom said to laughter. And it went on from there. The clear consensus from the adults in the room was that they were ill-equipped to answer the question. They believed that Jesus died for their sins, but they really had no idea why.

These Lutherans are not alone. Across the theological spectrum, Christians struggle to explain how Jesus' death worked on our behalf. Which, in a way, is surprising. It is surprising because when you ask people what the central event of the Christian faith is, most point to the cross. When Christians are asked how we know that God loves us, they point to Jesus' sacrifice on the cross. That's God's love. When forced to pick one symbol that best represents the entire faith, Christians throughout two thousand years of history have come up with the same answer: the cross. We see it used everywhere to represent Christianity—on steeples, in art, even on our bodies in jewelry and tattoos. So isn't it a little strange that it's hard to explain what transpired on the cross with Jesus and how it affects us?

Of course, some are like the earnest evangelist, cocksure that they know exactly why Jesus died and who was responsible.

As it turns out, his version—that God is terribly angry with you and kills his son in your place—is just one of the various answers that have been proffered over the past two thousand years. Although it's only a thousand years old, this version is the most popular today, but it also happens to have some major problems. For example, the preacher said that when God looks at us, God is disappointed, disgusted, or even irate about our sin. So I ask, what happens when you look in the mirror? Or when you look at your friend or spouse or child? If God finds us disgusting, and we're to seek after the heart of God, won't we find ourselves and our loved ones disgusting, too? Ah, you say, but aren't we supposed to pretend to see Jesus when looking at ourselves or at our loved ones? Ask yourself, is that how love works in your life? When I look at my children, I see *them* and love them as themselves. I don't have to pretend to see Jesus in them in order to love them.

To be sure, each of us at times struggles with self-loathing. And we sometimes struggle to see the best in our partners and children and friends. But most of us, most of the time, find myriad reasons to *love* those around us, in spite of their shortcomings. Surely this is what we try to do. And if we have a little grace with ourselves, we can even find ways to love the person in the mirror. And how about God? When I look deep within myself, when I examine my own feelings for God, what I find is love. It's love and gratitude and wonder and awe—and mostly love—that I have for God.

But if this popular model of the cross were true, then I am freer with my love than God is with his. And that can't be right.

Even without the Bible, what kind of sense does it make to believe that God would create you and me, only to be disgusted by us and wrathful at our inevitable shortcomings? But add in the Bible, and you can really see how misaligned this interpretation of the crucifixion is. If we look in the Bible for evidence of this overwhelming disgust God has for us, it's hard to come by. Sure, there's the occasional verse that talks of God's anger at particular sins or human behavior that God considers an abomination, but the overarching message of scripture is clear: God created us, God loves us, and God wants the best for us. In fact, the Bible is rife with stories of God going out of his way to set people on the right path—despite our failures, despite our sins. Indeed, the Apostle Paul assures us that God loved us "while we still were sinners."[3]

Before we study the Bible and even before we formulate and

wrestle with all the doctrines from church history, we intuitively know something fundamental: the message of Jesus, God's primary emissary, is that *God loves us.* That's what Jesus came to preach and to enact in his miracles. He referred to God as his "Father" and his "Abba"—intimate terms based in relationship. Theirs was a close and loving connection. Jesus came to open that loving relationship between himself and the Father to all of us. This event, the crucifixion, on which all of cosmic history pivots, forever changed both us and God.

This also means there can be no separation between God and Jesus; we cannot set a wrathful and vengeful God in opposition to a loving and gracious Jesus. Jesus repeatedly taught that he and the Father are one, that the best way to know and understand the Father is by knowing and understanding the Son. And the main message of both Father and Son is that they love us and want to be united with us. Even before we come to understand what happened on the cross, we know that whatever explanation we discover cannot contradict the eternal relationship of love that binds the Father and the Son, that binds God and us.[4]

The retreat evangelist's version of who God is and his related justification for the necessity of Jesus' death on the cross is not only inconsistent with the Bible, it's also dangerous. When embraced, it taints people's view of God, of others, and even of themselves. After two thousand years of Christian history, we wonder why our world is so flooded with war and violence and ethnic hate. We fret that church attendance is low and dropping. And we worry that many see the Christian faith as irrelevant or even bad for the world. Could viewing God as vengeful and wrathful and bloodthirsty be the source of our problems?

On that evening in 1992, I couldn't articulate these objections, but in my gut I felt that something was very wrong. Later that night, at the counselor meeting, I was livid. I protested that the entire thing was grotesque. The speaker, as you might guess, was mighty defensive in the face of my anger. He made his living giving this very talk over and over, to a different group of high school or junior high students every weekend. In fact, he was shocked at my criticism. He'd never had anyone raise similar concerns. He assumed that every true Christian agreed with him about why Jesus died: that God killed Jesus to appease his own wrath. But deep down I knew this model is not a message of God's love, and actually caused spiritual harm—I'd seen it in the faces of the kids in my youth group. They had arrived at that retreat assuming that God loves them, only to be told that God is disgusted by them.

But I did not know what alternative views of Jesus' cross might be, and that started me on a quest. This book is the fruit of that search.

I was not starting from scratch. The consensus among Jesus' earliest followers was clear: Jesus was the *love of God* in the flesh. In Jesus' own words, "As the Father has loved me, so I have loved you; abide in my love."⁵ In that same speech, Jesus comforts his followers by assuring them that he won't leave them as orphans, that he will continue to work with God the Father to give them what they need, and that he'll send the Holy Spirit to be humanity's advocate forever. This promise is claimed still by Christians today, two millennia after it was written.

These words are in the Gospel of John, one of the last books written in our New Testament. Scholars think it was penned around 95 CE, over sixty years after Jesus' death. With this hindsight, the author of the Fourth Gospel gives us an account of Jesus' life that is more theologically evolved and sophisticated than the previous three Gospels. And the message in John is clear: God loves us, and God showed that love for us by sending Jesus, his son, to live and die among us. This is an act of love, of solidarity with humankind—an act, as the Apostle Paul virtually sings in his letter to the Philippians, written four decades before the Gospel of John, of divine humility:

> *Let the same mind be in you that was in Christ Jesus,*
> *who, though he was in the form of God,*
> *   did not regard equality with God*
> *   as something to be exploited,*

but emptied himself,
 taking the form of a slave,
 being born in human likeness.
And being found in human form,
 he humbled himself
 and became obedient to the point of death—
 even death on a cross.[6]

From the first books of the New Testament to the last ones written, Jesus' life and death are portrayed as revealing, demonstrating, and modeling for us the meaning of love. Jesus' death on the cross not only revealed God's love for us but also exemplifies the love we are to have for one another.

Now here we sit, two millennia later, and survey after survey tells us that Christians are known not for our love, but for our fear: fear of gays, fear of change, fear of the "end-times," fear of science, fear of the Other—in whatever form the Other takes.

How did we get here? How did the act of following Jesus go from something that was a response to God's love in the first century to a bloody, fear-based, avoidance-of-hell decision in the twenty-first?

That is the question I will tackle in this book. My deepest wish is for the church to restore the central symbol of the Christian faith—the cross—so that it can once again become the symbol of humble love, pointing both back to the love that saved us and forward toward the love we are to embody. It's also a personal journey, because I've always loved the cross and what the event of the crucifixion means about God's relationship with the world. I've long been in awe of God's act of humility on the cross, and I've doubted that it could have really been about wrath. Yet I've lacked a good explanation for this, for the cross being about love. On that winter night at the retreat center, I couldn't articulate a better version of the meaning of the crucifixion. Now it's time that I have one, that we all have a better version.

To do that, we need to take an intellectual journey in order to understand not only what the Bible says about the cross but also how our ancestors in the church have contemplated this very question. Again, understanding what happens on the cross is not an arcane theological discussion. How we understand the cross also colors how we picture God, Jesus, ourselves, and our mission in the world and how we see others. Very much is at stake.

We will begin by looking at the Hebrew Bible, known as the Old Testament to most Christians. Jesus' ministry did not simply fall out of the sky but emerged out of the long history of Israel, the hopes and dreams of Judaism. We cannot understand Jesus' role without recourse to the Bible he used and quoted in his own ministry, and we cannot understand Jesus' first interpreter, Paul, without knowing about the Hebrew system of sacrifice that the Old Testament codified.

Of course, we'll study the New Testament also. Paul was the first writer to try to make sense of Jesus' death, and he wrote out his thoughts in several of his letters. Other letter writers, from those who wrote in the names of Peter and John to the anonymous preacher of Hebrews, also had their perspectives on Jesus' death. Then there are the Gospel writers, who wrote about Jesus' life and death. Clues to the meaning of Jesus' death can be found in each of their narratives.

The church is two thousand years old, and over that time various theologians and preachers have put forward various ideas about the death of Jesus, what it accomplished, and what it means to us today. Each of these can be judged against the biblical accounts and against our own experience and reason—especially the test of love, as we have already seen.

Ultimately, we will judge the crucifixion and its effects against what we know of God. For the death of Jesus cannot be a repudiation of God's love. It cannot pit God against Jesus. Nor can it be anything but good news.

In fact, it might be better news than we've ever imagined.

2

Why God Matters

I GREW UP in a nice Midwestern suburb at a centrist church that preached a centrist God. Some of my friends were reared in homes and churches that taught that God was so angry he skipped sinners across the lake of fire. But in my church, God wasn't so much angry with me as he was disappointed. I'd really let God down with my adolescent sins of lust and white lies. When God looked at the ledger of my sins, I imagined that he shook his head in sadness and maybe shed a tear about how I'd failed him.

Yes, I felt shame over the fact that I'd stolen a five-dollar bill off my brother's dresser and called a girl names at recess; still, even back then I wondered how these transgressions were worthy of the torture that Jesus endured on the cross. Yet that's what I was taught. Had I not committed those sins, God wouldn't have had to subject his son to death. *I* was the reason for the crucifixion of the son of God, Jesus, the one innocent man in all of history.

Mine was a fairly mild version of God, relatively speaking. In some of my friends' churches, God wasn't just disappointed in human behavior, he was downright furious. *Wrath.* That's the biblical word for it, and in those churches, God's primary characteristic seemed to be that all of our sin had really caught God by surprise, and God was out to even the score. "Turn or burn" goes the phrase. These church websites tout statements of faith that assure the "eternal, conscious torment of unrepentant sinners." I have never quite figured out why they call this "good news"—yes, God's honor is preserved, but most people end up getting tossed into the lake of fire. When asked about the many passages of scripture that speak of God's love, these Christians counter that this *is* love. God's love would be worthless, they claim, if God weren't holy, if God weren't just, if God weren't righteous.

From an early age, this troubled me. When I prayed, God didn't seem angry with me or even disappointed. Instead, it seemed that whether I prayed in joy or prayed in terror, God was there no matter what, listening, accepting, forgiving. When I read the Bible, I found God's loving-kindness. These characteristics of God were also preached at my church, so I didn't know quite how to fit all this together. On the one hand, God was terribly disappointed in me; on the other hand, he was always there with open arms, like the father in Jesus' parable of the prodigal son.

God seemed a bit schizophrenic, but for a long while I learned to accommodate his condition.

A lot of us are on a quest for God. We're trying to figure out just who God is, how God relates to us, and what God wants from us. This quest matters because, it turns out, how we think about God influences how we think about ourselves, others, and the world we live in. And here's the rub: many of our churches emphasize that God is disappointed or angry, which encourages us to be disappointed or angry with those who do not measure up, including ourselves. Still, many people's experiences of God are like mine, that God is loving, gracious, merciful. We hear about a God of wrath, but we experience a God of grace. How can God be both? Does he hate us, or does he love us? Does God love us only if we love him back the right way—and, if we don't, do we meet the wrathful God?

I've made mistakes in life. I've got broken relationships in my past, scars that don't seem to heal. I've failed friends, my spouse, my children. I have failed others and God, in "things done and left undone," as the Book of Common Prayer puts it. I often go to God in prayer over these failings, especially on nights when I can't sleep.

I lie in bed, staring into the darkness, and rehearse the joys and sorrows of my life. And as I ask God to forgive me my trespasses and help me be better tomorrow, I have a deep and very real sense that God forgives me, that God is *for* me, that God *loves* me, even when I fail. In other words, my deepest spiritual experience is that God loves me as I am. Yes, God longs for me to grow and become like Jesus, and God partners with me in this process of becoming more Christlike. But God also loves the current version of me.

Of course, it's possible that I'm deceiving myself, that in fact God is so disgusted by my sins that he can't even hear my prayers. But I don't think so. Both my experience and my reading of scripture tell me that God created me for good and that God loves me in spite of my flaws. In fact, I think that God created me knowing my flaws, even loving my flaws, because *God is love.*

I have a friend who says, "I think God has to be at least as nice as Jesus." His point is that Jesus was notorious for reaching out to those on the margins, for dining with sinners, and for hanging out with prostitutes and tax collectors. He spoke the truth, sometimes pointedly, but he wasn't an angry person. And, as God's representative and emissary, Jesus reflected God. "I and the Father are one," Jesus taught.[1] We can gauge a lot about God by looking at Jesus. So, my friend reasons, God must be at least as nice as Jesus was.

It's with confidence in this assessment that I confess my shortcomings to God. And I don't worry that God will reject me because of them. Instead, I'm quite sure that God loves me in spite of—or even because of—my failings.

If Jesus tells us anything about God, it's that God is love—not wrath or anger or vengeance, but pure love.

God: Violence or Peace?

Much violence has been perpetrated in the name of God, and unfortunately that's part of the story, too. Today, famous atheists bellow that religion leads to violence, and they're not wrong. Massive amounts of bloodshed have been justified with religious language and under the imprimatur of religious authorities.

Whenever you're reading this, violence in the name of religious belief is taking place somewhere in the world. One religion is battling another over a patch of land, or one sect is fighting another for control of a government. Some argue that religion is just a cover for tribalism and greed and power, but nevertheless, religion always seems to be at the center of the conflict.

All this leads us to ask, *If God is love, why is religion so violent?* And, more pointedly, *Is Christianity inherently violent?* We would like to think not, but there's a lot of evidence to the contrary. After all, we've got a bloody execution standing right at the center of our faith, memorialized in the crosses around our necks. A lot of us don't necessarily think about that when we look at the cross. We see it as a symbol of redemption and even resurrection. But long before it represented those things, it was a symbol of torture and death.

Jesus' death itself was rooted in a religious conflict. During his three years of itinerant ministry, Jesus preached a particular perspective on the future of Judaism and the nature of God. But his view was at odds with those of other religious and political groups of the day: the Pharisees, the Herodians, and the leaders in the Jerusalem temple. The Roman authorities got caught in between these rivals. The temple leaders had more power than Jesus and his band of Galileans, and the Romans sided with the powerful and sent Jesus to the cross. We tend to look at a crucifix and think of Jesus as a willing victim who died for our sins, but to the eyewitnesses—both Jew and Gentile—it surely must have been seen as an internecine religious disagreement. And in the years since, even more religious violence has been perpetrated as a result of that crucifixion, in the name of the crucifixion, most notably the extraordinarily heinous history of Christian anti-Semitism. The crucifixion, an event that we claim brings peace between God and humans, has also been used to justify pogroms and holocausts.

While we could look at a lot of aspects of Christianity to help us solve the problem of violence that besets our religion, the obvious place to start is with that bloody execution. What we do with that violence will help us figure out what to do with all of the subsequent violence in Christianity and in the world. And what we finally decide about God will have massive implications for these questions, because if God is wrath, then violence is inevitable.

But if God is love, then violence must be surmountable. And the crucifixion of Jesus, while violent, must be the key to ending violence.

What the Crucifixion Tells Us About God

The crucifixion of Jesus is the central act in the drama that is the Christian story, and its importance cannot be overstated. Therefore, it simply must tell us something very important about God. That's really what this book is about: God.

It's notoriously difficult to talk confidently about God, the Great and Unknowable. The ditches are many, and they're deep, and we will likely fall into a few of them along this journey. But nevertheless, we must endeavor to search the death of Jesus for clues about who God really is and how we can relate to God. Because how we think about God determines everything else: who we are, what we are to do, what we hope for, and who we hope to be.

Essential to the Christian story is that Jesus of Nazareth was God's unique son and that Jesus of Nazareth died a violent and unwarranted death. Looking back on Jesus' death and resurrection, his disciples and the subsequent apostle, Paul, attempted to make sense of that death. They looked to the Hebrew Bible, and they reminisced about Jesus' own words, looking for clues as to the significance of a crucified Messiah—a very different outcome than they had previously expected. Within a short time after his crucifixion, they'd determined that Jesus' death was the key that unlocked the door to understanding everything: God; the law; Jesus' life, teachings, and miracles; and, maybe most importantly, how Christians are to live.

Like the earliest followers of Jesus, every generation of the church since has been uniformly committed to the importance of the cruci-fixion. It's why a cross or crucifix hangs at the front of nearly every church in the world. But who is the God behind that cross? My ministers may have taught me that I'm responsible for Jesus' death, but at least some Christians have asked if it is God who bears the ultimate culpability: Did God kill Jesus?

In fact, we can't help but ask a whole litany of questions as we see Jesus hanging there:

- What kind of God lets his son die?
- What was accomplished when Jesus died?
- Was there another way?
- Was violence necessary to take away our sins?

Jesus dies on the cross, and all the dominoes start to fall. Was it God who pushed over the first one and started the chain reaction? Or did God demand it of his son?

These questions vex me—and maybe you, too. I've set out on a quest to understand the crucifixion so that I can better understand the God behind the crucifixion. Part of that is studying all of the ways that theologians have interpreted the crucifixion in the past. When we really dig into those interpretations, we find a particular version of God behind each of them. And part of it is looking for new explanations and interpretations that jibe both with our sacred text and with our experience that God is breathtakingly loving, not volcanically wrathful.

I suspect that as we journey through the history of thought about Jesus' crucifixion and look at the biblical accounts of that event, we will find a God who is not wrathful or disgusted. We won't find a God who killed his son, nor demanded that his son be executed to pay a penalty. Instead, I suspect that we will find a God of love who goes even to the most extreme lengths to identify with the human experience and to build a bridge between the human and the divine. We'll find a God who wants nothing more than to communicate his love to us.

It's a Multiple-Choice Question

It turns out that the reason for Jesus' death preached at that middle school retreat—embellished with the story about the blood and the woman trapped under the collapsed building—is not the only way that Christians have understood the death of Jesus. Instead, it's one of about half a dozen theories that preachers and theologians have used over the past two thousand years to explain why Jesus died. This fact wasn't advertised to me when I was growing up. Instead, I was taught that there was one and only one reason that Jesus died: because of my sin and God's anger and disappointment with me. Maybe you were told the same thing. But this sentiment would have been confounding to a second- or third-century Christian. They had entirely different ways of understanding Jesus' death, ways that we will explore in later chapters.

And behind each explanation of the crucifixion is an implied view of God. God is either strong or weak, in control or abdicating control, engaged or absent, gracious or vindictive. In the pages that follow, we will walk through the various views of Jesus' death, and we will look at the God who stands behind the cross in each.

The version that I heard that night at the retreat wasn't the first in history, but it is currently the most popular view in the Western world. It's called *penal substitution,* and at the heart of this view of the crucifixion is a God who is extremely wrathful.

A few years ago, I was lunching with a famous pastor of the Calvinist persuasion. The topic of the crucifixion came up—okay, I brought it up—and he proclaimed that *his* version of this doctrine is the only true and biblical version. His version, he confidently stated, *is* the gospel. I demurred, asking him if he didn't think that it was disingenuous for him to hide from his congregation the fact that Christians through the ages have had an array of beliefs about why Jesus died.

"You should never preach!" he nearly shouted at me across the table.

"People need fixed points of doctrine," he continued, holding up one index finger and circling it with his other index finger. "And to tell them about this historical relativism that you're suggesting would only confuse them."

Well, not only does that pastor have a low view of his congregants' intellectual abilities, he's doing a disservice to the Bible and to the doctrine of the atonement. That's the term that theologians use to talk about the question, Why did Jesus die? *Atonement* means reconciliation, in this case between God and humans. It comes from a Middle English word, *onement,* which means "harmony"—literally, the state of one thing being "at one" with another.[2] Interestingly, the main Greek word for atonement, *katallagé,* occurs only four times in the New Testament, and it's usually translated "reconciliation."[3] Atonement is a more common concept in the Hebrew Bible, as we will see when we investigate the history of sacrifice. Nevertheless, atonement has become one of the most contested doctrines of our day, as I found out at lunch with the Calvinist pastor.

This is actually in spite of its history. I was speaking at an evangelical college not long ago. I'd been booked by the campus chaplain to speak at a pastors' conference and at the weekly student chapel, but as word leaked out about my appearance, conservative alumni began to object. A couple of prominent alumni families even threatened to withhold their donations to the school if my invitation wasn't rescinded. Claiming academic freedom, the college administrators stood their ground, but in order to appease their critics somewhat, they canceled my last talk at the conference and scheduled a debate in its place. So there I sat, with members of the school's theological faculty on either side of me, and we all fielded questions from the audience.

One of the pastors in the crowd asked me how I could continue to be friends with another Christian author who had referred to the penal substitution version of atonement as "cosmic child abuse." In his question, he referred to my friend as a heretic. Before I could answer, one of the school's theology professors spoke up, and he was mad. "The atonement has never been a defining trait of theological orthodoxy," he said forcefully. "It was never debated in any church council nor formulated in a creed. Therefore, by definition, you are not able to call someone a heretic based on their view of the atonement."

Until he said it, that had not occurred to me. While the early church cast out as heretics those who didn't affirm the Trinity or didn't believe that Jesus was fully human and fully divine, the atonement never rose to that level. It's not that the early church fathers didn't think it was important that Jesus died to save sinners, it's that they didn't get hung up on the mechanics by which that happened. They recognized that the event of Jesus' death on the cross was much deeper and more mysterious than our explanations of it could describe—let alone there be one single explanation. Yes, we talk about it because we want to understand the God who loves us and the Son who saves us, but our accounts can never fully capture the mystery of that event.

That's not the case today. Today, the atonement is one of the most contentious theological issues in the church, and it's not hard to see why.[4] Many think that the salvation of every human who's ever lived hangs on one's explanation of the nature of the atonement. In one way, they're right: on the atonement hinges our understanding of human nature and the nature of God: Are we sinful? Lost without God's help? Do we play a role in our own salvation? Is God happy to offer us salvation? Or was God left with no choice but to allow the execution of his son? Was Jesus crucified to satisfy God's sense of justice? His wrath? A deeper law that binds even God? Or was Jesus setting an example of the sacrificial way that human beings are meant to live?

The importance of these questions, and what they have to say about the very nature of God and humans, cannot be overstated. That's why the aforementioned pastor with whom I had lunch said that the atonement *is* the gospel. But there's something else that the pastor got very wrong, and that's the belief that there is only one acceptable explanation of Jesus' death.

I remember exactly when I took my last multiple-choice test; it was the GRE, and I was applying to a Ph.D. program. Now I'm prepping my own children for the ACT and SAT as they look forward to college admissions. They've got lots of multiple-choice questions in their future. We've been led to believe that the questions that surround Jesus' death have one and only one answer. That's why so many preachers can so confidently state just why Jesus had to die and just why you need to accept that fact to gain access to heaven. But one of the more startling realizations we'll make as we journey into this topic is that it's not a true-false question, it's multiple-choice. And the answer just might be "all of the above."

What I mean is that the Bible and the Christian tradition are not unanimous about the reason that Jesus had to die and what his death accomplished. True, the Hebrew Bible set forth a system of sacrifice that gave a framework to the New Testament authors, but the Hebrew Bible itself is ambivalent about the how and why of blood sacrifice. The New Testament varies widely as well, with the Gospel writers understanding Jesus' death as a Passover sacrifice and the author of Hebrews considering it a Yom Kippur sacrifice. Mixing those two is a bit like putting a Christmas tree up on Easter, which is basically what Paul does in his various letters.

And then we'll get to the last two thousand years, during which different—and even contradictory—interpretations of Jesus' death have been considered the one and only answer to the question. Each of the theories about the crucifixion is historically contingent, reflecting the place and time of its invention and even the personality of its author. Each sets out to solve a particular problem, and in each case the death of Jesus is the solution.

Throughout Christian history, the death of Jesus has been the answer—it's the question that has changed.

This is all great news because it frees us from the pressure of getting the answer just right. It's quite likely that the answer is, in fact, a mixture of several answers—that the death of Jesus on the cross is so powerful because there is enough meaning in that event for all times, all places, and all people. That's not to say that everyone gets to make up their own answer; as we will see, some explanations are better than others. But we are given some agency—maybe more than we thought we had—in making sense of the violence that is memorialized in the crosses around our necks and atop our churches. We get to take part in a conversation that's been going on for centuries, and we get to contribute to that conversation.

Later in this book, I'll do just that and offer my own contribution to our understanding of Jesus' death. It's one that I think does justice to the magnitude of that event while preserving the eternal love between the Father and the Son. And even better, I think that the crucifixion opened the door so that you and I can enter that love ourselves.

The Bible itself provides multiple answers, as does church history. So it is not an option to proclaim that there is only one answer. And it should certainly raise many red flags when we hear that the one right answer was discovered a thousand years after Jesus died. But before we get to that, we've got to survey the territory—the Old and New Testaments and the history of the church. And even before we dive into that, we've got some preliminary ground to cover. But all the way through, our goal will be to ground our understanding of the cross in God's love and measure various theories by the standard we get from both the Bible and from our experience: *How does the crucifixion reveal the God of love that Jesus proclaimed?*

3

The Bible and the Smell Test

WHAT YOU BELIEVE matters. That is, *beliefs have consequences*.

Our culture is rife with examples. A young man believes all non-Muslims are the enemy of God and that God will reward all martyrs, and so we read of another suicide bomber. A Christian minister believes that the Koran is the work of Satan, so he publicly burns a copy, instantly insulting the faith of over a billion people. And we shake our heads at how people can be so deceived. What we believe matters.

Research shows that those who believe in a wrathful God are more likely to suffer from depression and anxiety disorders than those who believe in a loving, merciful God.[1] Our beliefs really do have consequences, for they structure how we live.

I tend to be a pretty logical person. I like debates, reasoned arguments, and rigorous thinking. But after many years of searching and studying the ways of God, theology, and the Bible, I've concluded the following:

Bad theology begets ugly Christianity.

Good theology begets beautiful Christianity.

I call it the *smell test*. It's an aesthetic argument. Like me, you've probably pulled that half-gallon of milk out of the back of the refrigerator, seen that the "best by" date is long past, and cautiously waved the open bottle under your nose. The result is either, "Smells fine to me!" or a sour stench strong enough to strip the bark off a tree.

That may seem an odd way to measure a faith system. We are used to matters being true or false, right or wrong, not beautiful or ugly, sweet or sour. Most prefer a more forensic approach: she who has the most logical doctrine wins. But, as we will see in the pages to come, many religious systems that are perfectly logical are nevertheless downright ugly. They're bad for the world and bad for people. In other words, you can devise a system of doctrine that makes perfect sense within its own little self-inscribed world, but when you take it out into the broader marketplace of ideas, it spoils, like dropping a teaspoon of vinegar into a gallon of milk.

Jesus himself taught us to use a "smell test" in the Sermon on the Mount:

> Beware of false prophets, who come to you in sheep's cloth-
> ing but inwardly are ravenous wolves. You will know them
> by their fruits. Are grapes gathered from thorns, or figs from
> thistles? In the same way, every good tree bears good fruit,
> but the bad tree bears bad fruit. A good tree cannot bear
> bad fruit, nor can a bad tree bear good fruit. Every tree that
> does not bear good fruit is cut down and thrown into the
> fire. Thus you will know them by their fruits.[2]

According to the Gospel of John, at the end of his ministry, Jesus told his followers to love one another, and that "by this everyone will know that you are my disciples, if you have love for one another."[3] Even Jesus declared that we can tell something about people's faith by looking at how they live their lives, so we're in good company.

The beauty of art is famously subjective. One person walks through a museum of modern art and sees masterpiece after master-piece, while another sees blobs and squiggles. Music is the same: to one, the latest pop song is a tour de force; to another, it's an assault on the eardrums. Nevertheless, I am proposing that we judge theol-ogy similarly. Jesus instructs us to do this. As you read this book—or any book dealing with God, Jesus, spirituality, or faith—stop every once in a while and take a whiff. Does it emit a sour stench? Or is it developing in a way that you find palatable, even wonderful? That's what Jesus is telling us to ask.

What I'm saying is that deciding what we believe is less like doing math or chemistry and more like making music or painting a portrait or composing a beautiful photograph.[4] And just like good art, mastering one's subject matter is important—i.e., one needs to proceed from the truth—but how we shade and color that truth makes all the difference. And if it's not beautiful or it smells bad, then we haven't got it right.

I'm also saying that the *outcome* of someone's belief is a fair criterion by which to judge the belief. Paul famously wrote, "The fruit of the Spirit is love, joy, peace, patience, kindness, generosity, faithfulness, gentleness, and self-control."[5] How often do we measure Christian ideas and beliefs by these criteria? Paul is saying that you can tell something about people's faith by how they behave in the world. To paraphrase: assholes have bad theology. Or, related to the point above, it doesn't matter how logically airtight some doctrinal system is if it results in an army of jerks.

This is a controversial point, to be sure, because you could then say that a church's financial or sexual scandal can be attributed to its doctrine. Yes, that's basically what I'm saying—at least that theology plays a role when things go bad in religion.

The early church members were not known as hateful and judging. Just the contrary. They got in trouble for being too loving, for calling one another "brother and sister" and greeting one another with a "holy kiss." As a result, some Roman government officials thought they were a sex cult.

The modern church, on the other hand, is considered hateful, judging, condemning, and obsessed with sex. Is this imprecision merely the result of persecution, the result of outsiders misperceiving a church that in reality is all about love, joy, peace, patience, kindness, generosity, faithfulness, gentleness, and self-control? No,

I'm afraid not. Many of us Christians have these negative impressions from within the church, because some of the loudest voices in modern Christianity have some of the worst doctrine (meanwhile, thousands of small communities of beautiful faith toil in relative obscurity).

I'm saying that the church that looks beautiful in the world has better doctrine than the church that is known for its ugly hate-mongering. And I'm saying that what someone thinks about the crucifixion of Jesus very much abides by this rule.

A lot of us have grown increasingly uncomfortable with the regnant interpretation of Jesus' death as primarily the propitiation of a wrathful God. For one thing, we don't experience God as uber-wrathful toward us. For another, it simply doesn't make sense that God would game the whole system so that he has to kill his own son just to vitiate this wrath.

It just doesn't smell right.

How an explanation of the crucifixion "smells" isn't our only criterion. We also need to measure our beliefs by other teachings we learn from scripture and from the great teachers throughout history. Jesus testified to a loving God, and we're going to search for that love in each of the explanations of the crucifixion that we encounter. We'll do that by asking a set of questions about each model:

- What does the model say about God?
- What does it say about Jesus?
- What does the model say about the relationship between God and Jesus?
- How does it make sense of violence?
- What does it mean for us spiritually?
- Where's the love?

Hopefully that rubric will help us sort through the many options that confront us.

What About the Bible?

As we look for a better way forward, for a new (or old) explanation of what really happened on the cross, we will of course have to deal with the Bible's voices on the subject. I say "voices" because the Bible is not exactly unanimous on Jesus' death—its causes or its consequences. The Bible is composed of 66 books, and many of those were edited several times before settling into their current form. With that many hands involved in its composition, it's no surprise that the Bible is rarely univocal on a subject. The variety found between the Bible's covers both keeps a lot of scholars employed and accounts for the myriad denominations we've got in the world today. It gives us plenty to talk about, even argue about.

The upside is that we can mine the Bible's depths for amazing insights into the nature of God and humanity and the relationship between us. The downside is that sometimes people can find anything they want in the Bible and even in the meaning of Jesus' death. Here's a case in point:

I teach a class at a local state university called "Introduction to the New Testament." The first half of the semester is taken up with the historical, religious, and literary context of first-century Palestine and the Gospels, and the second half of the semester is concerned with Acts, the letters of Paul, and the balance of the New Testament writings. Just before the midterm, having looked at all four Gospels, we spend one class session considering the "quest for the historical Jesus"—who was Jesus, *really,* and how much can we confidently say about him? So I'm always looking for examples of how the Bible and Jesus are used as if they're floating signifiers. Recently, two examples fell right into my lap.

The first was a *60 Minutes* interview with a right-wing TV personality. He'd just written a book about the death of Jesus, and he was doing the talk-show circuit, selling his book. He professed to *60 Minutes* that he'd written a book free of any religion or doctrine—"It's a history book," he claimed. Then he got to the crux of his argument, the thesis, he said, of his book: Jesus was killed by the Jewish and Roman authorities because he interrupted the flow of taxes from the "folks" to the elites. Jesus was a small-government revolutionary, shown most clearly when he stormed the Temple and overthrew the table of the money changers and those selling animals for sacrifice.

As I was sitting in the living room, watching this interview, my spouse, Courtney, started chuckling. "What?" I asked. "Well, I was just reading about that same episode." Courtney was sitting across the room, studying for her yoga teacher certification. She proceeded to read to me from one of her assigned books, *World Peace Diet: Eating for Spiritual Health and Social Harmony*, in which the author claims that Jesus' cleansing of the Temple was "an act of animal liberation" and that "it was for this flagrantly revolutionary act that Jesus had to be crucified by the herding culture's power elite."[6]

So, we've got two authors, both saying that Jesus' actions in the Temple got him killed. One claims it's because Jesus was a small government, anti-tax protestor. The other says it's because Jesus was an anti-herding animal liberationist.

I showed the *60 Minutes* interview to the class, and I read them the relevant paragraphs from *World Peace Diet*. We all had a laugh. Then I read them the passage about the cleansing of the Temple from the Gospel of Matthew. It's two verses long:

> Then Jesus entered the temple and drove out all who were selling and buying in the temple, and he overturned the tables of the money changers and the seats of those who sold doves. He said to them, "It is written,
> 'My house shall be called a house of prayer';
> but you are making it a den of robbers."[7]

Nothing about taxes, and nothing about a vegan diet.

There's an old saw that you hear a lot these days. If you read a newspaper report about the deleterious effects of coffee on your health, wait a week, because there's sure to be a study next week that touts coffee's wonderful benefits. The Bible has a similar role in

our society. One person reads it and finds God's love; another sees
God's wrath. One finds justification for gay marriage; another reads
condemnations of all homosexuality. And on and on it goes.

This is very much the case for Jesus' death. As we'll see below,
many diverse interpretations of the significance of that event have
been proposed over the centuries, each with biblical backing. The
Bible is rife with language about both God's love and God's wrath.
The Bible talks of sacrifice, for example, and of the penalties for sin.
Proponents of one version will tell you that their position has *more*
Bible verses in their favor, while another camp will tell you that they
have *better* verses. Quantity versus quality. And on and on it goes.

The authors of the New Testament say many things on the topic
of Jesus' death. They are not of one voice on the matter; they are
polyphonic. Thus, we will have to weigh the biblical evidence, but
we'll also have to run it through the gauntlet of our reason. Our
conclusions, too, will have to pass the smell test.

I once got mentioned in a sermon by Jerry Falwell. It was only
a couple of weeks before he died, and he was preaching a sermon
condemning me and my friends and what was called the "emergent
church movement." He was deeply offended, it seems, by something
I wrote about in a blog post about postmodern philosophy and the
Bible. Here's what I wrote:

> I am quite convinced that the Bible is a subversive text, that
> it constantly undermines our assumptions, transgresses our
> boundaries, and subverts our comforts. This may sound like
> academic mumbo-jumbo, but I really mean it. I think the
> Bible is a f***ing scary book (pardon my French, but that's
> the only way I know how to convey how strongly I feel
> about this). And I think that deconstruction is the only her-
> meneutical avenue that comes close to expressing the trans-
> gressive nature of our sacred text.[8]

In his sermon, Falwell read the sentence with the F-bomb, then
addressed me: "Really, Tony; don't you think it's rather pitiful that

your vocabulary is so limited that this is how you speak about the Word of God you are supposed to proclaim to your fellow 'Christ-followers'?"[9]

Jerry Falwell's distaste for vulgarity notwithstanding, I do find the Bible to be subversive and, quite honestly, a little frightening. That's because it's so unpredictable—the Bible has shown the capacity to be open to myriad interpretations, both beautiful and terrifying. And the stakes are high in these interpretations, since the four Gospels constitute our sole record of Jesus' life, death, and resurrection. That is why I think it's crucial we keep in mind that the Bible is the *second* most important revelation of God to humanity. The *most important* revelation of God is Jesus himself. The Bible is, among other things, our best record of who Jesus was and what he did. But Jesus comes to us in other ways as well. Jesus has been explicated and interpreted by church councils, theologians and popes, and countless everyday Christians. Jesus himself promised that his presence would continue with us through the advent of the Holy Spirit, who came to Jesus' followers immediately after this promise. Therefore, we can reliably count on our own experiences of Jesus to complement what we find in the Bible.

For a Christian, the Bible is primarily a record of (1) the experiences of the people of God who prepared the way for Jesus; (2) the testimony of the life, death, and resurrection of Jesus; and (3) the early church's interpretation of what Jesus was all about. The Bible is other things as well: a history of Israel's experiences with God, a catalog of the rules that bound a people to that God, various genres of ancient literature (histories, prophecies, poems, and apocalypses), and the early history of an upstart religion under the dominance of the Roman empire. The Bible is lots of things, and it is a great treasury on which we can draw in this investigation. But it's also contentious.

Conservatives tend to valorize the Bible to the point that it lords over everything. Liberals, put off by the Bible's seemingly primitive taboos and violence, too often minimize the Bible's role to the point of unusefulness. They've both got a point. The Bible does have authority, both because it's the sole primary source we've got when investigating Jesus' death and because the church has uniformly allowed the Bible to set the terms for the conversation about salvation. But the Bible also comes from a context—from a time and social location that is very distant from our own. In fact, it can be argued that the original context of the Bible's writing is virtually inaccessible to us. We know a lot less than we'd like about first-century Palestine—most of the history of that era comes from the capital of the empire, Rome.

Further, the books of the New Testament record the first wrestling with the meaning of Jesus' life and death. Each of the four Gospels was written to a different audience, with a slightly different purpose, and as such they hold different details: each, for example, has Jesus uttering different words from the cross. The Bible is neither a textbook nor a newspaper. Its purpose is not to present an objective account of a noteworthy event. Instead it is the record of a community of people trying to come to grips with the meaning of their leader's death.

As we journey into the meaning of Jesus' death ourselves, it will be supremely important that we bear this in mind. On the one hand, we should take a fresh look at the Bible and listen anew to what it has to say. On the other hand, a lot of smart and faithful people have looked at these same texts and proffered opinions about what they mean, so we should listen to them as well. Honestly, the most faithful thing we can do is wrestle with the Bible in the same spirit that the first Christians wrestled with their own thoughts and feelings about Jesus' death.

Our Working Assumptions

So we've got some working assumptions to begin this book. One is that theology can be "beautiful." Two, the life that results from doctrinal convictions is a fair way to determine how beautiful that doctrine is. Three, the Bible is of prime importance to this discussion, but it's got to be understood for what it is: the record of a group of people in search of answers about their Messiah's death and resurrection.

I write this by way of introduction. This is not a conclusive book on the crucifixion, meant to solve the riddle of Jesus' death for all time. In fact, I think that theologians who attempt to do that are fooling themselves and probably their readers. Theology is, by its very nature, an ongoing conversation across the ages. Some issues come up because culture brings them up, and we deal with them. Gay marriage is a current topic in this vein, just as indulgences were for Martin Luther in the sixteenth century and Neoplatonic Gnosticism was for Augustine in the fifth. Other issues have vexed the church since its inception, including the Trinity, the return of Christ, and, yes, the crucifixion.

As we'll discover, the way that Christians have understood the crucifixion has changed through the years. In fact, it has changed dramatically. That tells us two things. First, it reminds us that the event is more fundamental than our explanations of it. The cross compels us, moves us, and works on us before we can even put words to it. Second, this diversity of explanations also provides us some freedom. Yes, the history of these changes is both compelling and telling, giving us an insight into our forbears' understanding. But it also reminds us that we're allowed to change our minds on this issue. The very evolution of this doctrine testifies to the fact that there is no unanimous understanding of why Jesus died. But there are answers. Therefore, it is supremely faithful to ask questions like *Why did Jesus die?* and *Did God kill Jesus?* But we can't stop with the questions. We've got to press on toward faithful answers, because that's what the Christian journey is all about.

PART TWO

Sacrifice as Prelude

4

The Mystery of Sacrifice

THERE'S A FAMOUS story from the 1960s about the South Pacific. Several Westerners, stranded on an island, were overrun by natives from a nearby island. The natives' island was home to a volcano, and the volcano was showing signs of waking from its dormancy. The natives, led by King Kaliwani, needed a goddess to worship—specifically, a white goddess—and they demanded a woman from the Westerners. The American women considered the possibilities of being worshipped as a goddess, but it became clear that the goddess's fate was more dire: she was to be "married" to the volcano and then thrown in as a sacrifice, meant to calm and satisfy the volcano god. At that point, the Westerners dressed one of their men up as a woman and convinced the islanders that he was in fact the ideal candidate to serve as the white goddess.

Okay, this isn't exactly a "famous story." It's the plot of the final episode of the television sitcom, *Gilligan's Island*. First aired on April 17, 1967, and shown innumerable times in syndication since, episode 98 of *Gilligan's Island* incorporates a meme both ancient and modern—indeed, it's a trope so recognizable that modern writers, sitcom and otherwise, can utilize it without introduction. It can be found in everything from Woody Woodpecker cartoons to the Tom Hanks/ Meg Ryan movie *Joe Versus the Volcano* to a *Far Side* comic in which two clueless tourists are being dragged up a volcano by natives, and one says to the other, "They just perked right up when we told them we were Virginians!"

So what does *Gilligan's Island* and human sacrifice have to do with Jesus' death on the cross? Danger stalks us modern people when we try to understand something that happened so long ago and so far away. It's too easy for us to impose our assumptions and beliefs onto the events and the people whom we are seeking to understand. (That, for example, is why some Christians during the seventies and eighties taught that the cross is really about having good self-esteem.) To truly try to understand an event in its original setting and what it meant to its original audience, we have some work to do. As much as we can, we must explore the ideas, culture, history, and influences that shaped the original event. And Jesus' death on a cross demands that we go even deeper. Why? Two reasons. Because Christians believe that Jesus was the climax of Israel's story and so cannot be understood outside the context of Israel's history, especially its sacrificial system. And to understand that system, we must ask why humans first came up with the idea that we need to offer blood and sacrifice to appease the gods.

Even today, Suzanne Collins's blockbuster Hunger Games trilogy is based on a sacrificial system. Set in postapocalyptic North America, the country of Panem is made up of twelve districts. Decades earlier, the Capitol District had put down a rebellion, and as recompense, each of the twelve districts must offer one boy and one girl as "tributes" to fight to the death in the annual Hunger Games. The story is rife with both substitution—the heroine Katniss takes the place of her sister Primrose—and bloody vengeance. As evidenced by the millions of copies these books have sold and the accompanying movies, human sacrifice is a theme that still resonates with us in modern times.

Ancient archaeological and documentary evidence suggests that human sacrifice was relatively common in ancient societies. Walter Burkert, eminent scholar of ancient myth and ritual, has posited the beginnings of human religion and human sacrifice in the Upper Paleolithic era, at least fifty thousand years ago.[1] He and others agree that human sacrifice predates animal sacrifice in prehistoric human societies. And human sacrifice is inscribed in the founding myths of human civilization.

In ancient Greek mythology, Artemis is the goddess of the hunt, wildness, childbirth, and virginity. In one myth, a sacred bear whom she loved is killed by some young boys, and as compensation to the goddess, several young girls every year must be sacrificed to her service—the girls must act as her "bear," as atonement for their brothers' crime. In an even more famous myth, Agamemnon kills a sacred stag of Artemis and brags that he's a better hunter than she. Enraged, Artemis calms the wind just as the Greek fleet is about to set sail for the Trojan War. A seer advises Agamemnon that the goddess will only be satisfied if he sacrifices his daughter, Iphigenia, which he agrees to do. But just as she's about to be sacrificed, Artemis substitutes a deer in her place and takes Iphigenia to be her immortal companion—a story that has some obvious parallels to Abraham's near-sacrifice of Isaac in the Hebrew book of Genesis.

Tales of human sacrifice in ancient (and not-so-ancient) societies are too numerous to list in detail. The Celts used to run prisoners through with a sword and then have their wise men divine the future from the death spasms of the victims. In 1487, the Aztecs sacrificed tens of thousands of prisoners to mark the consecration of a pyramid. Egyptian pharaohs would have hundreds or thousands of victims slaughtered at their funerals, with the belief that these victims would serve them in the afterlife. In the eighteenth and nineteenth centuries, the wandering Thuggee tribe in India killed over a million people in an effort to impress Kali, the Hindu goddess of violence and sexuality; they were the original "thugs," notorious for their use of the garrote, a chair on which the victim is bound and strangled.

As recently as 1926, American explorer Armstrong Sperry posted a dispatch in *World Magazine* of a trip he made to the Solomon Islands. Rife with racist phrases like "great black savages," Sperry's dispatch reported that he convinced a couple dozen of the Islanders to take him and his crew to the top of their active volcano. They did, and atop the volcano, Sperry wrote,

Not a hundred feet below us lay a lake of living fire, a pit of hell, where waves of glowing lava writhed and twisted and dashed upon the rocky walls, just as the waves of the sea were beating the cliffs of Boukai. It drew you with a strange fascination, glowing with every devilish color of the spectrum, terrifying and alluring. You wanted to run, and you wanted to jump in.[2]

According to Sperry, his guides began by throwing pigs into the lava. But then their frenzy increased: They cut themselves with knives and shells, hoping their blood would appease the volcano god. "And then all pandemonium broke loose," Sperry reported, and they grabbed a man from another tribe. As Sperry watched in horror, "With one convulsive heave the cannibals shot the struggling victim out into the air. In horror I saw the poor screaming wretch descend into the fiery furnace and the livid, hissing lava closed over him."

Remember: this happened less than one hundred years ago.

Other examples of human sacrifice happen to this very day, though usually in similarly remote corners of the world. So-called honor killings sometimes make the news, in which a woman is killed by her own family for marrying a man other than the one they'd chosen for her. These girls and women are sacrificed to redeem their families' honor.

Frenzy and Pain

Some sacrifices are still made to get the attention of the gods.

In the late summer of 2012, I flew to the other side of the world with half a dozen bloggers. We were sent by World Vision to observe their charitable work in Sri Lanka, a bewitching, troubled country that hangs like an earring off the southern tip of India. Sri Lanka is a majority Buddhist country, but it also has significant populations of Hindus, Muslims, and Christians. On our first day there, after orientation and some shopping, our host asked if we'd like to see a Hindu festival nearby. We jumped at the chance, and not much later we were disembarking from our van amid throngs of Hindu Sri Lankans.

We were the only white people among thousands of people at the Munneswaram temple, celebrating the eponymous festival, a twenty-seven-day affair celebrated every August at the temple site in Chilaw, not far from Colombo. Foreign as we obviously were, everyone in our group was diffident, save Matthew Paul Turner, who had organized the trip and was serving as our photographer. With a combination of unabashed hand motions and a big Nikon that made him look like a journalist, Matthew gained access inside a rope barricade, and he beckoned us to follow him. A policeman waved us in. What followed was one of the oddest, most intense experiences of my life.

Once inside the cordoned-off area, we saw a pit dug into the sandy earth. Six feet wide and twenty feet long, the pit was full of huge logs and stumps, all on fire and being tended by several men. The men wore only sarongs; they stirred the fire with long, wooden poles, and they were sweating profusely. Occasionally, younger men would dump buckets of water over their heads. Even fifty feet away, the fire was uncomfortably hot on my face. The air temperature must have been over two hundred degrees near where the fire stirrers were standing.

Over the next hour, the fire tenders removed the larger stumps, leaving a pulsating bed of red hot coals. Dusk settled. A bull with long, sharp horns meandered through the crowd, brushing past us. His neck was decorated with flowers. He caused near panic among some in our group, yet he merited not even a sidelong glance from the Sri Lankans.

Then others were allowed into the inner sanctum with us. They were the family members of those who were about to walk the fire. Moments later the fire walking began. The entire scene became a complete frenzy, and the formerly ubiquitous policemen were now nowhere to be found. Men and boys and men carrying boys began walking and running across the coals. Someone yelled at us, and we all squatted or sat so that those behind us could see. The stream of men and boys continued, each walking briskly across the coals, and people yelled and screamed, and the temple's PA system blasted Hindu music so loud that the speakers crackled with distortion.

We found someone who spoke English. Our new bilingual friend told us that many of the men walked the coals because they'd made a vow to the god Shiva. Those who carried their sons over the fire had vowed that if they were given a son, they'd walk the fire in gratitude. Others were making sacrifice to Shiva in hopes of getting a blessing. Some carried pots of milk, a common Hindu symbol of atonement; others had massive pins piercing their cheeks, lips, and ears, meant to show Shiva extra devotion.

The crowd's fever grew, and there was no longer any barrier between us and the entire throng. Thousands of devotees pressed in toward the fire, and members of our group shouted above the din to stay together. With wild eyes, we scanned the crowd for one another. I linked arms with a couple of people, and we forced ourselves to the outskirts of the horde. Others did the same; we reunited as a group and headed for the van.

For the rest of the week, we processed what had happened, what we'd seen, and how we understood it—the sacrifice, the danger, the religious devotion, the frenzy. It was as far from your average Lutheran or Presbyterian worship service as you could imagine.

The Munneswaram festival didn't end with the fire walking ceremony. It continued with other calm and frantic activities, culminating in a massive animal sacrifice. On the final day of the festival every year, hundreds of goats and thousands of chickens are sacrificed, beheaded on a concrete slab. The chief priest of the temple asserts that this is not conventional Hindu practice, but he allows the tradition to proceed. The Sri Lankan government, however, does not. In 2011, a government minister arrived on the eve of the sacrifice and loaded every animal he could find onto a truck, calling the mass sacrifice an act of animal cruelty.[3]

In Nepal, animal rights activists have succeeded in reducing the number of animals sacrificed at the annual Gadhimai festival from over two hundred thousand in 2009 to about half of that in 2014. "I really look forward to this," said forty-four-year-old Joginder Patel, who kills over two hundred water buffaloes at the festival each year. "God will bless me for it. It is as easy as cutting vegetables."[4]

Holy Violence to Fight Violence

Sacrifice, both animal and human, has been a part of religious practice as long as there's been religion, as far back as 50,000 BCE and maybe even earlier. As twenty-first-century Westerners, we tend to find such things primitive and barbaric. How did our human ancestors convince themselves that the death of an animal or, worse, a fellow human would appease an angry deity? And why did they seem to think that the bloodier the death the better? For that matter, why did they think that the gods were mad at them?

No one has provided a better answer to the first of these three questions than René Girard. We will consider Girard's work more extensively in a later chapter, but here it is in brief: As human societies developed, tribes formed. With more people living together, rivalries increased, as did violence. Primitive religions—we might call them protoreligions—sought to deal with ever-increasing violence by setting up a pressure-release valve in society: violence would be perpetrated on an innocent victim in the form of a bloody sacrifice, and everyone would feel better, at least temporarily. In a somewhat ironic twist, the sacrificial victim in this process becomes sacred—maybe even divine—because he or she seems to have a magical power to quell violence in the community. Girard calls this the "scapegoat mechanism."

Among other interesting and challenging claims, Girard accuses most scholars of ancient myth as being mistaken about how literally these stories were acted out in a community's life. For example, the Babylonian creation myth tells the story of the god Marduk defeating the goddess Tiamat, splitting her body, and laying one half over the sky and the other under the earth. He then kills Tiamat's lover, Kingu, and creates humankind out of Kingu's blood. It's a fantastical myth, to be sure, but Girard insists that the Babylonians used this myth to justify a real murder.[5] Their creation story takes real violence and covers it with the patina of sacredness.

While I didn't witness a sacrifice involving death in Sri Lanka, the fire walking ritual was definitely sacrificial. Every year, participants are injured and sometimes killed. And it takes no stretch of the imagination for me to consider that same festival killing scores of animals days later. In Hinduism, Shiva is both a fearful destroyer holding a three-bladed weapon and a kind benefactor looking after those who please him. In the Hindu pantheon, he is one of the primary forms of god and considered to be a supreme manifestation of the divine. As such, he demands sacrifice from his followers. He demands that they show their commitment to him by enduring pain and by shedding animal blood.

Sacrifice runs deep in our evolutionary past. And while as Western Christians we may not practice it in the way that Sri Lankan Hindus do, we still value it highly. A football player who's injured on the field has made a "sacrifice for the team," and a soldier who's killed in battle has made the "ultimate sacrifice." Every Sunday, millions of Christians around the world echo this call-and-response with their priest as the priest holds the eucharistic bread and wine aloft:

Priest: "Christ our passover is sacrificed for us."

Congregation: "Therefore let us keep the feast."[6]

But just how that sacrifice works is more difficult to figure out. The uniqueness of Christ's sacrifice is what we claim sets Christianity apart from other belief systems. But the sacrifice of Jesus on the cross did not happen *ex novo*. Instead, it came out of the story of Jesus' people, the Jews. And they had a long history of sacrifices to God, recorded in the portion of the Bible that we share, the Hebrew Bible.

5

An Acceptable Sacrifice

J ews and Christians share an origin story. While not quite as violent as the Babylonian version, it too is rife with bloodshed, including a famous original murder.

But before that murder, we first turn to the creation of the world. As Genesis tells it, God separated the water from the land and the earth from the sky and the light from the dark. And, according to the third-century Jewish teaching called the Mishnah, even before the world was created, God was busy: "Seven things were created before the world, viz., The Torah, repentance, the Garden of Eden, Gehenna, the Throne of Glory, the Temple, and the name of the Messiah."[1] Repentance seems odd in that list. The teaching continues, "Repentance, for it is written, Before the mountains were brought forth, or ever thou hadst formed the earth and the world. Thou turnest man to destruction, and sayest, Repent, ye sons of men."[2]

This tradition holds that early on the sixth day of creation, the Lord created *repentance*. Before the original humans had done anything to repent of—indeed, before they were even created—God already knew that repentance was going to be part of the equation. When Eve and Adam ate the fruit from the tree of moral knowledge, it was both inevitable and terrible. Prior to eating the fruit, they lived lives of stasis, of inertia. They walked with the Lord in the cool of the day. They had everything they needed. As my friend

Rabbi Joseph Edelheit says, "Before they ate the fruit, Adam and
Eve were sociopaths. Literally. They did not know the difference
between good and evil."[3] That ended with two bites, and suddenly
they became fully human. They knew good from evil, and they
were confronted with moral choice, which has vexed every subsequent member of their species.

But in this scenario, the Lord had already built into the system
a way for the human beings to repair their relationship with their
God. The Hebrew word for repentance is *shwb*, and it means "to
turn." However, that's not what Adam and Eve did after their original sin. They were cast out of Eden immediately, before they could
eat from another magical tree that would grant them immortality,
and the very next story recorded in the Book of Genesis is of their
sons and the original murder. Adam and Eve never look back. They
do not turn. They do not repent, and neither does their son after
killing his brother.

And that murder is over an issue none other than blood sacrifice.

Sacrifice had not yet been commanded by the Lord in the earliest
days recounted in Genesis. But it seems there was an inherent desire to sacrifice something to God, which drove these protohumans
(and, more importantly, those who generations later told the stories
of these protohumans) to bring a sacrifice to the God who created
them. For some mysterious reason, sacrifice seemed like the right
thing to do.

Adam and Eve's sons brought to the Lord what they had. Cain
brought fruit of the ground, for he was a farmer; he was given no in-
struction nor direction as to what God wanted. Abel brought sheep,
for he was a shepherd. They each brought their sacrifice in the spirit
of thanksgiving. It was, the text tells us, an "offering."

For some inexplicable reason, the Lord liked what Abel brought
(bloody meat), but not what Cain brought (vegetarian's delight).
So jealous was Cain of his brother's success that he killed Abel—
ironically, the farmer murdered the butcher—and this act deeply
upset the Lord, even though it is arguably God who incited the
murder by choosing one brother over the other. So the Lord both

punished Cain by sending him out into the wilderness as a wanderer and protected him by marking him and ensuring that no one would do to him what he had done to his brother.

And thus the story begins. Within the first few pages of the biblical epic, there is disobedience and murder, acceptable sacrifice and unacceptable sacrifice. And it is quite clear from the story that we, too, are descended from these disobedient, murderous, confused people. As we explore the tradition of sacrifice in the Old Testament, we need to keep in mind what relationship it implies between God and humanity and what role offering sacrifice played in that relationship. Did God ask for these sacrifices, and if so, why?

Abraham and Isaac

One of the unique characteristics of Solomon's Porch in Minneapolis, the faith community of which I'm a part, is that we don't have sermons in the conventional sense, delivered by a clergyperson from behind a pulpit or a lectern. Instead, we read through books of the Bible together, over several weeks. Usually we read a chapter a week. After a brief introduction, a paragraph will be shown on a video screen. Someone from the congregation will read that paragraph aloud, and a discussion will ensue, sometimes brief, sometimes lengthy. Then the next paragraph goes on the screen, and so on.

Recently, we were reading through the book of Genesis, and I must have drawn the short straw, because I was asked to lead the Bible discussion on Genesis 22. Arguably the climax of Genesis, this chapter is what biblical scholars call a "text of terror." After decades of waiting for a long-promised son, Abraham and Sarah finally give birth to Isaac. The angelic announcement of Sarah's pregnancy was so unlikely that she chuckled; when the child came, she named him "laughter."

But then something terrible happens. In order to test Abraham, God tells him to take his son to the land of Moriah and "offer him there as a burnt offering on one of the mountains that I shall show you."[4] Abraham doesn't argue; he doesn't even flinch. He just saddles up his donkey with his son and some dry wood and sets off for the mountains. When Isaac asks, "Where is the lamb for a burnt offering?" Abraham hedges his bets, saying, "God himself will provide the lamb for a burnt offering, my son."[5] Abraham neglects to tell the boy about the Lord's command.

When they arrive at the appointed spot, Abraham binds Isaac atop the altar and woodpile and draws his knife to cut the boy's throat. At the last second, a messenger of the Lord appears and says, "Abraham, Abraham! . . . Do not lay your hand on the boy or do anything to him; for now I know that you fear God, since you have not withheld your son, your only son, from me."[6] Abraham sees a ram caught in a thicket and sacrifices it instead.

After reading this aloud at Solomon's Porch, an intense conversation broke out. Many in the congregation looked for ways to let God off the hook. "This story didn't actually happen," someone protested, "so we don't need to take it that seriously." But it's in the Bible, so we must deal with it, was my rejoinder. "Abraham knew that God was going to provide another sacrifice," said another. The Bible doesn't say that, I said, and we've only got the text we've got; we can't superimpose thoughts into Abraham's head. "God's ways are greater than ours," said another. "Who are we to question God?" How can you read this episode and not question God? I asked in reply.

These are all common responses to this text: a quest for a loophole, a desire to avoid the terrible implications of this terrifying story. The rabbis in the Midrash said that this happened so that Mount Moriah could be consecrated as the future site of the Temple. One medieval rabbi argued that Abraham was deluded and misheard God. The author of the New Testament book of Hebrews wrote that Abraham believed God would resurrect Isaac after the murder, thus it shows that father Abraham pre-believed in the resurrection of Jesus. And philosopher Søren Kierkegaard argued that, while the sacrifice of Isaac was ethically wrong, it was religiously right: Abraham was correct to think that God's religious commands trump human ethics when he agreed without argument to kill his son.

Many have tried to make excuses for God, and many tried the same thing in our congregation. But I kept pressing them to deal with the story as it actually is: a man we uphold as the father of three religions is ready to slit his son's throat. Deal with it.

Then a young mom in her twenties, Danielle, raised her hand. She was nursing her newborn child. I can remember exactly where she was sitting, in the middle of the room. I called on her. "I fucking hate this story," she said. I swallowed hard—it felt like the air had been sucked out of the room. "I wish it weren't in the Bible. If God asked me or Mark to climb on the roof of our house and kill one of our children, there's no way we would do it. This story is craziness."

Well, I thought, at least she's being honest.

As you might guess, the conversation turned on a pivot at that point. Instead of trying to defend God, we started to talk about what this incident must have done to Abraham's relationship with God and to Isaac's relationship with Abraham (*nota bene*, Abraham and Isaac never speak again in the biblical text). I'll admit, God didn't fare too well in that discussion. Twice in the early chapters of the Bible, God seems arbitrary in relation to sacrifice. First, God accepts one sacrifice and rejects the other, and then he demands a father sacrifice his son, only to step in at the last minute. The earliest history of sacrifice between God and Israel, with the exception of Noah's sacrifice upon leaving the ark, isn't great.

The Pesach Paradigm

For the last several years, my wife, my children, and I have been invited to the Passover Seder dinner at the home of Rabbi Joseph. There, we've sat alongside his grown children, college students, fellow professors, friends, and a Catholic priest. The Seder dinner is long and full of tradition. The meal begins with extended readings, and Joseph calls on different people around the table to read aloud from the prayer book. His children occasionally sing parts of the liturgy. And there is ceremonial eating, of *maror* (horseradish, a bitter herb to recall the bitterness of the Israelites' bondage in Egypt), *charoset* (a sweet mixture of nuts and fruit, reminiscent of the mortar that the slaves used to build for the Egyptians), and *karpas* (parsley that's dipped into salt water, representing the tears of the Hebrew slaves). Three whole *matzot* (unleavened bread) are stacked near the plate. Bread is unleavened during Passover because the Israelites didn't have time for yeast to do its work while they were fleeing Egypt.

Each of these is an ancient element on the plate. Rabbi Joe supplements these with modern additions, each with a meaning of its own. One year, there were tomatoes, there in solidarity with migrant farmworkers, many of whom labor in near-slavery conditions and at risk of deportation. Another year it was olives, as a sign of repentance for how Israelis have treated Palestinians, including bulldozing ancient olive trees to make way for Jewish settlements. And an orange, placed for GLBT Jews and in response to an apocryphal story of a rabbi shouting, "There's as much room in Judaism for a lesbian as there is for an orange on the Seder plate!" I've been fascinated to watch this ancient ritual evolve, even in the few years that I've been a guest.

Two more items grace the plate. Both are ancient, and both denote sacrifice. The first is *z'roa*, a roasted shank bone of a lamb—a symbol of the roasted lamb sacrifice in the Temple and the first animal sacrificed in Egypt and then consumed entirely that night—but now it is neither eaten nor touched during the Seder dinner. That's because since the Temple was destroyed by Roman forces, Jews have not been able to sacrifice, which leads to the final element on the table: *beitzah* is a hard-boiled egg that is charred with a flame, representing the destruction of the Temple. Eggs, traditionally the first food served at a Jewish funeral, are a food of mourning.

Jews around the world hold Passover Seder with these very same elements on the plate, as they have for centuries. Passover—also known as Pesach—is the holiest time in the Jewish year.

It would be difficult to overstate the change at the very heart of Judaism that took place when the Temple was razed by the Roman general Titus in 70 CE. In fact, it can be argued that Judaism as we know it is a result of that event—that the religion of the Hebrews that preceded the destruction of the Temple cannot rightly be called Judaism.

The religion that Jesus knew, and what had been known by Hebrews for generations, was centered on worship in the Temple. Everyone who was able would journey to Jerusalem for the several festivals per year, but none matched Pesach, the festival that happened each spring, for the Israelites' exodus from Egypt is considered the single most important event in all of their history.

In that well-known story, Moses is raised as Pharaoh's son, even though he's a Hebrew. When this fact is discovered, he escapes to the wilderness, where he finds a tribe, a wife, and a fiery bush through which the Lord speaks to him. Moses' task from the Lord is to rescue his people from slavery. He returns to Egypt, but his demand of freedom for the Hebrews is met with a scoff from Pharaoh. So, in a show of strength, God inflicts ten plagues upon the Egyptian people. Though his people moan, Pharaoh stays strong. That is, until the final plague.

On the night of Pesach, Moses tells the Hebrews to kill an unblemished lamb at midnight and spread its blood on their doorposts and lintels. They are then to eat the lamb, along with unleavened bread and bitter herbs. At midnight, just as had been promised, the Lord murdered the firstborn son in every home in Egypt, except those marked with lamb's blood—those he passed over.

"There was a loud cry in Egypt, for there was not a house without someone dead."[7]

That very night, Pharaoh demanded that Moses and the Hebrews leave. And, though Pharaoh later changed his mind and pursued the slaves, the Hebrew people did escape and eventually made it to the land that God had promised to them.

Embedded in the chapter-long story in the book of Exodus are Moses' commandments for keeping the Passover, including some of the very elements that Rabbi Joseph has on his plate. Also embedded in that story is the genesis of the Jewish rite of sacrifice. From that day forward, according to Moses, the Israelites were to sacrifice the firstborn of everything—"you shall set apart to the Lord all that first opens the womb."[8] That goes for all except firstborn human sons, which are redeemed by the Lord.

Moses does not introduce sacrifice in the Hebrew Bible. We've already seen Cain and Abel sacrificing to the Lord, as did Noah after the ark runs aground—it's said that Noah burned animals from the ark, and the Lord found the odor pleasant.[9] And, of course, we've got God's demand that Abraham sacrifice Isaac. Each of these played a part in launching the practice of sacrifice. But the Mosaic moment marks the inauguration of regular, systematic sacrifice. And this command to sacrifice—unlike the command that Abraham sacrifice his son—is accompanied by an explanation: the sacrifice of the firstborn is an act of thanksgiving and remembrance: "It shall serve as a sign on your hand and as an emblem on your forehead that by strength of hand the LORD brought us out of Egypt."[10] In this first instance, "sacrifice" did not carry the connotation of surrender that we now think of. Instead, the word means a thanksgiving meat offering.

Sacrifice, it turns out, is about blood. And there's no blood without violence.

Jews are very specific about the fact that there was only one Pesach. Every Passover celebration since—whether an animal sacrifice prior to 70 CE, or a Seder dinner since—has been an imitation and commemoration of that one Pesach. When Christians take communion, we don't think we're at the Last Supper; we are performing an act of remembrance of that singular event. Similarly, the Passover Festival was and is an act of remembrance. And what Jews are remembering is a deliverance from bondage, bound up in a rite of animal sacrifice. The blood on their doorposts played a pivotal role in their freedom from slavery, and so the rehearsal of that night every year on Passover is laden with the hope of future deliverance. And that is fundamentally *messianic* in nature.

6

Sacred Blood

UNFORTUNATELY, CHILD SACRIFICE is never condemned in the Bible. I wish it were. God could have included it in the Ten Commandments, or in any of the other 613 laws in the Torah, but God didn't. It would have been perfectly appropriate, too, since child sacrifice was well known among Israel's rivals. The closest God comes are in commands like this one from Leviticus: "You shall not give any of your offspring to sacrifice them to Molech, and so profane the name of your God: I am the LORD."[1] Molech was an Ammonite god, worshipped by Israel's neighbors in Canaan and Phoenicia. Parents who worshipped Molech were often required to sacrifice a child to the god. In fact, ancient documents state that if the parents shed any tears while their child's throat was being slit on the altar, Molech would consider the sacrifice unworthy.

Commands in 2 Kings and Jeremiah are similar, but nowhere in the Torah is child sacrifice—or, better yet, all human sacrifice—explicitly and universally condemned.

Nevertheless, there's no evidence to show that the Israelites sacrificed their children, except in rare instances.[2] Animal sacrifice, on the other hand, was an integral part of worship in the early days of Israel. Following Abel's introduction and Moses' institution, the Torah is rife with regulations about ritual animal sacrifice:

- Any animal that meets the criteria should be sacrificed rather than simply slaughtered (Leviticus 17:3–4).
- The hard fat on the entrails of the animal (aka, suet) and the kidneys belong exclusively to the Lord and should be burned on the altar (Leviticus 3:16).
- Only a priest can perform an animal sacrifice, and as compensation he gets some of the meat (Leviticus 3:5,11).
- Cattle, sheep, goats, doves, and pigeons are the animals to be sacrificed (various).
- One sacrifice requires an unblemished red heifer (Numbers 19).
- The sacrificial animals have to be without disease or injury and must be uncastrated (Leviticus 22:17–25).
- All offerings must be salted (Leviticus 2:13; Ezekiel 43:24).

The most important part of a sacrifice was the blood. Whether smeared down the side of the altar, splashed against it, or slathered on the animal's horns, the blood is what made the sacrifice valid. Here are God's words to Moses about blood:

> If anyone of the house of Israel or of the aliens who reside among them eats any blood, I will set my face against that person who eats blood, and will cut that person off from the people. For the life of the flesh is in the blood; and I have given it to you for making atonement for your lives on the altar; for, as life, *it is the blood that makes atonement.* Therefore I have said to the people of Israel: No person among you shall eat blood, nor shall any alien who resides among you eat blood. And anyone of the people of Israel, or of the aliens who reside among them, who hunts down an animal or bird that may be eaten shall pour out its blood and cover it with earth.
>
> For the life of every creature—its blood is its life; therefore I have said to the people of Israel: You shall not eat the blood of any creature, for the life of every creature is its

blood; whoever eats it shall be cut off. All persons, citizens or aliens, who eat what dies of itself or what has been torn by wild animals, shall wash their clothes, and bathe themselves in water, and be unclean until the evening; then they shall be clean. But if they do not wash themselves or bathe their body, they shall bear their guilt.[3]

The misuse of blood was considered criminal because blood is sacred. Since the blood is the stuff of life, the most precious fluid of all, the Lord deemed it the only acceptable offering (if only Cain had known this!). Under the various blood offerings explicated in the Hebrew scripture, two in particular were meant to appease God. One was called the *guilt offering*, brought when a person had desecrated a holy thing or perjured himself. Always a private offering, a guilt offering was meant as reparation—the guilty party repaid the damages plus 20 percent and made an offering in which the meat was split between the offended party and the officiating priest.

The other was called the *sin offering*. That's not to be confused with the Christian understanding of sin, for Christians tend to think of sin as an inherited darkness that stains the human soul. Jewish doctrine, however, doesn't consider sin in the abstract but is instead concerned with specific sins. Sin isn't a condition, it's an action (or inaction). Judaism teaches that sinning against God is inevitable. When a sin is committed, the sinner repents, and reunification takes place through a process of atonement.

This cycle isn't seen as bad or good; it just is. It's what it means to be human. It's the cycle that we're in because we're human, and like Eve and Adam, we have the blessing and curse of moral choice. Remember, according to the rabbis, before there was sin there was repentance. So first came repentance, then came sin, and finally came the mechanism to reunite humans with God: atonement, via a blood sacrifice.

Contrary to its name, the sin offering didn't really cleanse an individual of her or his sin. Torah is replete with punishment standards for crimes against other people, and it's also clear that sins against God cannot be atoned for, even by sacrifice.[4] Our common conception may be that sacrifice in the Hebrew Bible is to make things right between God and humans, but that's not what the text says. Instead, the sin offering atoned for sins committed unintentionally, and it cleansed the sanctuary of any remnant impurities. That's why it was used before just about every festival. A public rite, the sin offering was often a collective sacrifice by the people, and on the national Day of Atonement (Yom Kippur), the high priest brought a bull and two goats for the sin offering. Unlike the sacrifices on Pesach, which were memorial in nature, the sacrifices on Yom Kippur were real and active and timely. The bull and the unblemished goat were slaughtered on the altar in the Temple, their blood making atonement for the sin of the people over the past year.

The other goat brought by the high priest on Yom Kippur offers an interesting key to the Jewish understanding of atonement. While the bull and one goat were sacrificed as sin offerings on the altar in the Temple, the other goat had a different fate:

> Aaron shall offer the bull as a sin offering for himself, and shall make atonement for himself and for his house. He shall take the two goats and set them before the LORD at the entrance of the tent of meeting; and Aaron shall cast lots on the two goats, one lot for the LORD and the other lot for Azazel. Aaron shall present the goat on which the lot fell for the LORD, and offer it as a sin offering; but the goat on which the lot fell for Azazel shall be presented alive before the LORD to make atonement over it, that it may be sent away into the wilderness to Azazel.[5]

Azazel is commonly translated "scapegoat," but in fact the word's meaning is less than certain. A more detailed description of the rite from the Second Temple period is found in the Mishnah: the high priest cast lots—one was inscribed "for the Lord" and the other "for Azazel." The goat chosen for Azazel was bound with a crimson wool thread and brought to the city gates. As the high priest placed his hands on the goat, he prayed that all of Israel's transgressions would be put on the goat. Then the goat was sent to the wilderness.[6]

Some Christians prefer the scapegoat image of Jewish atonement because it's seemingly bloodless and without violence. Unfortunately, it's not that simple. For one thing, no one knows what the Hebrew word *Azazel* actually means. Some take it to mean the place to which the goat was sent, "a land which is cut off," a land of rocks and cliffs. But there's another opinion that takes *Azazel* to mean some kind of demonic power. This latter opinion is substantiated by the Levitical passage that draws a parallel between the Lord and Azazel—God gets a goat as a burnt offering, and Azazel gets one as a sin offering. Many rabbis follow this thinking and say that Azazel is a fallen angel—the one who taught human beings to create weapons, slept with their daughters, and was ultimately cast into the wilderness by the angel Raphael. Still others say that *Azazel* refers to the goat itself, a "scapegoat."

Then there's the often-overlooked fact that the goat was killed. History is a little foggy during the era of the original Temple, but not so during the Second Temple period. During those years, documentary evidence makes it clear that after the ceremony at the city gates, the goat was taken to a cliff, whereupon it was pushed off backward. By the time it was halfway down the cliff, the goat had been torn limb from limb.[7]

On Yom Kippur, the bull and both goats were killed. It was bloody. There's no way around that.

A Cycle of Bloody Worship

And so Israel got into a pattern with two great sacrificial feasts every year: Pesach in the spring and Yom Kippur in the fall. At each, animals were sacrificed, and their blood was spread, sprinkled, and scattered across an altar. One was historical, memorial, and messianic in nature, and one was timely and atonement-based.

Once the Israelites settled in the Promised Land of Canaan, the sacrificial rites and ceremonies became increasingly elaborate, prompting criticism from prophets: "For I desire steadfast love and not sacrifice, the knowledge of God rather than burnt offerings," said the Lord through Hosea.[8] Nevertheless, sacrifices continued, becoming an integral part of Hebrew life.

In the seventh century BCE, King Josiah assumed the throne of Israel and set about a major program of reform.[9] In fact, it seems that parts of the Torah had been misplaced and were recovered when the Temple was cleaned up. Josiah read the dire warnings of what would happen to those who did not keep the sacrificial commandments, and he renewed the covenant between Israel and God. Among his reforms were banning the worship of any god other than Yahweh and declaring that sacrifices could be performed only in the Temple.

As long as Israel lived in Canaan and had the Temple, that was no problem. But when they were exiled and the Temple destroyed in 586 BCE, it was a major problem. They were cut off from the ritual that had become central to their identity. Upon their return to Jerusalem in 516 BCE, they rebuilt the Temple and reconstituted sacrifice, until the Temple was once again destroyed, this time by the Romans in 70 CE. An identity crisis ensued—leading, as we've seen, to modern Judaism—because for the Hebrews, worship and sacrifice were inextricable from one another. There was no worship without blood sacrifice, and there was no blood sacrifice outside of worship. The importance of their connection is preeminent.

It was into this religious world that Jesus was born. Yet, oddly, Jesus says virtually nothing about the sacrificial system, neither condemning it nor praising it. To the early church, however, sacrifice was a major sticking point. One of the biggest debates in the first-century church was whether or not Christians could eat meat that had previously been sacrificed to idols, and the author of the New Testament book of Hebrews is consumed with the idea that Jesus' death is a repudiation of Hebrew sacrifice.

If nothing else, we've got to at least acknowledge how deeply ingrained the idea of blood sacrifice was to every Jew of the first century, including Jesus, Peter, and Paul. Almost immediately, the death of Jesus was seen by his followers as fitting into the framework of sacrifice that had been part of the Hebrew tradition since the beginning of time. And at the core of the sacrificial ritual was the relationship between God and humanity. So if Jesus was a part of that sacrificial framework, then his death must activate something unique in God's relationship with us. That's definitely what the early Christians thought, which we will see as we turn to the New Testament. But what we'll discover that's really interesting is that the Gospel writers and Paul chose to see the bloody death of Jesus in two different sacrificial frameworks.

What's a Christian to Do with All That Blood?

Blood sacrifice played an important and unavoidable role in the religion that birthed Christianity. But it is far from clear how we should understand the mechanics behind blood sacrifice and its effect on the God-human relationship. Christians tend to take one of three positions on the sacrificial system of the Hebrew Bible, each with different repercussions for how to understand the divine-human relationship.

The first posture some Christians take is to simply write off Israel's obsession with sacrifice and blood as remnants of primitive, tribal religion. They consider the practice a primitive holdover from an earlier time in which God was seen as a frightening deity who had to be appeased. Humans lived in fear of this primordial deity and sated his appetite with blood so he would not punish them. God's plan was to reject and overcome this ancient conception. Many Christians essentially commend the Hebrew Scripture for taking a major step forward in not requiring child sacrifice—the bloody slaughter of animals is bad, the thinking goes, but at least the Hebrews weren't killing their children and throwing virgins into volcanoes! These Christians prefer to essentially write off the Old

Testament as an interesting artifact of ancient folklore, but with little relevance for today.[10]

But this ignores the sacrificial system that is the very fabric of worship in the Hebrew scripture. For the Israelites, there was no worship without sacrifice. Today, a Christian might be able to imagine a worship service without a hymn or a sermon or a prayer, but an Israelite in the sixth century BCE could not have imagined worship in the Temple without the death of an animal. To put it quite plainly, God wanted blood sacrifice. Either the Israelites got it wrong—and very wrong for a lot of years—or else that's what God wanted.

The second position Christians take is that God really wants blood. Blood is the God-ordained way that humans can reorder their relationship with the Divine, and the Hebrew Bible unequivocally testifies to that. These Christians take the Old Testament at its most literal, setting up a system of blood sacrifice to appease God that ultimately sets the table for Jesus' crucifixion. We should fear this God, and we owe God our blood. Only by the sacrifice of God's Son on our behalf, and the shedding of Jesus' blood, can this debt be paid.

A third way that Christians make sense of Hebrew blood sacrifice is to consider that violence between human beings preceded religion. As religion took hold among humans, they used these evolving religious systems to make sense of everything in their lives: food, sex, offspring, tribes, and land. Each of these elements of life became sacred—that is, infused with meaning and holiness from the divine being. Violence is no different. Certain types of violence took on the tinge of sacredness.[11] For the worshippers of Molech, child sacrifice became sacred. For the followers of Yahweh, it was the slaughter of bulls, goats, and doves.

In this interpretation, it's not God who demands blood sacrifice. Instead, God takes something that human beings were already doing—being violent and shedding blood—and makes it sacred.[12] God does improve it by taking human sacrifice out of the equation, but still, God basically accepts violence, almost against his better judgment. God provides a system that we humans can understand, but it's not the perfect ideal that God wants to reveal "at the appointed time." The sacrificial system serves to organize and control violence, to give it boundaries. Priests are the gatekeepers of the system, and the inevitability of bloodshed is administered by them.

There is a fourth position, held by only a minority, but it's worthy of consideration. The basis for this position is that God is moving through time and history with us, and that God's responses to his relationship with humanity evolve as humanity evolves. We change, and God changes. As God's relationship with Israel developed, he anointed the sacrifice of animals as a key element in that relationship. In spite of its obvious shortcomings, God accepted it, perhaps because God knew that at this stage we needed it. From the prehistoric stories of Abel and Cain and of Noah disembarking from the ark, humans have had an impulse to offer something valuable to the Lord, even to offer the life of an animal. God built upon our impulse, regulating it through the law and the priesthood.

But when it didn't work anymore, then God knew that something had to change. And that's where Jesus comes in.

PART THREE

The Violence
on the Cross

7

History's Most Famous Execution

JESUS LOVES US, as the song goes, "This we know." But that's not all we need to know if we want to understand why he came, what he taught, and why—and by whom—he was executed. Over the centuries, several bad ideas about Jesus have arisen, some becoming very popular, and we will need to wade through these as well.

On our living room wall at home, we have a framed poster of one of my favorite works of art. It's called *The Census at Bethlehem* by the Flemish Renaissance painter Pieter Bruegel the Elder. Painted in 1566, it shows Joseph leading a donkey carrying pregnant Mary toward an inn. But the setting is not first-century Palestine. Instead, it's set in a sixteenth-century Flemish village: snow covers the ground; children ice skate on a frozen river; adults in topcoats and hats are gathered outside a pub; in the foreground, chickens peck food from the ground. Mary, Joseph, and their donkey are anachronisms in the painting.

Visit any major museum in Europe and you'll find paintings like this, in which the masters took biblical scenes and reimagined them in their own times, dressing biblical characters in the provincial garments of their own day, surrounding them with contemporary architecture. Art critics suspect that Bruegel was using this biblical scene to criticize bureaucracy in general, and possibly the severe administration of Spanish rule in the southern Netherlands during his time. The baby Jesus is dragged into sixteenth-century Flemish politics.

That's one of the problems in trying to figure out who Jesus was. Jesus seems to be everything to everyone. Walk into a hipster T-shirt shop on Venice Beach, and you're likely to find a shirt with the face of Jesus in the famous Jim Fitzpatrick portrait of Che Guevara, equating the Savior with the twentieth-century Marxist revolutionary. Go to the Christian store around the corner, and you'll find Jesus, wrapped in an American flag, riding a bald eagle, under a banner declaring, "One Nation Under God." If Jesus can be a Marxist to one person and a patriotic American to the next, then Jesus can be just about anything to just about anyone.

The tendency to turn Jesus into whatever we want him to be has been going on a long time. In the second half of the nineteenth century, German scholars were locked in the "quest for the historical Jesus," each attempting to strip away the mythologies that had accumulated around Jesus the literary and religious figure. They wanted to get back to the actual man, Jesus of Nazareth. In 1906, Albert Schweitzer published a book in which he claimed to conclusively end the debate. One by one, he picked off the theories of his rivals, showing that each was mistaken, being merely the projections by the scholars of who they wanted Jesus to be. Then he reached the apogee of his argument: Jesus of Nazareth was an itinerant, apocalyptic rabbi (who, by the way, was not divine). In one of the most famous paragraphs of theology ever written, Schweitzer concludes:

> There is silence all around. The Baptist appears, and cries: "Repent, for the Kingdom of Heaven is at hand." Soon after that comes Jesus, and in the knowledge that He is the coming Son of Man lays hold of the wheel of the world to set it moving on that last revolution which is to bring all ordinary history to a close. It refuses to turn, and He throws Himself

upon it. Then it does turn; and crushes Him. Instead of bringing in the eschatological conditions, He has destroyed them. The wheel rolls onward, and the mangled body of the one immeasurably great Man, who was strong enough to think of Himself as the spiritual ruler of mankind and to bend history to His purpose, is hanging upon it still. That is His victory and His reign.[1]

The irony is that Schweitzer himself found Jesus to be exactly who he wanted Jesus to be: a human prophet crying out for social justice for the disenfranchised and envisioning a new world of equality and tolerance. To the question, *Why did Jesus die?*, Schweitzer answers, "Because he was on a fool's errand." Schweitzer looked at Jesus and found an apocalyptic rabbi who was not divine, who was misunderstood, and who was later mythically deified by his followers. Like everyone else in the quest for the historical Jesus, Schweitzer made Jesus who he wanted Jesus to be: a very human man who preached brotherhood.

Shaping Jesus into one's own image is not just a modern phenomenon. Ancient emperors and medieval kings were happy to see Jesus as a Messianic High King, which perfectly supported these royals when they claimed to be Jesus' representatives on Earth. All this to say that from earliest times, Jesus has been everything from a general's vanguard in battle to a peripatetic peasant rabbi who was incapable of inaugurating the end times he preached.

I've already mentioned that I teach a class on Jesus, the Gospels, and the New Testament at a state university, and I can tell you that even undergrads who show up for class with dog-eared and highlighted Bibles need a primer in the outline of Jesus' life and death. So it's valuable for us to rehearse the facts about the life and death of Jesus, even though he's surely the most written-about figure in the history of literature. Only then can we draw some initial conclusions about what his life—and death—meant, and not end up with a Jesus of our own creation.

How Jesus Lived

Jesus was probably born in 6 or 4 BCE. Despite jokes to the contrary, there was no Year 0. And the medieval monk who counted backward to arrive at Jesus' birthday in 1 CE, the date by which we now number our lives, was off by a few years.

The most reliable accounts of Jesus' life come from three Gospels: Mark, Luke, and Matthew. Although they are unquestionably documents with theological agendas, they are nevertheless concerned with historical accuracy. Mark, the first, shortest, and rawest Gospel, was written in the early fifties. Luke and Matthew were both written within a decade of Mark, and each used Mark as a source, copying whole sections while making both minor and wholesale edits. The Gospel of John was written significantly later, probably between 90 and 100; while less reliable as a history of Jesus' actual life, it is more valuable in establishing Jesus' role and purpose, especially in the eyes of the early church.

Jesus grew up in obscurity. The Gospels tell us that Jesus was reared in Nazareth, a town in the region called Galilee. Little is known of Nazareth from Jesus' day—it isn't mentioned in any other historic source until the third century. So it was small—probably less than a thousand residents—and unimportant. Galilee itself is in the northern reaches of Israel, the historic home of the Israelite tribes of Dan and Naphtali. Primarily a rocky and mountainous region, Galilee is rich in orchards and farms and has abundant rainfall.

The Gospels also tell us that Jesus was a *tekton* and the son of a *tekton*. Tradition has taken that to mean that Joseph and Jesus were carpenters, but in fact *tekton* simply means "craftsman." Jesus could have just as well been a stonemason or a bricklayer. And although popular culture has portrayed Jesus as little more than a peasant, the region of Galilee in which Jesus grew up was relatively prosperous.

All four Gospels agree that at about age thirty, Jesus emerged from obscurity. In a rather dramatic fashion, his baptism by his locust-eating cousin, John, was accompanied by a voice from heaven, declaring, "You are my Son, the Beloved; with you I am well pleased."[2] After a lengthy, forty-day fast, Jesus walked out of the wilderness and into the public eye. Among his first acts, along with choosing some men and eventually women to follow him as he preached, was a dramatic episode in his hometown synagogue. Here's how Luke recounts it:

> *When he came to Nazareth, where he had been brought up, he went*
> *to the synagogue on the sabbath day, as was his custom. He stood*
> *up to read, and the scroll of the prophet Isaiah was given to him. He*
> *unrolled the scroll and found the place where it was written:*
> *"The Spirit of the Lord is upon me,*
> *because he has anointed me*
> *to bring good news to the poor.*
> *He has sent me to proclaim release to the captives*
> *and recovery of sight to the blind,*
> *to let the oppressed go free,*
> *to proclaim the year of the Lord's favor."*
> *And he rolled up the scroll, gave it back to the attendant, and sat*
> *down. The eyes of all in the synagogue were fixed on him. Then he*
> *began to say to them, "Today this scripture has been fulfilled in your*
> *hearing." All spoke well of him and were amazed at the gracious*
> *words that came from his mouth.*[3]

This is Jesus' inauguration speech. In it, he sets the course for the next three years of his life—indeed, this short homily lays out the plan for much of what's been done and said in his name for the past two millennia.

For the next three years, Jesus traveled on foot around Galilee, preaching sermons, performing miracles, and collecting followers. His message ranged from the compassionate:

> *Blessed are the poor in spirit, for theirs is the kingdom of heaven.*
> *Blessed are those who mourn, for they will be comforted.*
> *Blessed are the meek, for they will inherit the earth.*

*Blessed are those who hunger and thirst for righteousness, for they will
     be filled.*
Blessed are the merciful, for they will receive mercy.
Blessed are the pure in heart, for they will see God.
Blessed are the peacemakers, for they will be called children of God.[4]

to the apocalyptic:

> But when you see the desolating sacrilege set up where it
> ought not to be . . . , then those in Judea must flee to the
> mountains; the one on the housetop must not go down or
> enter the house to take anything away; the one in the field
> must not turn back to get a coat. Woe to those who are
> pregnant and to those who are nursing infants in those days!
> Pray that it may not be in winter. For in those days there will
> be suffering, such as has not been from the beginning of the
> creation that God created until now, no, and never will be.[5]

It's a treacherous exercise to sum up the teaching of Jesus, for it
was wide-ranging and not entirely consistent. But, if pressed, I'd say
that this is the core of Jesus' message: *a new age is dawning—the rules
by which followers of Yahweh lived their lives, while not irrelevant, are in
need of a serious overhaul; the spirit of those rules has been forgotten amid the
attempts to keep those rules; I've come to redefine the relationship between
God and humanity.*

Jesus, uniquely at one with God, taught that the ultimate rule
is love and that any other religious rule that did not extend God's
reign of love needed to be reconsidered. Jesus hinted that this rule of
love was even to be extended to non-Jews, and this became a major
theme of Paul's ministry and writing a couple of decades later.

As for the apocalyptic elements of Jesus' teaching, one has to remember that the apocalyptic was a common genre of preaching and
writing in the first century. When Jesus speaks about the "desolating
sacrilege" and warns pregnant women about the suffering they must
endure, he is both hearkening back to the prophets of the Hebrew

Bible and speaking in a style that people of his day understood. Just as many science fiction novels, movies, and TV shows today are really political commentaries on issues of the day, so were apocalyptic pronouncements in Jesus' day masked indictments of the Roman empire (the book of Revelation is a prime example of this). The ultimate message of Jesus' apocalyptic statements ends up being the same as that of his comforting Sermon on the Mount: *God is in charge, God will win the battle against evil, and, even if it seems scary at points, everything will turn out all right.*

Jesus' miracles can be understood in a similar way. Contrary to popular belief, they were not carnival acts meant to wow the crowds and convince everyone of his divinity—if that were the case, the miracles failed miserably, since none of Jesus' followers seemed to consider him a divine being until after his resurrection. Instead, the miracles showed in action what Jesus was teaching in his sermons and parables. With the nature miracles—calming a storm, walking on water, killing a fig tree, feeding large crowds—Jesus is showing God's power over nature.

And with the even more important people miracles—healing lepers, paralytics, blind men, and a bleeding woman; exorcizing demons; raising the dead—Jesus is reaching out to people who had been literally and figuratively cast out of God's kingdom, and he's bringing them back into God's kingdom. In fact, he is saying that bringing in the poor and outcast is a characteristic of the new kingdom that God is inaugurating.

Cleanliness really was next to godliness in first-century Judaism. Religious life centered on the Temple in Jerusalem—Yahweh himself was believed to be especially present there. But only "whole" persons were allowed to enter the Temple courts to experience Yahweh. People who were in any way "unclean" were prohibited from Temple worship—this included anyone who was physically infirm: the blind, the lame, the leprous, the bleeding, persons with mental illness and/or demons, and anyone who'd touched a dead body but not yet gone through a ritual bath. When Jesus healed these people, he was effectively ushering them back into the center of life with God and bypassing all the rules that had been set up to keep them out.

So when Jesus defended his disciples for picking grain on the Sabbath, he was essentially telling his interrogators that they misunderstood God's relationship with human beings. He was saying, in effect, *Yes, there are rules, but don't let the rules get in the way of loving God and others*. And when Jesus healed a leper, he was giving an object lesson in the same: by the power of God's Spirit, the people who have been excluded are now included.

Be it apocalyptic preaching or nature miracles or cryptic parables or miraculous healings, the entirety of Jesus' ministry—his three years on the road—was about telling and showing what the kingdom of God is really like. He was, in speech and action—indeed, in his very being—inaugurating something new, a new configuration of the relationship between God and humans. And Jesus himself was to become the very linchpin in this relationship.

Jesus' Passion

After about three years of peripatetic preaching and healing, Jesus and his followers set their sights on Jerusalem. No place was more important than Jerusalem for a follower of Yahweh in the year 30 CE. Today that city is still important in an unparalleled sense for all three Abrahamic religions. At the time, however, it was exclusively the capital of Judaism.

As we've learned, the Judaism we experience today did not exist in the first century. Jesus' era was a time of complex transition from the biblical Israelite religious practices of sacrifice and the priesthood to the early foundation of rabbinic Judaism, characterized by textual interpretation and the legal observance of the law as established by the rabbis and sages. Jesus' interlocutors, the Pharisees, were among the first of these rabbis. There were synagogues—houses of gathering—in which there was the public study and discussion of the Torah and prayer, but not yet any worship outside of the Temple.

The local synagogue played a relatively minor role in the religious life of most people.

When the Roman general Titus sacked Jerusalem and destroyed the Second Temple in 70 CE, however, these Jews had an identity crisis. Without the Temple, in which they observed their biblical religion, they were forced to reconsider everything. Local synagogues took on much greater meaning in peoples' lives, and the other books of the Hebrew Bible beyond the Pentateuch were codified. By the end of the first century, just as Christianity was forming a distinct identity, rabbinic Judaism—the basis of the religion that we know today as Judaism—had been born.

But before the fall of the Temple, Jerusalem was the capital of religious practice in a way that no place on Earth is today. Jerusalem was also where Jesus' passion would play out.

The Greek word for passion, *pascho* ("to have an experience," or, when used negatively, "to suffer") is used several times in the Gospels and Acts to refer to Jesus' final days, and it is similarly found in the Septuagint (the Greek translation of the Hebrew Bible) in passages that have traditionally been interpreted to predict Jesus' arrest, torture, and execution. (It should be noted that the contemporaries of Jesus, including his disciples, did not seem to have been expecting an executed Messiah. So these interpretations of Hebrew prophecy by Paul and the Gospel writers were all done in hindsight.) From that word, Christians have used the term *passion* to indicate the period in Jesus' life from his triumphal entry into Jerusalem—celebrated annually on Palm Sunday—up to his crucifixion.

In each of the four Gospels, Jesus' passion is the longest and most detailed sequence recounted in Jesus' life. The Gospel writers spend more ink on those six days than on anything else in Jesus' thirty-three years of life. In John, it's presented very much as a drama, leading to the common practice since the Middle Ages of passion plays. Each of the Gospel writers presents the passion as such, with John even giving scene settings that sound almost directorial. It is clearly a dramatic narrative they're presenting—maybe even a narrative drama.

As they recount the last week of Jesus' life, the Gospel writers have different emphases in their narratives.[6] Mark and Matthew share a perspective, and they probably shared source material as well. In their telling, Jesus is abandoned by his followers, left to die agonizingly alone. Framed by two prayers—in the Garden of Gethsemane, Jesus prays in Aramaic and Greek that his suffering might be avoided, and on the cross he prays in Aramaic, asking why God has abandoned him—the passion in Mark and Matthew seems to indicate the absence of God, but then God arrives just at the moment of Jesus' death. In both Gospels, the Temple curtain is torn in two, and in Matthew, there is an earthquake and dead bodies rise from graves. A strong theme leading up to the passion in both Gospels is that Jesus' followers themselves will have to follow his path, carry their own crosses, and endure suffering in his name. So it is significant both that the passion is excruciating in these Gospels and that God, albeit hidden, is not entirely absent.

In contrast, Luke's Gospel depicts God and Jesus in a less tortured relationship. When Jesus prays in the Garden, angels answer him back. And on the cross, Jesus offers entrance to paradise to a fellow victim and breathes his last after praying, "Father, into your hands I commend my spirit." Throughout Luke's Gospel, the focus is on healing, on Jesus' ministry to women, and on forgiveness, and these themes continue through the passion and crucifixion. In Luke, the passion and crucifixion of Jesus are more salutary than in Matthew and Mark.

In John, the passion of Jesus is not so much tragic as it is triumphant. Written decades later than the other Gospels, the Fourth Gospel is both more theologically sophisticated and more hopeful than the Synoptics. In John's telling, Jesus' passion is leading him toward his ultimate destination: eternal glory at the right hand of the Father. Jesus is portrayed as a king, though a hidden one, throughout the passion of the Fourth Gospel, even concluding with a somewhat regal entombment, as opposed to the hasty burial of the first three Gospels. The Johannine passion can best be summarized by a passage from another New Testament book, 1 John: "For whatever is born of God conquers the world. And this is the victory that con-quers the world, our faith."[7]

In spite of their different emphases, the four Gospels are largely in agreement on the outline of the passion. On Sunday, Jesus came into Jerusalem to great acclaim. Jews at the time expected a Mes-siah, just as many do today. And they expected certain things of that Messiah: he would be a great military or political leader or both; he would unite the people; he would reclaim King David's throne in the Temple; and he would expel the Roman oppressors. Based on the Gospels' portrayal of Jesus' entry into Jerusalem, it seems that a collection of his followers and that city's residents thought that Jesus might be just the Messiah they'd been hoping for. With shouts of "Hosanna!" and coats and palm branches laid at his feet, Jesus was welcomed into Jerusalem as a prophet and possibly as a liberator.

But as the week wore on, it became increasingly clear that, if Jesus was a Messiah, he wasn't the kind of Messiah that they'd been hop-ing for. Early in the week, Jesus threw a fit in the Temple, castigating the money changers and animal peddlers therein. He ate meals with his followers, and at one of those meals a woman anointed his feet with oil over the disciples' objections, a clear precursor to his death. He continued to preach and heal. All the while, the Gospel writers tell us, the religious leaders in Jerusalem were plotting to silence the wild-eyed Nazarene preacher.

Ultimately, those leaders convinced one of Jesus' compatriots, Judas, to betray him. On or around the Passover celebration, Jesus celebrated one last dinner with his followers, from which Judas ex-cused himself to complete his transaction as betrayer. While we have a lot of detail about this dinner, the nature of Jesus' comments are something of a conundrum. Paul, who was not present at the din-ner, wrote to the Christians in Corinth that Jesus connected that dinner—and every subsequent commemoration of that dinner—to his own death, indeed, to the tearing of his flesh and spilling of his blood. Three of the four Gospels also record Jesus' words, each with slight variations. The connection of the Last Supper to the blood sacrifice of Pesach is clear.

Following dinner, Jesus and his disciples retreated to a grove of olive trees, where Jesus prayed and the disciples slept. The Gospel writers give us some of Jesus' most poignant words in this scene. He is deeply distressed. He prays that God will take away the cup of suffering that he is about to experience, and he chides his disciples for not staying awake during his hour of need. Judas arrives in the grove with a coterie of soldiers, indicating to them which Galilean is the marked man by kissing Jesus. From there, Jesus is taken, jailed, beaten, mocked, and bandied back and forth between Jewish and Roman officials. Everyone wants him silenced, but no one, it seems, wants to be responsible for his fate.

The Gospels tell us that Jesus was tried before a Sanhedrin court and that he also stood before Herod, the Jewish governor, and Pontius Pilate, the Roman prefect.[8] Through it all, Jesus is portrayed as carrying himself stoically, answering his inquisitors rarely and briefly, and even evoking a slap across the face from a soldier and the high priest who demanded, "Have you no answer?"

In the end, Pilate assents to the demands of the crowd—a crowd that has turned on Jesus in less than a week—and, though he washes his hands and attempts to deny responsibility, Pilate sentences Jesus to be executed by crucifixion.

How Jesus Died

In the famous closing scene from Stanley Kubrick's cast-of-thousands epic, *Spartacus*, Varinia (Jean Simmons) visits her slave lover, Spartacus (Kirk Douglas), with their newborn son. Spartacus, having earned the ire of the Roman general Crassus (Laurence Olivier), is hanging on a cross, dying the long, slow death of crucifixion. As Varinia and the child roll away in a wagon, the camera pulls back to reveal hundreds, if not thousands, of men hanging from crosses on either side of the road. The viewer is left with the feeling that this great hero warrior is dying an anonymous and ignominious death, just another slave, one among thousands. The scene also serves to shatter the illusion that Jesus' death on a cross was somehow unique. Historians think that about six thousand men were crucified when Rome defeated the rebelling slaves in the Third Servile War in 71 BCE. That's a lot of crosses.

Crucifixion was a common form of execution for over a millennium, from at least the sixth century BCE until the Emperor Constantine banned it in 337 CE out of respect for Jesus. After one battle, Alexander the Great (356–323 BCE) crucified two thousand defeated Tyrian soldiers. Three centuries later, the Roman Empire embraced crucifixion; it was considered a particularly humiliating way to die and thus was used for slaves, pirates, and insurrectionists. Roman citizens were exempt from the ignominy of crucifixion.

Unlike a firing squad or lethal injection or the gallows, crucifixion does not kill in an instant. Instead, it's a long, torturous death. The ancient church wasn't concerned with the medical explanation of how Jesus died; it wasn't until 1805 that there was any published account hypothesizing about the cause of death. In 1847, J. C. Stroud, M.D., proposed that Jesus died from a violent rupture of the heart; this theory long held sway, making for many imaginative sermons. But as cardiac medicine advanced, doctors discovered that heart valves rupture due to disease, not mental anguish.

In 1950, a French surgeon suggested that victims of crucifixion actually die from asphyxia. Pulling up on the spikes through the arms, and pushing on the spike through the legs, the victim can take in breath. But as exhaustion sets in, the victim cannot rise enough to breathe; the muscles that facilitate inhalation and exhalation similarly become exhausted; ultimately, exhalation of carbon dioxide from the lungs becomes impossible, suffocating the victim.

There are other, equally horrible aspects of crucifixion that, while they may not have killed Jesus, surely accelerated his death. For one, he likely lost a great deal of blood from the scourging he suffered at the hands of Roman guards and the crown of thorns they pressed into his scalp, since cuts to the head cause significant blood loss.

Some recent studies have cast doubt on the asphyxiation thesis, positing the cause of death as shock and dehydration. Indeed, a crucifixion would likely send anyone into shock. Popular depictions most often show Jesus with a spike through each hand, and one through his stacked feet. But in fact it's most likely that the spikes went through his wrists or forearms, between the radius and ulna bones, and that each of his heels was nailed to a side of the upright beam of the cross.

Whatever the medical cause of death, crucifixion was just as the Romans intended: long, agonizing, humiliating (the victims were often naked), and excruciating (a word that is derived from *crucifixion*).

The Gospels differ somewhat on the details of Jesus' crucifixion—in Mark and Matthew, he is abandoned; in John, his mother and others keep vigil as he dies. In Mark and Matthew, a fellow Jew mockingly offers Jesus some vinegary wine on a sponge; in Luke, Roman soldiers offer the wine; in John, an unspecified "they" offer it.

But in each, Jesus dies. Unequivocally. Even the apocryphal gospels, written in the second and third centuries, agree on this:

Jesus died.

He died on a cross.

He died at the hands of the Roman Empire.

He died at the provocation of his coreligionists.

And in his death, the disciples' hopes for a military-general-messiah were dashed. On Good Friday, all they've got is a dead messiah. In fact, they likely thought that they had a dead pretender-to-the-throne.

And just as quickly as Jesus of Nazareth came to Rome's attention, he was forgotten. Merely a blip on the imperial radar screen.

To his followers, however, his death became an event of unparalleled importance, due primarily to his resurrection. As reported by three of the four Gospels, Jesus appeared to his followers in the days and weeks following his death, inciting them to interpret his death differently than every other crucifixion they had witnessed. It led them and succeeding generations to reinterpret the words he'd said predicting his death. They began to understand his death cosmically and theologically.

They began to see his death as an act of God.

Who Killed Jesus?

We're trying to solve a mystery. Can we find any answers—even preliminary ones—looking at just the Gospel accounts of Jesus' life? Without turning to Paul or to the other New Testament writers, and without cataloging the various answers proffered by theologians over the past two thousand years, who do the Gospels say killed Jesus, and why?

As it turns out, the Gospels are not acutely interested in our question. Mark, as we've noted, is the earliest, shortest, and most stylistically primitive Gospel. It is also relatively unconcerned with pinning responsibility for Jesus' death on one party or another.

After Jesus enters Jerusalem during passion week, he cleanses the Temple, and Mark reports, "And when the chief priests and the scribes heard it, they kept looking for a way to kill him; for they were afraid of him, because the whole crowd was spellbound by his teaching."[9] But Jesus and his disciples had retreated from the city for the night. Later in the week, Jesus publicly condemns the scribes, saying they act nice in religious settings but are actually faking their prayers and stealing the houses of widows.[10] By the end of the week, the chief priests and scribes had cooked up a plot to have Jesus killed.[11]

The Jewish priests of the first century can basically be understood in three levels: the everyday priests, which Jesus never mentions; the chief priests, a kind of aristocratic class; and the high priest, Caiaphas at the time of Jesus' passion. The chief priests were in Rome's pocket; they had money and power in Jerusalem, and the Roman government let them run the city as long as peace was kept. Jesus was a clear threat to the status quo, prompting their retaliation against him.

There are various other actors in the scenes leading to Jesus' death. The Pharisees were a religiopolitical party in Jerusalem that propagated a particular interpretation and application of the law, and they seem to have been the most powerful political force in the city in 30 CE. The scribes were teachers of the law and aligned with the Pharisees, and they fiercely opposed Jesus at every turn, both in his home region of Galilee and in the capital, Jerusalem. Presbyters ("elders") came up against Jesus, too, and these were probably local synagogue leaders, in Jerusalem for Pesach.

Together, the chief priests, scribes, and presbyters form the Sanhedrin, a court convened to judge matters both religious and legal, since the two were very much intertwined at the time. They considered their job to guard Jewish religious and political life, though all their decisions were also made with an eye toward Rome. In their view, Jesus was fomenting a revolution by breaking Sabbath and cleanliness laws, teaching new forms of prayer, and generally introducing a novel posture toward God. It was the Sanhedrin court that made the pact with Judas, had Jesus arrested, and tried him for blasphemy. But their guilty verdict was the extent of their jurisdiction. Only the Romans could put a person to death in cases like this, so the court turned Jesus over to Pilate, who reluctantly ordered his soldiers to crucify him.

In a strictly historical sense, Jesus was killed by Jewish and Roman leaders working in collusion with one another. But in the early church, the blame was poured mainly on the Jews; and in the subsequent centuries, blame has been placed exclusively on the Jews. Matthew, breaking with Mark and Luke, takes up the issue of responsibility for Jesus' death, and he lays it at the feet of the Jewish leaders. Matthew co-opts passages from the Hebrew Bible about the innocent blood being on the hands of the executioners. And in a scene unique to Matthew, Judas repents of his betrayal, saying, "I have sinned by betraying innocent blood." When he tries to give back the money he was paid for turning on Jesus, he is rebuffed, and he hangs himself.[12]

The more troubling quote comes later in the chapter. Pilate, upset that the crowd was threatening to riot if he didn't execute this innocent man, symbolically washes his hands—a Jewish custom—and declares, "I am innocent of this man's blood; see to it yourselves."[13] Matthew writes, "Then the people as a whole declared, 'His blood be on us and on our children!' "[14] No longer is it just the Jewish leaders who want Jesus dead. Now it seems to be all Jews.

No verse has a more terrible legacy in all the Bible than this one. And the Gospel of John has reinforced this as well, since that Gospel is far less precise about who plotted Jesus' death, preferring the phrase "the Jews" to any talk about chief priests, scribes, and presbyters.

To our question *Who killed Jesus?* the answer too often has been *The Jews!* The unconscionable anti-Semitism and anti-Judaism promulgated by this verse started in the early church and runs through the Crusades and Hitler to white supremacy in our own day. In 240 CE, the early church father Origen wrote, "For this reason the blood of Jesus is not only on those who lived at the moment but on all the generations of Jews that followed till the end of time."[15] Even earlier than that, in about 170 CE, Melito, the bishop of Sardis, preached, "God has been murdered; the King of Israel has been removed by an Israelite hand."[16] These sentiments have been tragically repeated by some of the greatest theologians in church history.[17] For centuries, Jews have been accused of deicide, and they've paid mightily in blood and anguish.

But the accusations against the Jews in the Gospels of Matthew and John must be understood in their historical context. First, those were brutal times. Religious and political violence was terribly common, and proto-Judaism itself was not exempt. In the two centuries leading up to Jesus' birth, various factions of Jews had fought for control of the religion, razed one another's temples, and assassinated rival priests. In the Judean Civil War in the first century BCE, over fifty thousand Jews were killed. When it ended, the victorious King Alexander Jannaeus crucified eight hundred Pharisee men, slaughtering their wives and children before their eyes as they hung on crosses. As I said, it was a brutal time, and religious violence was well known outside and inside Judaism.

More to the point, Jesus was a religious revolutionary. Even scholars who reject his divinity, his miracles, and his resurrection concede that Jesus' preaching was a radical departure from the dominant religiopolitical parties in first-century Jerusalem. So out of step with traditional interpretations of the law was Jesus that he was opposed by the Pharisees, the Sadducees, the Herodians, the scribes, the presbyters, and the chief priests. In other words, he was opposed by everyone in power. Even when they agreed on nothing else, they agreed that Jesus should be silenced.

When he entered Jerusalem on Palm Sunday, Jesus had at least part of the festival crowd on his side. By Friday, most of the crowd had turned on him. Maybe it was because he hadn't fulfilled their expectations of a military leader. Maybe it was because the leaders had convinced them otherwise. No matter the reason, the people didn't turn on Jesus because they were Jews. They turned on Jesus because they were human.

No matter the cultural, political, and religious system into which God incarnated himself in Jesus, he would have faced massive and violent opposition. Religious people in any time and any place would have rejected Jesus' message, and religious leaders of any age would have silenced him. Today, those of us who live in the West tolerate religious difference, but that's a recent and local phenomenon. And as we know from history, no religion has been more violent in quashing dissenting voices than Christianity.

Passover Undertones

It's one thing to look at the historical record and pin the responsibility for Jesus' death on a group of people who were part of a particular religiopolitical system. But their responsibility is historically contingent, and it doesn't make them guilty of the death of God. The four Gospels are relatively silent on the question of guilt, and even more so on the question *What did Jesus' death accomplish?* The first person to really grapple with that question wrote before the Gospels were written, but he came to faith in Jesus after all of the disciples. That person is Paul, and he more than anyone else set the framework by which we will attempt to solve the mystery of the meaning of Jesus' death.

But the Gospel writers do make one thing explicit in that they tie Jesus' death to Passover. The entire passion narrative in all four Gospels takes place leading up to the celebration of Pesach. Jerusalem is crowded with hordes of people in town to celebrate. And instead of defying or ignoring this Jewish custom, Jesus plunges headfirst into the throng. He verbally and physically attacks the apparatus of blood sacrifice when he cleanses the Temple, and this more than any other act leads to his arrest and execution. Jesus' final meal with his disciples, described at length in the Fourth Gospel, is a Passover meal. Mark, Luke, and Matthew agree that the Last Supper took place "on the first day of unleavened bread, when they sacrificed the Passover lamb."[18] And he is crucified on Pesach.

The blood of Jesus, according to the Gospels, is the blood of deliverance. Like the original Passover lamb, whose blood saved Israel from the plague of death and freed them from bondage, the Gospels cast the blood of Jesus as liberating the people by bringing new life. Through blood, the Lord saved Israel on Pesach, and through blood the Lord saved humanity through Jesus.

The Gospels honestly don't have an explicit theological view of this. It's more implied than anything. Paul, on the other hand, does have a very sophisticated view of *why Jesus died,* and his view is not always consonant with the Gospels.

8

Paul's Cross-Centered Life

I KNOW THIS guy who, as a teenager, read an article in *Popular Science*—one of those articles that says we use only 15 percent of our brains and speculates about what the human race might be capable of if we figured out how to use more of it. As proof of this claim, the article suggested this: try reading a novel upside down and from back to front. Your brain, the article claimed, is amazing and will be able to decode the novel. You will understand the book by the time you finish it.

Being a nerdy fourteen-year-old living in the moonscape of West Texas, my friend decided to give it a try. And lo and behold, it worked. He understood the book, even though he'd read it upside down and backward. Now, as a result of training his brain, this guy can read four hundred pages per hour. You might call my friend "scary smart." The more I read the letters of the Apostle Paul, I suspect that his contemporaries would use the same words to describe him.

And, as it turns out, Paul came to understand Jesus' life the same way—in reverse.

Getting the Story Backward

Mostly, we hear stories from beginning to end. That's how we make sense of a plot. The three-act play, on which almost every movie is based, follows the beginning to end format: 1) cat gets stuck in tree; 2) several unsuccessful attempts are made to get cat out of tree; 3) cat gets rescued from tree. But occasionally a story comes along that's told in reverse—like the film *Memento* or the *Seinfeld* episode in which the cast attends a wedding in India—and we realize that we can, in fact, make sense of stories that are told in reverse or in other discombobulated ways. We mentally rearrange the parts, and the story goes from nonsensical to comprehensible.

Peter, John, Mary, Martha, and the other disciples had seen Jesus' life unfold in a conventional manner. They'd joined him on his journeys, heard him teach and seen him perform miracles, watched his popularity grow among the crowds and the opposition harden among the leaders of the Temple. They'd witnessed his betrayal, arrest, and crucifixion. He'd appeared to them—bodily—after his death, and he was ultimately swept into the clouds before their eyes.

The Gospels and Acts are rife with examples of the disciples slowly getting it, understanding who Jesus was and what his mission was. It dawned on them over time that Jesus was the Messiah, albeit an unexpected Messiah. In the Gospel of Mark, this transition from nonunderstanding to understanding is explained with a story. A blind man is brought to Jesus when he's in Bethsaida. Jesus puts saliva on his hands and places his hands on the man's eyes.[1]

"Can you see anything?" Jesus asks.

"I can see people, but they look like trees, walking," the man responds.

Jesus touches the man's eyes again, and the blind man's sight is completely restored. Mark reports, "And he saw everything clearly."

This story stands right at the center of Mark's Gospel, and the author is sending his readers a message. The disciples, portrayed as bumbling fools in the first half of the Gospel, don't see who Jesus really is. But in the second half, the scales begin to fall from their eyes, and over time they see clearly that Jesus is the Messiah. The Gospels, written in the sixties (Mark), seventies (Matthew and Luke), and nineties (John), tell the story of Jesus much the way that the disciples experienced it, from beginning to end. And most of us learn the story in just that way, starting with Jesus' birth in a stable and ending with his death on a cross.

Paul had no such luxury. He didn't meet Jesus during Jesus' life. He never saw a miracle, heard a sermon, or witnessed a debate with the Pharisees (his own political party). Instead, he met the Risen Christ on the road as he was making his way to Damascus, intent on persecuting Christians. In an instant, sometime in the midthirties, Paul went from a persecutor of Christians to a Christian himself. He immediately began preaching Jesus as the Messiah but was quickly set upon by his former compatriots.

Even Christians doubted him; in Acts, Luke reports that shortly after the Damascus Road conversion, Paul went to Jerusalem to meet the disciples—in Galatians, Paul writes that this is three years after his conversion—but "they were all afraid of him, for they did not believe that he was a disciple."[2] At that point, Paul exits the scene, and he's not heard from again for several years.

We know nothing of the "lost years" of Paul. But in the decade between his dramatic conversion and his first missionary journey, Paul clearly did a lot of thinking about the meaning of Jesus' life, death, and resurrection. Based on the dozen or so letters of his that we have, he concluded that the death and resurrection of Jesus were of supreme importance. Jesus' life? Not so much. In all of Paul's letters, there's not one mention of Jesus teaching a parable, nothing about the miracles, no allusion to his birth in a manger. Maybe Paul didn't know about these aspects of Jesus' life—the Gospels likely weren't written until after Paul's letters were completed—or maybe he heard the stories of Jesus' life and considered them unimportant. In either case, Paul pays the life of Jesus no heed. The death and resurrection of Jesus, on the other hand, are Paul's foremost concern. When he looked back on Jesus, that's all that mattered to him.

Paul's epiphany was that the long-awaited Jewish Messiah had come as expected, but he'd come in a *way* that was totally unexpected. Paul could have turned his back on Judaism altogether. That's what most people do when they convert: they go from one religion to another, taking nothing with them. When I visited Sri Lanka,

I asked a couple of Christians who had converted from Hinduism what they maintained from the religion of their youth. "Nothing!" they assured me, going on to tell me that the gods of the Hindu religion are demonic. I get much the same response from several of my friends who grew up Christian but are now atheists. There is *nothing* about Christianity that they embrace.

Paul could have done this same thing. He could have rejected Judaism in toto. He could have embraced Jesus as the savior of the world without also considering Jesus the Jewish Messiah—many converts since Paul have made this very choice.

But that's not what Paul did. Instead, he racked his brain and his spirit to figure out a way that Jesus' death and resurrection fit into Israel's longstanding story about themselves and God. What he came up with shaped Christianity indelibly and irreversibly.

N. T. Wright, the preeminent Bible scholar working today, says that one verse in all of Paul's letters says more about the meaning of Jesus' death than any other—Romans 8:3: "For God has done what the law (being weak because of human flesh) was incapable of doing. God sent his own son in the likeness of sinful flesh, and as a sin-offering; and, right there in the flesh, he condemned sin." [3]

To Paul's way of thinking, after the torturous prehistory of Eve and Adam, Abel and Cain, the Tower of Babel, and the ark and the rainbow, God made an everlasting covenant with Abraham and his descendants. They, the Israelites, were uniquely bound to God, in particular through the rite of circumcision and later through the law of Moses.

But after his conversion, Paul saw the law differently. As he spells out most explicitly in his letter to the Galatian church, Paul came to believe that the purpose of the law was not to bring Israel closer to God, but to show Israel how impossible it is to do what God wants.[4] The law, it turns out, is not the savior; the law shows us our need for a savior.

The law does this by 1) defining sin, and 2) establishing the means of mitigating the consequences of sin through food laws and the sacrificial system. "Through the law comes the knowledge of sin,"

Paul writes to the Romans.[5] The Israelites had a unique understanding of God's Law because it had been delivered only to them, but consequently they were uniquely accountable for upholding it. Even Moses, to whom the law was delivered, warned the Israelites that their knowledge of the law meant that the curse of the law would fall uniquely on them.[6] Indeed, Paul writes, even Christ himself was cursed by the law—more accurately, he became the curse of the law.[7] In other words, even Jesus was not exempt from the consequences of the law.

According to Paul, the law killed Jesus.

Paul on the Crucifixion

The cross is everything to Paul.

For Paul, the "cross of Christ" is a metonym, a word or phrase that acts as a substitute for another, like when journalists use "Washington" as shorthand for the U.S. federal government.[8] According to Paul, the cross *is* the gospel, and he uses the "cross of Christ" as a stand-in for the gospel throughout his letters, just as he uses "Christ crucified" as a primary identifier of Jesus. For example: "May I never boast of anything except the cross of our Lord Jesus Christ, by which the world has been crucified to me, and I to the world."[9]

The cross is also the primary interpretive lens through which Paul understands most everything: his former life, his new life, the law, the Hebrew scripture, and the life of Jesus. It is Jesus' death on the cross that reveals the righteousness of God, and Jesus' death on the cross that results in our justification. The cross both fulfills and shows the limits of the law. The cross culminates the various covenants that God has made with Israel through Adam, Noah, Abraham, and Moses. The cross fulfills Old Testament prophecies. The cross discloses the self-sacrificial nature of God. The cross exhibits the love-bond between the Father and the Son. And the cross shows followers of Jesus and lovers of God how they are to live.

The cross is like a giant reset button that God pushed in his relationship with humans and with all of creation. As a result, new things were revealed about God and humanity. Some elements of that relationship, like blood sacrifices and circumcision, were made unnecessary; other elements, like hospitality to the stranger and love of neighbor, were amplified. The whole cosmic state of affairs was rejiggered by Jesus' death.

Paul's letters make up over half of the New Testament, and out of all that, two passages stand above the rest in explicating Paul's view of the cross: Romans 3 and Romans 7–8.

Paul's letter to the Romans is unique in that it's the only time he wrote to a church that he hadn't visited—all of his other congregational correspondence is to churches that he launched himself. He writes to the Romans with a much less paternalistic tone than he does to, say, the Corinthians or Thessalonians. His purpose in writing is to introduce himself—he's planning to visit the church in Rome on his way to Spain, and he wants to collect from them an offering for the church in Jerusalem—and to establish his theological bona fides. As such, the first eight chapters of Romans are the closest thing we have to Paul's system of theology.

We don't know how his letter was received by the church in Rome. Paul did wind up in Rome, but not as he'd planned. He was brought there under house arrest and spent two years pleading his case—and probably teaching the Roman Christians—before he was beheaded by imperial soldiers. Over the spot of his burial today stands the magnificent church San Paulo Fuori le Mura (St. Paul Outside the Walls).

Now let's look a little more closely at those two passages.

Romans 3

The backdrop to Paul's famous lines in Romans 3 comes a chapter earlier.[10] The promises of God were delivered to the Jews—they are God's covenant people. But, Paul argues, God's promises were not exclusively *for* the Jews; they came *through* the Jews. "God shows no partiality," Paul writes, after saying that both good and bad come through the law, to "the Jew first and also to the Greek."[11] Israel was "entrusted with the oracles of God," Paul goes on to say, but he continues to make clear that that was for the sake of all humanity.[12] Israel is the conduit through which God achieves the redemption of the world.

Many books have been written by commentators on two words in this chapter, each of which, when read correctly, redirects the entire narrative plumb line of Romans. The first dispute is over a mere preposition. The traditional translation of Romans 3:21–22 reads, "But now, apart from the law, the righteousness of God has been disclosed, and is attested by the law and the prophets, the righteousness of God through faith in Jesus Christ for all who believe." But the Greek genitive case doesn't necessarily mean "in." It can also mean "of." Thus, with one slight change, this passage and much of Paul's theology takes a turn: " . . . the righteousness of God through the faith *of* Jesus Christ for all who believe."[13] Now we see this narrative arc differently: God is faithful. That's the message. And that's a big part of Paul's message in all of Romans. God's redemptive plans will not be thwarted, even though Israel has consistently stumbled over the law.

Then Paul reaches his crescendo: in Jesus the Messiah, all of God's promises are funneled and fulfilled. It is God's faithfulness to his plan, and Jesus' faithfulness to that same plan, that is the good news for both Jews and Gentiles. N. T. Wright explains it this way:

(A) The covenantal God promises to rescue and bless the world through Israel.
(B) Israel as it stands is faithless to this commission.
(C) The covenantal God, however, *is* faithful, and will provide a faithful Israelite—*the* faithful Israelite, the Messiah.[14]

The other disputed word comes in the very next sentence. Paul continues his thoughts, "They are now justified by his grace as a gift, through the redemption that is in Christ Jesus, whom God put forward as a sacrifice of atonement by his blood, effective through faith."[15]

The word translated "sacrifice of atonement" doesn't mean exactly that. Actually, it refers not to a concept or idea, but to a place: the spot in the Temple where sacrifices were made. "Place of atonement" is a better translation, or even "Mercy Seat." Again, Paul is saying that everything that's gone before, the entire history of Israel—the Passover, the Exodus, the Temple sacrifices—is concentrated into the person of Jesus. God's faithfulness comes to its climax in the life of Jesus and, ultimately, in his death and resurrection.

Romans 7–8

Again we have to back up a bit since Paul hits this chapter already running full speed. In his on-ramp in the previous chapter, Paul again makes clear that the problem in the triangular relationship of God, the law, and humans wasn't God, and it wasn't the law. It was the humans. Because of our frailty, which we inherited from Adam, human beings are incapable of keeping the law. Paul writes that our flesh has weakened the law, rendering it impotent to save us. All the law is able to do is to remind us that we're frail, also known as "sinful." This could be seen as a weakness of the law, but Paul thinks it's a strength, for the law is doing its job perfectly, namely, showing us our need for a savior.

According to Paul, the law had been misunderstood by his fellow Jews, just as it had by him when he was a Pharisee. The law cannot save; the law can only show us that we need to be saved. Indeed, the law brings human sinfulness and our need of salvation into their most fully concentrated form, to a single focal point, so that it can be dealt with once and for all.[16]

In Romans 3, the entire sacrificial history of Israel is concentrated in Jesus the Messiah, so in Romans 7–8 is all of human sin concentrated in him. Then, on the cross and in the person who represented Israel most perfectly, all sin is condemned.

What this *doesn't* mean is that Jesus died because you and I sinned. Instead, it means that sin is endemic to the human condition, that it needed to be conquered, and that on the cross it was. What some see here—that God demanded sacrificial recompense because his holy honor had been disparaged—isn't really there. Yes, Jesus acts as a substitute for us, but it's not to appease a wrathful God. Instead, it is to vanquish sin.

Like all Jews of his day, Paul both expected and longed for the Messiah. Exactly no one, Paul included, expected the Messiah to be defeated and executed by the Romans. They expected just the opposite. The Messiah was going to free Israel from oppression, expel the foreign colonizers, and finally bring about the national sovereignty that had long been promised. This very expectation is what prompted the leaders of the Temple in Jerusalem to reject the claims of Jesus' followers that Jesus was the Messiah, so they colluded with the Roman governor to have him killed.

Therefore, when Paul was confronted by the Risen Christ on the road to Damascus, he had to recalibrate himself intellectually, spiritually, and theologically. He went away for a few years to get his head straight, and he did a one-eighty. When he emerged as a Christian preacher and church planter, as described in the second half of Acts, he had made sense of a crucified Messiah. His theological rationale for an executed savior consumes much of his writing, and the outworking of that—the ethics of the Christian life, how a Christian is to live in the shadow of the crucifixion—can rightly be said to comprise his entire corpus.

It can be argued that Paul was the *first* theologian, that he *invented* theology. Athens had its philosophers, and Jerusalem had its priests and prophets, but Paul was the first person to really theologize about religious events. And the prime event about which he theologized was the crucifixion and the puzzle of an executed Messiah.

When I teach "Introduction to the New Testament" at the state university, I always give the undergrads the same assignment for the final essay. After a semester of the Gospels and Acts and Paul and the other letters of the New Testament, I ask the students to take a position on this question and explain their answer: "Did Paul continue the religion that was started by Jesus, or did he use an aspect of Jesus' life to launch a new religion?"

There are two reasons that I can even ask this question: (1) the Gospel writers are almost completely uninterested in the meaning of Jesus' death, and (2) Paul is almost completely uninterested in the meaning of Jesus' life.

Some look at Paul's theologizing about the crucifixion and see an exclusively substitutionary view. But N. T. Wright cautions us not to impute this to Paul. Paul's view of the efficacy of Jesus' death, Wright argues, is far more complex than many would like to admit. In fact, Paul is anything but unequivocal, and Wright sees at least six aspects to Paul's understanding of the atonement: representation, substitution, sacrifice, judicial punishment, Israel's purpose, and divine victory.[17] Each of these themes can be found in Paul's letters and sermons. As we've already discovered, the death of Jesus contains a surplus of meaning, and surely there is not one single take on his death that answers every question or exhausts all possibilities, at least not for Paul.

However, Paul does introduce an innovation that we didn't see in the Gospels. For the writers of Mark, Luke, Matthew, and John, the death of Jesus was seen exclusively through the lens of the Passover sacrifice—a Messiah leading the people into liberation. While Paul acknowledges this, he also introduces the idea that Jesus was the Yom Kippur sacrifice, an atonement in blood, meant to cleanse sin. It's not that Paul disagrees with the Gospels; it's that he emphasizes a very different part of Jewish sacrificial life. And Paul stresses individual human sin as making Jesus' atoning blood necessary, an idea that is absent from the Gospels.

Living the Crucifixion

God revealed something essential about himself in the crucifixion. That's central for Paul. What God revealed is that he is unequivocally on the side of human beings—*all* human beings, both Jew and Gentile. And if the crucifixion tells us something central about

God, it also tells us something about how we're supposed to live as followers of God. Several of Paul's more memorable lines continue this theme:

> Romans 6:6—"We know that our old self was crucified with him so that the body of sin might be destroyed, and we might no longer be enslaved to sin."
>
> Galatians 2:20—"It is no longer I who live, but it is Christ who lives in me. And the life I now live in the flesh I live by faith in the Son of God, who loved me and gave himself for me."
>
> Galatians 5:24—"And those who belong to Christ Jesus have crucified the flesh with its passions and desires."

I was talking to Rabbi Joseph recently, and he said, "You know, Paul was right—the cross *is* a stumbling block for the Jews!"[18] What he meant is that for Jews, the Lord is unseeable and ineffable. For God to pour himself into human flesh is unthinkable for Jews. For that human flesh to be nailed to a tree is beyond unthinkable. According to Rabbi Joseph, the crucifixion, and Paul's take on it, is exactly why nascent Christianity grew so much more quickly among Gentiles than it did among Jews.

For Paul, everything is implicated by the crucifixion. Life itself, life in the flesh, is to be crucified. When Paul wrote letters back to the congregations that he'd founded, they were full of exhortations that the people were to subjugate themselves in every way, just as God had subjugated himself on the cross. A godly life means forsaking pleasures, practicing self-control, even punishing your body until you bring it into submission. Similarly, human relationships—between husband and wife, parent and child, master and slave, business associates—are to be characterized by submission. In the church, members were taught to share their money, food, and possessions. And all of this stems from the crucifixion of Jesus, the impetus for every aspect of life.

For all the words that have been written trying to uncover Paul's theology of the cross, it was the ethics of the cross that most interested him. What he hoped for the people he'd led to faith and the congregations he'd founded was that they would live out the example that God set on the cross: self-limitation, humility, and submission. That, for Paul, was the lesson in Jesus' death.

Throughout this journey, we're looking for love in the event of the crucifixion. We've seen humanity's and Israel's history with sacrifice, and we've looked at how the Gospels portray the life and death of Jesus. Now we have considered Paul's contribution—the first overtly *theological* contribution to the understanding of the crucifixion. For Paul, the love of God is shown in the cross because God confronts sin head-on. No more food laws or animal sacrifices—now it's personal. In a passage we've already read and will read again later, Paul virtually sings that in Christ and particularly on the cross, God's humble love for us is on full display:

> *Let the same mind be in you that was in Christ Jesus,*
> *who, though he was in the form of God,*
> *did not regard equality with God*
> *as something to be exploited,*
> *but emptied himself,*
> *taking the form of a slave,*
> *being born in human likeness.*
> *And being found in human form,*
> *he humbled himself*
> *and became obedient to the point of death—*
> *even death on a cross.*[19]

9

Reunited with God

WHEN I VISITED Malaysia, I was amazed to find out that the country includes 878 islands as well as two large sections of mainland. My host, Pastor Arul, hailed from the island of Borneo, and he tried to figure out a way for me to visit his home. But the schedule was too tight, and I spent my entire visit in the capital city, Kuala Lumpur.

That's how a lot of people travel around the New Testament. They spend their time on the two sections of mainland called the Gospels and Paul's Letters. But look at the very end of the Bible, just before the maps, and you'll see a few small, independent islands—books that are only tangentially related to the mainland. We should take a brief tour of some of these islands and see if they shed any light on the question *Did God kill Jesus?*

Hebrews

Hebrews is an odd book. Included in the New Testament because fourth-century Christians thought it was written by Paul, it most surely was not. The vocabulary, the style, and the theology do not match the apostle's, and it does not even claim to be written by him.

It reads more like a sermon than a letter, and over the course of this sermon, seven different Old Testament passages are interpreted at some length.

The occasion for the sermon seems to be that some Gentiles who had converted to Christianity were now flirting with becoming Jews.[1] You can see why they'd consider it: Why not join the religion that their savior belonged to? Plus, if they were Jews, then the Roman authorities would be less likely to persecute them for refusing to worship the gods of the state, since the Romans were already familiar with Jewish customs. But the preacher of Hebrews warns that this would be a dire mistake. In Jesus, God did something far greater than anything that had gone before. Jesus is better than the law, higher than the angels, and more potent than Moses, Joshua, and the entire priesthood. Jesus transcends Judaism. Jesus is God's final word.

In making the case for Jesus' superiority, the author of Hebrews unearths one of the most enigmatic figures of the Old Testament. Melchizedek is mentioned only twice in the Hebrew Bible: first when he interrupts a scene to minister to Abraham with bread and wine and is called the "priest of the most high God." Abraham responds by giving him a tithe, 10 percent of what he had. The second mention is in a psalm in which he is again called a priest.[2] The author of Hebrews makes hay with those two verses, writing a hundred times more about Melchizedek than the entire Old Testament has about the man.

Jesus is *the* high priest, Hebrews argues, in the order of Melchizedek. And because Jesus' lineage traces back to Abraham's priest, Melchizedek predates and supersedes the priestly line of Aaron, the brother of Moses. In other words, Jesus skips all the problems of the Mosaic law and its sacrifices and goes right back to the first, uncorrupted priest.

But make no mistake. To the preacher of Hebrews, this connection has everything to do with blood sacrifice. One of the more intriguing paragraphs of Hebrews reads,

In the days of his flesh, Jesus offered up prayers and suppli-
cations, with loud cries and tears, to the one who was able
to save him from death, and he was heard because of his
reverent submission. Although he was a Son, *he learned obedience through what he suffered;* and having been made perfect,
he became the source of eternal salvation for all who obey
him, having been designated by God a high priest according
to the order of Melchizedek.[3]

So we've got a couple of interesting ideas to note: first, that Jesus
prayerfully begged God to save him, and God was able to save him
(though God obviously did not); and second, Jesus *learned.* Hebrews,
more explicitly than any other book of the Bible, refers to Jesus as
God, and here Hebrews also tells us something of the relationship
between Jesus and God, particularly when Jesus is at death's door.

A bit later in the sermon, the anonymous preacher returns to the
issue of priests. The priestly line of Aaron failed, goes the argument. If those priests had succeeded, they would have produced a
perfect sacrifice to the Lord and delivered Israel. But they could not,
because they themselves were imperfect. Instead, it fell to Jesus, "a
high priest, holy, blameless, undefiled, separated from sinners, and
exalted above the heavens," to make the perfect sacrifice, and that
sacrifice happened to be himself.[4]

"It is impossible for the blood of bulls and goats to take away sins,"
the sermon reads.[5] Jesus' blood supersedes the blood of bulls and
goats, bringing not annual forgiveness on the Day of Atonement,
but ultimate, once-and-for-all redemption. An analogy is made to
wills, which only come into effect upon death. Blood is the key to
forgiveness, for blood is what causes the covenant between God and
human beings to take effect. The blood of animals was fine, for a
time, but the blood of Jesus is the supreme sacrifice.

More even than Paul, Hebrews makes the case that Jesus' death
was a death of atonement. It's Yom Kippur, not Pesach. It's to pay
God for sins, not to pave a way for deliverance.

At least according to the author of Hebrews, God demands a sacrifice on account of human sin. Jesus is both the priest and the sacrifice, and with his sacrifice, all other sacrifices end.

Peter

Two letters are attributed to Peter, though it's doubtful that he wrote them. First Peter is written to churches under the persecution of Rome, likely after the destruction of the Temple in 70. The main theme of the letter is that Christians will unjustly suffer. This should neither be surprising nor a cause for despair, the author says. Instead, the faithful should follow the example of Jesus:

> When he was abused, he did not return abuse; when he suffered, he did not threaten; but he entrusted himself to the one who judges justly. He himself bore our sins in his body on the cross, so that, free from sins, we might live for righteousness; by his wounds you have been healed.[6]

Innocent suffering is the mark of the Christian—"Rejoice insofar as you are sharing in Christ's sufferings."[7] Yes, Jesus' death frees us from sin, but more so it acts as an example of what the Christian life ought to be. His death on the cross calls out to us to suffer quietly and without complaint. This runs counter to what we read in Hebrews, that Jesus did in fact cry out "with loud cries and tears" of prayer and supplication.

John

We know not whether the three letters of John were written by the same hand as the Fourth Gospel, though they do sound similar in theology and style. The first letter of John begins with a reminder that Jesus is "the atoning sacrifice for our sins, and not for ours only but also for the sins of the whole world"; and later, "In this is love, not that we loved God but that he loved us and sent his Son to be the atoning sacrifice for our sins."[8]

Here we must take a brief sojourn deep in the weeds. Believe it or not, these two verses represent the only times that another Greek word for "atonement" appears in the New Testament. The word *hilasmos* is ancient in its origin. The root word *hileo* goes back to Homer, and it means "cheerful"; our word *hilarious* derives from the same root. Over time, the word evolved to mean "favorable" and "gracious." In the Septuagint, the Greek translation of the Hebrew Bible favored by many at the time of Jesus, it is a common predicate of God, meaning "gracious God" and "merciful God."

Hilasmos is a relatively uncommon noun in ancient Greek literature, making it even more challenging for us to determine its meaning in these two New Testament instances. In modern times, the jury has been hung. On the one side sit scholars who think it means the requirement God has for forgiveness of sin—they translate it "propitiation." On the other side sit those who argue that it indicates the means by which God himself wipes away sin—they translate it "expiation."

Maybe we've entered "how many angels can dance on the head of a pin" territory, but you can see how much hinges on the translation of this one word. If John is saying that God required a sacrifice to free us from sin, then God is standing with his arms crossed, shaking his head at every sacrifice humans have offered until finally his own son meets the requirement. But if instead God looks at sin as separate from humanity and acts himself to end the tyranny of sin by sweeping it away in one loving and self-sacrificial act, well, that's a whole different story.

Looking more broadly at 1 John, it seems clear that the latter is implied. The entire letter, and these two passages in particular, are predicated on God's *love,* not God's requirements. Reading 1 John, God's love drips from every page. Sin, in the view of this letter, is a lack of love for God, and Jesus' atonement is the wiping away of that lack of love and replacing it with love.[9] Notably, this is not about Jesus' death—John nods to the resurrection and to the mission of Jesus, but he does not tie the atoning sacrifice specifically to Jesus' death. Here we don't find any of the blood that we found in Hebrews. Jesus' entire life is the atoning sacrifice, not just his death.

The bottom line in 1 John is that God acted out of love. Jesus *was* that act of love, sweeping away the sin that separated God and humanity, and when we embrace this, we, like Jesus, are swept up in God's love and made sinless. John admits that we still sin, but he responds by exhorting us to look again to Jesus to be lifted out of that sin.

Revelation

If you're looking for a book awash in blood, this is it. Revelation, or the Apocalypse of John, is the science fiction novel of the New Testament. As a piece of ancient literature, it's impossible to understand without knowing a bit about the genre in which it was written. We've already learned about apocalyptic writing and its popularity in the first centuries BCE and CE. Revelation is the apex of the genre, a book rife with fantastical imagery of dragons, angels, horsemen, beasts, and whores. It is best understood as a Christian version of an ancient warfare scroll, comparable to those found in Qumran Caves known as the Dead Sea Scrolls. And Revelation's ultimate message is twofold: (1) God will finally triumph over all oppressors (Babylon, Rome, etc.); and (2) Christians can expect persecution and even martyrdom for following the Risen Lord.

The book opens with a greeting that includes an intriguing line: "To him who loves us and freed us from our sins by his blood, and made us to be a kingdom, priests serving his God and Father, to him be glory and dominion forever and ever. Amen."[10]

At first blush, this seems to propound a traditional view of the atoning work of Jesus' death: his blood washed away our sins. But let's not rush to judgment. Many scholars consider this line to have been added later, in the scribal era of early Christianity, because the rest of Revelation does not talk about Jesus' blood in this way.[11] And this is the only time that the sinfulness of humanity is mentioned in the entire book. Also, the greeting is addressed, "To him who loves us," which couches Jesus' death in God's love, not in God's requirement for a sacrificial death of an innocent victim.

In fact, in the context of the whole book of Revelation, Jesus' death is of utmost importance, and it effectively does two things. First, Jesus' crucifixion defeats the powers of evil and death in the world. In Revelation, the big problem in the world is not sin, it's evil. And Jesus conquered evil in his death, opening the door for his followers to conquer as well: "To the one who conquers I will give a place with me on my throne, just as I myself conquered and sat down with my Father on his throne."[12]

Second, and relatedly, Jesus' death is an example of the suffering that is sure to come to any who follow him. Revelation seems consumed with the people's subjugation by Babylon, but that had taken place centuries before. While some have read this as a prophecy about the future, Babylon is clearly a literary stand-in for the Roman Empire, the persecutor of God's people. Rome put Jesus to death; Rome was persecuting Christians; Rome had destroyed the Jewish Temple; and the readers of Revelation were told to expect more of the same. Jesus is called the "firstborn of the dead,"[13] and many of the scrolls that are read by the Lamb throughout the book are full of portents of terrible deaths for those who follow Christ.

In Revelation, Jesus is both the terrifying, powerful Lion and the slaughtered, sacrificed Lamb. When the author writes of a vision in chapter 5, he bemoans the lack of anyone who can break the seven seals and read the prophetic scrolls. Then the one appears, the only one "in heaven or on earth or under the earth" who can break the scrolls. This one, obviously Jesus, is both the "Lion of the tribe of Judah" and the "Lamb standing as if it had been slaughtered." When this one takes the scrolls, an otherworldly choir begins to sing,

> *"You are worthy to take the scroll*
> *and to open its seals,*
> *for you were slaughtered and by your blood you ransomed for God*

saints from every tribe and language and people and nation;
you have made them to be a kingdom and priests serving our God,
and they will reign on earth."[14]

Take heed of what this ransoming does. This does not pay God for a sin committed. Instead, people of every corner of the Earth are rescued from the power of evil and put into the service of God as a "kingdom and priests." Those who were slaves of Rome are now servants of God. Here the blood of Jesus rescues humanity from worldly forces of evil for use in God's good kingdom.

One more insight comes in a phrase that's repeated a couple of times in Revelation, including this verse: "Then he said to me, 'These are they who have come out of the great ordeal; they have washed their robes and made them white in the blood of the Lamb.' "[15]

To wash one's robes in blood was a practice of those going to fight a holy war, seen in various other examples in ancient literature.[16] Again, the implication is that Christians are to gird themselves up for a battle that will cost them everything, even their own lives. The rest of Revelation is replete with vivid descriptions of this battle, including dragons and devils descending to Earth to reign, and the Lord victorious, with a sword and riding a horse chest deep in blood. Jesus is both the humble Lamb and the fierce Lion, and Jesus-followers can expect to experience both the crushing defeat now (like the Lamb) and the awesome victory in the future (with the Lion).

A Surplus of Meaning

So we've toured four of the islands that sit just off the mainland of the Gospels and Paul. They are far from unanimous in their depiction of Jesus' death, or of the God who stands behind the cross. But in none do we find an angry, vengeful God, standing with arms crossed, awaiting a sacrifice equal to the weight of all human sin. Instead, we hear a chorus of polyphonous voices, each singing from his own perspective about how the death of Jesus is efficacious at reuniting God and humanity. In one, the ultimate high priest makes the final sacrifice, in another he suffers unjustly as a humble example, in another he fills the world with love, and in another he calls us to join him in a battle against evil. We've already mentioned the *surplus of meaning* in the cross, and here we see it in spades. We also see that even in the first century, the meaning of Jesus' death was understood differently by different people.

In fact, we've surveyed the entire Bible, from Genesis through Revelation, and we've found the very same thing. The Bible lacks one single perspective on the meaning of sacrifice in general and Jesus' death specifically. Instead, the sixty-six books that make up the Bible display a trajectory that evolves over thousands of years. From the sacrifices of Abel and Cain and the resulting murder to the apocalyptic poetry of Revelation, violence, blood, and sacrifice play a central role in the self-identity of Israelites and early Christians. Just how the death of Jesus fits in this trajectory has perplexed the church since its inception. And being that the sacred text of Christianity has multiple perspectives on the subject, it won't surprise us that theologians have similarly put forward many theories of their own.

Based on this survey and summary of what the Bible says about how to explain what happened at the cross, it might come as a surprise to hear how some schools of thought in the church claim that they have found the one and only way to understand Jesus' death. It's to one such theory that we now turn.

PART FOUR

The Majority Opinion

The Payment Model

10

God Is Very Angry with You

T HERE'S AN OLD church joke. Maybe you've heard it before. A Sunday school teacher is standing in front of her third-grade class, and she says, "I'm thinking of something that has a bushy tail, climbs trees, and stores nuts for the winter. What is it?"

An earnest little boy raises his hand and says, "It sounds like a squirrel, but I'll say *Jesus*!"

That's the epitome of the "Sunday school answer." Whatever the question, *Jesus* is the answer. Some graffiti artists have had a little fun with this: a well-meaning evangelist will spray-paint "Jesus is the answer" on a railroad trestle or bridge abutment, and a smart aleck will follow up with, "So what's the question?"

That's pretty much how the crucifixion of Jesus has played in the history of the church: Jesus' death is the answer in search of a question. Or to put it another way, in any given era, whatever the problem, the crucifixion is the solution.

As time moved from the Apostolic Age—when Jesus' apostles were still alive and the books of the New Testament were being written—into the era of the early church, the crucifixion of Jesus remained as important as Paul hoped it would be. The church fathers, as they came to be called, all agreed on the centrality of Jesus' death to understanding everything about Christianity. They debated the dual nature (human and divine) of Jesus, they argued over which books should go in the Bible, and they called each other heretics regarding the Trinity, but there was unanimity regarding the cross: Jesus died on it, and that was the most important event in history.

That same pattern has continued through every age of the church since. Theologians and preachers have debated various points of doctrine and dogma, but the death of Jesus has remained the hinge on which everything swings. That's not to say there haven't been debates about the *nature* of that death; just that there's been consensus on the *importance* of it. It is, indeed, *the* answer.

What's changed over the years has been the question, because the affliction that vexes one era does not concern another. And as we've already seen, the Bible lacks one particular perspective on the cross, instead offering us a plethora of ways to understand Jesus' death—a surplus of meaning. That means the church has had a lot to draw on when trying to make sense of this event.

Having investigated the Bible's various perspectives, we now turn ourselves to the twenty centuries since. It's a history full of colorful characters and heartfelt answers to sincere questions. And you might be surprised at just how many interpretations of the cross there are. If we could get in a time machine and motor back through history, we could pop out at various points and ask, *Just what did Jesus' death accomplish?*, the theologians and preachers of each era would confidently give us an answer, but each of those answers would be different.

This shouldn't be worrisome, leading us to fear that there's no answer. Instead, it frees us to do what Christians have done for centuries: namely, to meditate on the life and death of Jesus from our own context; to listen for the whispers of God's Spirit in making sense of that extraordinary event; and to allow ourselves to come to our own conclusions without fear of getting the answer wrong. In thinking this through and applying it to our own spiritual lives, we are doing just what our forebears in the faith have done.

So now it's time to turn to those who've gone before us and see what they've thought and said about Jesus' death. As I mentioned in chapter 3, after we look at each theory of the cross, we'll ask a set of six questions meant to get to the heart of the meaning of the crucifixion:

- What does the model say about God?
- What does it say about Jesus?
- What does the model say about the relationship between God and Jesus?
- How does it make sense of violence?
- What does it mean for us spiritually?
- Where's the love?

Our sensitivity to the question of violence, for instance, didn't worry earlier generations of Christians, so that will play a role in how we judge between these theories. We will also be looking for a view of the cross that doesn't pit Jesus against God, for both scripture and our experience tell us that their relationship is always one of love. We've also got to find a perspective on the cross that doesn't make Jesus or God helpless or beholden to a system of justice that's bigger than they are. Jesus' sacrifice was made out of love, not out of obligation, and his death must free us to love in new ways. It's got to open a door into a relationship with God that was previously unavailable.

In the end, how we understand the death of Jesus must make us better people. It's got to draw us closer to God and fill us with love. Too few of us experience that when we hear sermons on Good Friday or read about Jesus' passion in the Bible. We hear judgment; we're told that we disappoint God. But the crucifixion was God's ultimate act of love, so it should motivate us toward love and action, not fill us with dread and remorse.

We will start not with the oldest theory, but with the most popular today. It's about a thousand years old, which is old, but not ancient. And as we will see, there are reasons that it's gained such a rabid following of late. Because it's so popular, we'll spend more time on it than we will on the others. I will try to present it as sympathetically and objectively as possible—even though I disagree with it. Later, once we understand the history and arguments for why so many feel it's so compelling, we will judge how well it answers the smell/love questions we developed earlier.

We Owe God a Debt That Can't Be Paid

Unfortunately, I've got some experience in the American legal system. Most Americans do, whether it's contesting a parking ticket or something more serious. Mine has been due to a divorce, a very unpleasant experience. As I went through the divorce, I met weekly with a gifted therapist. In one session, she stopped me midsentence. I'd been complaining—again—about the family justice system, about how no one seemed to care about our case, about how everyone was incompetent, and about how totally frustrated and helpless I felt. She interrupted me and said, "How about this? Let's stop calling it the 'family justice system' and instead refer to it as the 'family legal system.' That might make it easier for you, since there really isn't any justice there." And she was right, it did help, because that whole system of lawyers and judges and custody and child support personnel isn't about justice, per se. The whole system is about laws. And laws aren't necessarily about justice.

Laws attempt to be about justice. That's what they're after. And that's what the legislators who pass them and the cops who enforce them hope for. But between the ideal of justice and the reality of laws, something is lost. It may be human fallibility, our own shortcomings making it impossible to turn the ideal into the real. We're faced with the gap between law and justice every time someone is released after years on death row, exonerated by DNA evidence.

And yet, we long for justice. I wanted justice during my divorce—sometimes I got it, sometimes I didn't.

A sense of justice traces back to ancient civilizations. Aristotle wrote about justice being a virtue, but one that was impossible to achieve in its absolute form. In its place, he said, we should strive for equity. But anyone who looks honestly at the classical world, a world that considered women property and that had an economy largely based on slavery, has to admit that justice was hard to come by in those days. We've made strides in the centuries since, but justice still eludes us. We pass more laws, but are we any closer to justice?

The quest for justice has culminated in the United States of America being the most litigious society in human history. As an American, I live under a corpus of laws—federal, state, and local—that is more voluminous than any in world history.[1] America is "a nation of laws, not of men," John Adams wrote in 1774, and that has been a guiding premise in the past two and a half centuries. The first view of Jesus' death we'll investigate is the most popular today, largely because it appeals to our sense of justice and our understanding of law and penalties.

Most of us in Western Christianity were raised with the same version of the atonement that the dynamic youth speaker at the junior high retreat—the version with the blood and the collapsed building—assumed was the only version. Theologians call it the *substitution* or the *satisfaction* theory of the atonement. We will call it the Payment model. There are reasons, both cultural and theological, that this understanding of the atonement has grown in dominance over the past thousand years. Although there were hints of this view of the cross in the early church, it wasn't until the eleventh century that it was really developed, by Anselm of Canterbury.

Anselm was a powerful churchman in his day. Reared in a wealthy family in the Italian Alps, he wanted to enter the monastery at age fifteen, but his father wouldn't allow it. So it wasn't until age twenty-seven, after many years of wandering through Europe, that he finally entered the abbey. He rose quickly through the ranks, becoming a prior in the abbey just three years later, and he became the abbot in 1078 at age forty-five. From there, he got the plum assignment of Archbishop of Canterbury in England. But that got him mixed up in English politics, and he was exiled by King William II from 1079 until the king's death in 1100 because the two men disagreed on who was the real pope. During his exile, Anselm wrote *Cur Deus Homo* (*Why a God-Man?*), one of the most famous books in history—and the book that put Payment atonement on the map.

In that book, Anselm argued that Jesus died as a substitute for human beings and as a satisfaction for the sin-debt that humans owe God. Here's how that works.

God is *holy,* and we are less-than-holy. The God of the universe is perfect in every way. But as we learn in the book of Genesis, the first humans sinned against God by eating the fruit that taught them right from wrong. This broke a direct command given to them by God. It showed human hubris and offended God's honor. As a result, God expelled them from the Garden, and every subsequent human has followed the lead of Adam and Eve and sinned against God. "Every inclination of the rational creature ought to be subject to the will of God," Anselm wrote, but our sinfulness precludes that humility. We are incapable of doing what we're required to do.

God is also *just.* In fact, God is *perfectly just,* so God cannot forgive human sin without some recompense, some payment; to do so would undermine God's perfect justice. He can't just let us off the hook, because that would be unjust. And since every human being has sinned, there's not a single person available who's lived a life of perfect holiness. God demands from humans a life of perfect holy sacrifice, but we repeatedly fail him, racking up more debt every day.

This debt, incurred by humans, can only be paid off by a human. We created the debt, and we've got to pay it. But no human being is perfect. So who can satisfy the requirement of perfection? Who can make the payment? Only a perfect, sinless God-man can pay the price that we owe to God. Anything less would be unjust. So God does just that, sending his perfect Son to Earth, then letting him—or making him—die as a substitute for the billions of human beings past and future who are incapable of paying off the debt incurred by their sin. That's the Payment model.

Subsequent to Anselm, some of his acolytes say that God isn't just disappointed, he's mad at us for our sin. Our sin makes God angry. So angry, in fact, that God cannot possibly accept us into his presence. These people say it's not just a payment that God demands, but also a punishment. Someone needs to pay a penalty for the sin of the world, and that penalty is a torturous, bloody death, since that's what we all deserve. What Anselm started as a Payment model of Jesus' death has evolved into a Penalty/Punishment model.

A Legal Framework for a Litigious People

The Payment/Penalty/Punishment theory lends itself to metaphors, allegories, and parables that appeal to us. For example, there's this old standby: *A judge passes a sentence of death on a criminal who deserves nothing less; the judge then stands, removes his robe, and goes to the electric chair in the criminal's place.* I heard this one about a dozen times at Christian camps and retreats in my youth.

Any honest look at the genesis of Payment atonement must take account of the era in which Anselm was writing. He was on the front end of the development of the Western legal mind. There weren't judges and juries in Anselm's day, there were lords and vassals. If you were a serf and you crossed the king on the hill, you had to make it right by sacrificing something. You had to make a payment for your error.

Anselm was a man of his time in articulating a sense of justice, on the crest of a wave that was to sweep across all of Europe and, eventually, to the New World. Just over a century after Anselm's book, in 1215, the Western world witnessed a revolution with the writing of the Magna Carta, the predecessor of the constitutions that now govern Western democracies. The Magna Carta was an attempt to limit the power of King John of England and to convince the English people that his decisions were based on law, not on the arbitrary whims of a monarch who inherited his throne by divine right. The English monarchy remained strong for centuries after this, but the beginnings of its eventual devolution were inscribed in the Magna Carta.

Anselm's explanation of the life and death of Jesus captured people's attention even during his lifetime, and the Payment model was subsequently embraced by the leading theologians of the Scholastic era (Thomas Aquinas), the Reformation (Martin Luther and John Calvin), and the Great Awakening (Jonathan Edwards). With theological heirs like this, we can see why Anselm's Payment model has so many fans today, for these four men are responsible for a large portion of modern Christianity.

Appealing to the Western mind and championed by leading intellectuals, Anselm's view took off. While Anselm saw Christ's death as a *replacement* for the punishment that humans deserved, five centuries later John Calvin said that the crucifixion is the *penalty* that humans deserve. Calvin wrote that Christ had "to undergo the severity of God's vengeance, to appease his wrath and satisfy his just judgment."[2] God's holiness is both unremitting and demanding. What it demands is that a penalty be paid. This is how Calvin and others upped the ante from Anselm. Now it's not just that Jesus made our payment for us, but that he pays a penalty on our behalf—a penalty that we cannot pay. In theological jargon, this is how it goes from *substitution* to *penal substitution*, the "penal" connoting the penalty. This change happened during the Reformation, and it remains popular today.

So this Payment/Penalty/Punishment version of the atonement appeals to us because it resonates with our sense of law and justice—some even argue that it appeals to a *universal* sense of justice. But there is more reason than this resonance for its dominance. It also accords with a certain conception of God that we find in the Bible. At times, God is depicted as wrathful in both the Hebrew and Christian Scriptures, as when Paul writes, "For the wrath of God is revealed from heaven against all ungodliness and wickedness of those who by their wickedness suppress the truth."[3] Paul also writes that anyone who doesn't fulfill the law perfectly is under a curse.[4] The extension of these verses, and others, is that God's wrath burns against all who dishonor him, and that's everyone except Jesus.

This brings us to two related terms that we've already seen dominate this understanding of Jesus' death: *satisfaction* and *substitution*. They're strung together in a sentence like this: God's wrath was *satisfied* by Jesus' *substitutionary* death (that is, Jesus *substitutes* for us when he *satisfies* the debt we owe). Core to the Payment theory of the atonement are two premises: (1) human sin is a terrible offense to God; and (2) God is governed by a sense of justice that will not allow him to overlook even one sin. Here's how John Stott, the preeminent articulator of this position in the twentieth century, said it: "God loves us sinners and longs to save us, but cannot do so by violating the law which has justly condemned us."[5]

Stott sees the possible problem with his logic: how can you say that God *cannot do* something? Can't God do anything? Can't God just declare the law of justice satisfied without a bloody crucifixion? No, Stott argues, because the relationship that God has with the law isn't like a president or prime minister—those persons are first among equals in being *under* the law. In God's case, God *is* the law, and the law *is* God. This leads Stott back to Anselm, who decided that the real tragedy of sin is that it insults God's honor. God is holy and is "unable to condone any violation of his honor."[6] Every time we dishonor God, we incur a debt that we cannot pay.

But according to Stott, it's not a law or some concept of justice to which God is beholden. It's God's very nature that holds God back from granting us merciful forgiveness without some payment:

> God is always himself and never inconsistent. If he were ever to behave "uncharacteristically," in a way that is out of character with himself, he would cease to be God and the world would be thrown into moral confusion. No, God is God; he never deviates one iota, even one tiny hair's breadth, from being entirely himself.[7]

The holiness of God is preeminent for Stott, as it is for all who abide by the Payment model of the atonement. And the stakes are high, because if God didn't do it this way, as Stott says, "he would cease to be God."

We've got to put our list of questions to this view, as we will for every view. But before we do that, we're going to take a jaunt through history. Remember, every view sees the death of Jesus as the solution, but each tries to solve a different problem. For the Payment view, the problem is *original sin*, a concept that's so ingrained in most versions of Christianity that it may seem strange to question it. But like any other doctrine, it was developed by particular people and over time. And as we'll see, its history is telling.

11

—

The Invention of Original Sin

W HEN I WAS growing up in that moderate, centrist church—somewhere between mainline Christianity and evangelicalism—original sin was a given. I first learned about it in youth group, and we regularly talked about it. In truth, it's more accurate to say that we talked about a life with Christ, and the notion of original sin was ever-present in the background. It was assumed. And I cannot remember that it was ever debated.

In other words, I assumed that the doctrine of original sin was a biblical notion and that all Christians accepted it as gospel truth.

As it turns out, neither is true.

In college, original sin was also assumed by the Campus Crusaders and Navigators, parachurch groups of which I was a part, as well as in the little country Bible church that I attended. Here's a telling section from that church's current web page on doctrine:

Man (Anthropology)
Man was created in the image of God to enjoy friendship with Him (Genesis 1:26). Man sinned and his fellowship with God was broken (Genesis 3). Man is now deceitful and desperately wicked (Jeremiah 17:9). He has the capacity for all sin and lives his life independent of his

Creator. In his natural rebellious state, his destiny is to spend eternity totally separated from God in the lake of fire prepared for the devil and his angels (II Thessalonians 1:8; Revelation 20:11–15).[1]

But while in college, I also took at class on the theology of Augustine from an eccentric professor who taught us that the great father of Western theology was the originator of the doctrine of original sin. Augustine did not make up the doctrine *ex novo*, but took as his inspiration the account of creation in Genesis 3 and certain Pauline texts.

Then in seminary I learned from another professor that John Calvin and his theological heirs doubled down on the notion of original sin and that it hadn't played much of a role in the medieval and Scholastic theology that preceded them.

And sometime later, I discovered that whole branches of the Christian family tree—most notably, the Orthodox Church—have never embraced the doctrine of original sin. Nor do Jews, even though we share the texts in Genesis that supposedly make the doctrine so abundantly clear.

What I've come to realize is that the idea of original sin is not, in fact, God's Eternal Truth. It is, instead, like so many other items of faith, historically conditioned.

I remember some late-night dorm conversations in college in which half a dozen of us would stay up debating the biggest ideas in the universe: the existence of God; the meaning of life; which fraternity to pledge. One that took a great deal of our time was the question of whether human beings are inherently good or inherently bad. It may sound like a philosophically silly question now, but it was all-consuming to us as eighteen-year-olds. Reared as a Protestant Christian, my answer was always the same: human beings are inherently bad, from birth. We start bad, and we get worse. That answer was based on my notion of original sin, taught, as I said, as a matter of biblical fact in all of my various Sunday school and youth group experiences.

But I must admit, I always felt a bit uncomfortable with my own response. I really had nothing on which to base my "humans are bad" concept except what I'd been taught. Although I was surely aware of my own sin, I didn't really get the impression that I or anyone else was inherently evil. In fact, my experience was the contrary: I generally felt that people were good, kind, and generous. I still feel this way. Since then, I've become increasingly uncomfortable with the notion that people are inherently bad. I don't deny the reality of sin. But I do reject the notion that human beings are depraved from birth.

The classic doctrine of original sin says that everyone is born sinful. We inherit this condition, and we also inherit the condemnation of God that goes with it. Everyone has it—no one escapes. Even the innocent infant in the hospital nursery is unacceptable in the eyes of God.[2] Telling the story of this doctrine's development might help us to see how it's become virtually unassailable by many in the church today.

The Origins of Original Sin

Back in the beginning, Adam and Eve were forbidden by God to eat the fruit of the tree of the knowledge of good and evil, but they were bidden to eat it by the serpent. Eve listened to the latter and passed the fruit to her partner. He partook as well. God discovered their disobedience, and they had to pay the consequences. They were expelled from the Garden, never to return.

A couple of noteworthy phrases ring out in the narrative. One is that the serpent tells Eve that the magic fruit will allow her to know "good and evil," and Eve decides to eat the fruit, in part because it was "desirable for gaining wisdom." "Then the eyes of both were opened," they became ashamed of their nakedness, sewed themselves fig-leaf garments, and subsequently their choice was noticed by God.

Let's consider the consequences of their actions. Because of their fruity indulgence, Adam and Eve became aware and ashamed of their nakedness. God, in turn, laid some penalties on them: the woman will have pain in childbirth and be physically subservient to the man; the man will toil to bring food from the Earth; they are cast out of the Garden; and, the biggest penalty of all, they are condemned to die.

In the biblical account, this is surely *the* original sin. It's clearly meant to be paradigmatic of the human condition. The passage teaches that given the choice, each of us would choose the fruit that opens our eyes rather than trusting God who tells us we don't need our eyes opened.

But is this *original sin*? Is there anything in the passage that says that Adam and Eve might have *not* chosen to eat the fruit or, more to the point of the Western theological notion of original sin, that the consequences of their sin has been passed down to every subsequent human via the act of intercourse (thus exempting only Jesus of Nazareth from this inheritance)? Is there something in the passage that would lead us to believe that this is an "inherited spiritual disease or defect in human nature," as original sin is sometimes defined?

No. The account of the original sin in Genesis 3 teaches us a lot about the state of human nature, our freedom to know right from wrong, and our proclivity not to trust God. But it does not teach that the sin of Adam and Eve is responsible for the sins of subsequent generations. Many have drawn this out of the narrative, but it's simply not there.

Jesus' Ambivalence

Jesus is not recorded in the Gospels as saying anything that can be construed as particularly supportive of the doctrine of original sin. Jesus did talk about sin, to be sure. Probably the closest he came to tackling the idea of inherited sin is the story of Jesus healing a man born blind in John 9:1–12, which begins:

As he walked along, he saw a man blind from birth. His disciples asked him, "Rabbi, who sinned, this man or his parents, that he was born blind?" Jesus answered, "Neither this man nor his parents sinned; he was born blind so that God's works might be revealed in him. We must work the works of him who sent me while it is day; night is coming when no one can work. As long as I am in the world, I am the light of the world." When he had said this, he spat on the ground and made mud with the saliva and spread the mud on the man's eyes, saying to him, "Go, wash in the pool of Siloam" (which means Sent). Then he went and washed and came back able to see.

As usual with Jesus, his primary point is to subvert the conventional wisdom of the day. His interlocutors assume that the man's blindness is a direct result of either (A) his own sin or (B) his parents' sin.

Option A indicates that Jesus' questioners did consider it quite possible that sin was present in an infant: this man was born blind, and they wonder if it was his own sin that caused his blindness; since we can assume that they did not mean that the man volitionally sinned in utero, they are asking Jesus about some inherited sin passed down through the generations.

Option B indicates that the man's blindness is a direct result of his parents' sins, whatever they may be.

The ideas of inherited and generational sin were topics of debate among rabbis in Jesus' day, so it isn't that surprising that Jesus' disciples would want him to weigh in on the matter. The Hebrew Bible itself is ambivalent on this notion. In Exodus 34, just after Moses received the chiseled commandments, we read,

And [the Lord] passed in front of Moses, proclaiming, "The Lord, the Lord, the compassionate and gracious God, slow to anger, abounding in love and faithfulness, maintaining love to thousands, and forgiving wickedness, rebellion and sin. Yet he does not leave the guilty unpunished; he punishes the children and their children for the sin of the parents to the third and fourth generation."[3]

Yet in <u>Ezekiel 18</u>, the Lord repeatedly announces through the prophet that the sins of the parents are not imputed to the children,

> Yet you ask, "Why does the son not share the guilt of his father?" Since the son has done what is just and right and has been careful to keep all my decrees, he will surely live. The one who sins is the one who will die. The child will not share the guilt of the parent, nor will the parent share the guilt of the child. The righteousness of the righteous will be credited to them, and the wickedness of the wicked will be charged against them.[4]

The Hebrew scriptures are ambivalent on the matter; so we can understand why the disciples wanted Jesus' opinion.

As was his custom, Jesus didn't pick A or B, but instead replied, "Neither this man nor his parents sinned, but this happened so that the works of God might be displayed in him." It's an odd response raising all sorts of other theological questions, but surely Jesus' answer does not support the notion of inherited guilt or total depravity. And nothing else Jesus says or teaches directly supports such an idea.

Romans 5 and the Heart of the Issue

Paul was less ambiguous about the matter than Jesus. In his letter to the Romans, Paul writes specifically about the inherited nature of sin, and it is from this passage that the two most articulate proponents of inherited guilt (Augustine) and the total depravity of humankind (Calvin) get their material.

Romans is Paul's magnum opus, as we've already seen. He writes in chapter 15 that he is concerned about the conflict between Jewish and Gentile followers of Jesus the Christ in the Roman church, and this letter is his attempt to clear up some of the issues that have provoked the conflict—their understanding of sin, justification, guilt, and salvation seems to be the source of the dispute. In other words, while this is a letter about how the human being is justified before God, it is primarily a letter about the relationship between Jewish and Gentile Christ-followers.

Although Paul was, famously, a Roman citizen, he was first and foremost a Jew. Jews in his day, as today, consider Jewishness to be a matter of matrilineal descent: if your mom is Jewish, you are Jewish. In Jesus and Paul's day, there was much debate among rabbis about how, exactly, this happened and even about how semen was involved. One New Testament scholar recently told me that in the air at the time of Jesus and Paul was a Jewish belief in the physical transmission of one's status through reproduction.

So, with that in mind, let's look at what Paul wrote.

> Therefore, just as sin came into the world through one man, and death came through sin, and so death spread to all because all have sinned—sin was indeed in the world before the law, but sin is not reckoned when there is no law. Yet death exercised dominion from Adam to Moses, even over those whose sins were not like the transgression of Adam, who is a type of the one who was to come. . . .
>
> If, because of the one man's trespass, death exercised dominion through that one, much more surely will those who receive the abundance of grace and the free gift of righteousness exercise dominion in life through the one man, Jesus Christ.
>
> Therefore just as one man's trespass led to condemnation for all, so one man's act of righteousness leads to justification and life for all. For just as by the one man's disobedience the many were made sinners, so by the one man's obedience the many will be made righteous.[5]

We can see why Augustine, Calvin, and so many others propose that Paul is writing about inherited guilt. Paul states clearly that Adam's sin resulted in every one of his descendants being sinful, too. So it seems that part of our interpretation of this passage in Romans hinges on exactly how we interpret and understand Genesis 2–3. Were Adam and Eve real, historic persons? Are they, indeed, the father and mother of the entire human race? (Did they really live into their nine hundreds? Who was Cain's wife? The list of questions about the first few chapters of the Bible is long.)

If one believes that there is some kind of spiritual nature that is passed from mother (or father) to child by a biological process, as Paul likely believed, then this passage will be taken one way. If, however, one does not believe that the taint of Adam's sin is genetic but is instead an archetypal account of the human condition, then it will be taken another way. There's a fork in the road here, and two of the great theologians of the church took a different path than I do.

Augustine's Addendum: Adam's Aphrodisia

The shadow of Augustine of Hippo looms large over the entire subsequent development of the doctrine of original sin. If Paul was a Jew's Jew, Augustine was a Neoplatonist's Neoplatonist. Schooled in the philosophy of Plotinus, Augustine even converted to a Neoplatonic religion, Manichaeism, in his twenties.

As you might guess by its name, Neoplatonism magnified strands of Plato—most significantly, dualism. Prior to his conversion to Christianity, Augustine's philosophy and religion both held to a strict separation between God and humanity, good and evil, spiritual and material. Thus, Augustine's version of the world didn't necessarily jibe with the Hebrew worldview of Jesus and the apostles. Augustine's dramatic conversion to a religion in which God (good) took on human flesh (evil) was a tough one for him to swallow, and much of his writing can be seen as an attempt to reconcile Plato's ideas with the biblical narrative.

When it comes to the doctrine of original sin, Augustine's influence cannot be overstated.[6] Augustine first uses the phrase in his spiritual memoir, *Confessions,* in which he makes it clear that Adam's sin means that every human being has a hostile disposition toward God.[7] Augustine's thinking on the issue reaches full boil in his debates with Pelagius, an English monk, whose name is now spat at those who question Augustine's version of the doctrine of original sin. It's impossible to know what Pelagius really thought and wrote, since we know him almost exclusively through Augustine's refutations of him—Pelagius's own writings did not survive; he survives only as a literary foil for Augustine.

Supposedly, Pelagius blamed the moral laxity that he saw around Rome on Augustine's doctrine of original sin. According to Augustine, human beings have all inherited guilt from Adam and Eve and are completely reliant upon God's grace for any good work. Pelagius thought that this contradicted the biblical account, in which human beings are again and again told to behave in ways that accord with God's ways and are subsequently rewarded or punished based on their behavior. Pelagius believed that Augustine's views made people too passive and resulted in Christians ignoring the Bible's many injunctions to *do* things.

Augustine, on the other hand, argued that human beings are incapable of the good works that the Bible commands. It's only by God's grace, held in absolute sovereignty by God, that human beings are capable of any good works. Augustine does not deny free will, per se, but he does believe that human beings have lost our *moral* free will as a result of Adam's sin.

It should be noted that neither Pelagius nor his subsequent followers, the so-called Semi-Pelagians, deny the reality of sin. So it turns out that we're dealing with two nuanced positions that are not really as far apart as some make them out to be. What we should recognize, however, is how Augustine took the notion of inherited sin further than Paul had in Romans 5.

Interpreting Paul is the crux of the issue on the question of original sin. Humans inherited something from Adam, as Paul says, but just what we inherited is in dispute. Here's a thumbnail sketch of how Paul is understood:

- Eastern (Orthodox, Coptic, and Byzantine Rite Catholic) Christians take Paul to mean that what we inherited from Adam is *death*.
- Western (Augustinian) Christians take Paul to mean that our inheritance from Adam is death *and guilt*.
- Reformed (Calvinist) Christians take Paul to mean that from Adam we inherent death and guilt *and total depravity*.

We'll get to Calvin next, but still in the background is this lingering question: Do you believe that God would punish you for the sin of another person, namely Adam? For Augustine and Calvin, the answer is a full-throated yes.

There's one more salient point. Augustine believed that the human body and soul were formed in the uterus of a woman by the transmission of semen. He also said that Adam's original sin was passed from generation to generation by semen, and Jesus is without sin because there was no human semen involved in his conception. Later Roman Catholic dogma doubled down on this by inventing the doctrine of the Immaculate Conception—the belief that Jesus' mother, Mary, was also conceived without the involvement of any semen. That way, there couldn't even be a trace of original sin in Mary's womb to rub off on Jesus in utero. In 1544, the Council of Trent made this official Catholic doctrine: original sin is spread by semen.[8]

Calvin's Conundrum: Crammed with Concupiscence

So Augustine took Paul's interpretation of Genesis 2–3 and extended that to mean that Adam's sin conferred not only death on the entire human race, but also guilt. This was a big step, and it hinges on a particular reading of the second creation narrative in Genesis and on a particular biology of the transmission of moral standing via semen.

A thousand years after Augustine, John Calvin came along and ginned up the Reformation that Martin Luther had inaugurated. In his monumental *Institutes of the Christian Religion,* Calvin took the doctrine of original sin one step further than even Augustine, arguing that our inherited sinfulness has erased virtually all remnants of the image of God in us. In Genesis, God said, "Let us make humankind in our image, according to our likeness," but the subsequent sin of Adam expunged that image, according to Calvin:

> Therefore original sin is seen to be an hereditary depravity and corruption of our nature diffused into all parts of the soul. . . . For our nature is not merely bereft of good, but is so productive of every kind of evil that it cannot be inactive. Those who have called it concupiscence [a strong, especially sexual desire] have used a word by no means wide of the mark, if it were added (and this is what many do not concede) that whatever is in man from intellect to will, from the soul to the flesh, is all defiled and crammed with concupiscence; or, to sum it up briefly, that the whole man is in himself nothing but concupiscence.[9]

Calvin's acolytes seized upon the idea of "hereditary depravity" and made it the opening salvo of the TULIP doctrine, a popular acronym that summarizes the beliefs of many of those in the Reformed tradition:

Total Depravity
Unconditional Election
Limited Atonement
Irresistible Grace
Perseverance of the Saints[10]

In their defense, Calvinists make clear that total depravity is not the same as absolute depravity. While the latter allows for no good ever coming from humans, the former merely means that though every aspect of the human being is besmirched, good is still possible within a human. But total depravity does mean that the human being is not capable of producing anything good, nor capable of doing anything that is pleasing to God.

What this promotes is the sovereignty of God, a doctrine that, it must be noted, Calvinists value more highly than any other. Acknowledging the sovereignty of God, they argue, necessitates the doctrine of human depravity because if God is totally sovereign, then we are completely lacking in sovereignty. Sovereignty is a zero-sum game to Calvinists: God has it all, and there's none left for humans.

Where We Stand

Yes, it is hard to conceive of orthodox Christian faith without the idea of original sin. That's a sign of just how successful Augustine's ideas have been in the Western church. But that does not make the idea biblical or right. One can acknowledge the universality of the human proclivity toward sin without affirming either Calvin's total depravity or Augustine's original sin. One merely has to accept simple human fallibility. We're neither immortal nor perfect. We're fallible. We make mistakes. And we die. It's not such a big hurdle to accept those facts, and we can do so without the theological gymnastics required for the doctrine of original sin and all of the corollary doctrines that flow out of it.

In fact, if we simply embrace the Eastern notion that we inherit death but not guilt from Adam, then many of our theological problems are solved.

When we trace the doctrine of original sin, it seems like a runaway train. Paul adds something to Genesis; Augustine adds to Paul; and Calvin adds to Augustine. Each took the notion that we have inherited sin from Adam, and each ratcheted it up another notch. Each added more consequences for us.

But if they were wrong about the meaning of the creation accounts in Genesis, then they sent this train down the wrong track from the beginning. And it should give us pause that original sin and total depravity weren't even on Jesus' radar.

Speaking of Jesus, whether or not we buy the notion of original sin has everything to do with how we understand what happened to Jesus on the cross. If we think that God is bound by perfect justice, and therefore demands a pound of flesh for this sin that we inherited, then the death of God's son on the cross is the perfect—the only—fix.

But if I did not inherit sinfulness from my father's semen, then I'm suddenly open to considering other reasons that the crucifixion matters. And we're all open to finding a better atonement.

12

Does God Demand a Payment We Can't Afford?

H ERE'S ANOTHER STORY I heard multiple times in youth
group: There's a man who operates a train switching station. He sits all day in the switch house, watching trains
come and go, and he operates the switch that makes them go down
one track or another. Both of the tracks he oversees send trains over
bridges. At the time this story takes place, one of the bridges is out,
so he can only send trains down the other set of tracks.

The man has a young son, a toddler. One day, the man looks out
of his window and sees his son playing on the tracks. He also sees a
train barreling down the tracks. The train conductor is drunk, as are
many of the train's passengers. They're also gambling and fornicat-
ing and lying and cheating one another and fighting. It's a train of
debauchery.

The man looks at his son on the tracks, and he looks at the train
steaming toward the boy. There's not enough time for him to leave
the switch house, run down the hill, and move his son off the tracks.
He's got a choice: he can either switch the tracks, sending the train
plummeting over the broken bridge and all of the passengers to certain death, or he can let the train go on its way, crushing his son to
death before his very eyes. The switchman chooses the latter.

The youth pastor concludes this anecdote by saying, "The drunken, lying, cheating, stealing fornicators rolled right over the innocent son. They didn't even have any idea that they were responsible for his death. But the father knew, and he chose to save them instead of his own son.

"It's the same with Jesus. God made the choice to let his own son die because it was the only way to save us, even in the midst of our own sin."

When we hear metaphors of Jesus' death like that one, we can see why feminist theologians have called the Payment/Penalty/Punishment view of the atonement "cosmic child abuse" and "divine child abuse."[1] You can also see why youth pastors and preachers like it so much—whether it's the judge with the electric chair or the dad in the switch house, it really lends itself to some dramatic sermon illustrations. But rather than winning us over, maybe these metaphors should make us squeamish.

Earlier we learned the rather bulky theological phrase *penal substitutionary atonement*. The *penal* part is the more recent development, communicating the idea that Jesus didn't just have to stand in as a substitute for all of us sinners but also had to pay the *penalty* that our sin incurs: the first sin I commit excludes me from heaven, and every subsequent sin only adds more years to my sentence, more dollars to my fine; it would be impossible for me to pay enough of a penalty even for that first sin, much less to make up for the myriad sins that I've committed since that first one. So in order to preserve his perfect sense of justice, God needs to find someone who can pay that penalty in full, and the only one capable is Jesus, God's perfect son. In the words of Anselm, "Everyone who sins is under an obligation to repay to God the honour which he has violently taken from him, and this is the satisfaction that every sinner is obliged to give to God."[2] This, according to Anselm and his heirs, is the demand of justice.

The problem with this whole scheme is not that difficult to see: it makes justice more powerful than God. Or, to put it conversely, it makes God subservient to justice. Our sin forces God to respond in a certain way.

Another problem is that this understanding of the atonement is built on a human sense of justice. It is surprisingly difficult to suss out God's sense of justice from the Bible, because in the Bible God is not particularly consistent in his application of justice. Sometimes God demands an eye for an eye and a tooth for a tooth, and other times God decides to let sinners off the hook in a twist we call *grace* (in the New Testament) or *steadfast love* (in the Hebrew Bible).

In fact, God is not subservient to anything—not justice, not law, not commandments. God can do whatever God wants (making it all the more confounding that God would choose to save the world through the death of his Son—that's a mystery that we'll continue to unravel in coming pages).

Lately, evangelicals have been turning up the volume on the Penalty/Punishment aspect of this version of the atonement. In 2011, outspoken Seattle pastor Mark Driscoll shouted this at his congregation:

> Some of you, God hates you. Some of you, God is sick of you. . . . God hates, right now—personally, objectively— hates some of you. . . . The Bible speaks of God not just hating sin, but sinners. Because sin is of our nature. Sin is not just a mistake that we make. . . .
>
> You are the problem, not the solution. You and I are sinners, and by our nature are objects of wrath. That's a quote from the Bible. . . . God doesn't just hate what you do, he hates who you are. My job is to tell the truth, your job is to make a decision.[3]

Or consider Driscoll's compatriot, John Piper, pastor emeritus of Bethlehem Baptist Church in Minneapolis, who preached to his congregation, "Consider that any offense and any dishonor to an infinitely honorable and infinitely worthy God, is an infinite offense and an infinite dishonor. Therefore, an infinite punishment is deserved."[4] Or this: in May, 2006, the flagship magazine of American evangelicalism, *Christianity Today,* planted its flag in the sand with a cover that heralded, "No Substitute for the Substitute." In the cover story, Washington, D.C., pastor Mark Dever made a vociferous defense of Penalty/Punishment as the only true and biblical understanding of Christ's death: "Apart from Christ's atoning work, we would be forever guilty, ashamed, and condemned before God. But not everyone these days sees it that way."[5]

Controversy has reared its head on the other end of the Protestant spectrum as well. In 2013, the Presbyterian Committee on Congregational song decided to leave a song out of its new hymnal. The song, "In Christ Alone," contains the stanza, "Till on that cross as Jesus died / the wrath of God was satisfied." The committee asked the song's authors if they could change those lines to "Till on that cross as Jesus died / the love of God was magnified." The songwriters rejected the change, leaving the committee to debate the merits of the hymn and of that particular stanza. One committee member reported, "It would do a disservice to this educational mission, the argument ran, to perpetuate . . . the view that the cross is primarily about God's need to assuage God's anger."[6] The committee voted to remove the song from the hymnal.

Six Questions for Payment

It's time to put our list of questions to this version of the atonement.

What does the Payment model say about God?

The Payment model requires a God who, paradoxically, both knows the future perfectly (predestination), but is also sorely disappointed that humans sin. In some versions, that disappointment evolves into wrath. This does not paint an appealing image of God, nor is it very reasonable.

Centuries ago, Augustine argued that if God knows something's going to happen, then it necessarily has to happen, because God is never wrong. And because it has to happen the way God knows it's going to happen, then God is actually *causing* that thing to happen.

Augustine said foreknowledge equals forecausal.[7] So, according to the progenitor of Payment atonement, God caused Adam and Eve to sin, caused original sin to enter humanity, and caused the ultimate death of his son to satisfy his own wrath. That's right: God set up the whole system, including his own wrath and the death of his son.

If we are supposed to learn about love from God, then the idea that God predestined us to sin, which results in our eternal damnation and requires God's Son to die on the cross, teaches us very little about love.

What does it say about Jesus?

The main facts of this drama are God's wrath and justice, our sin, and the need for Jesus to die to appease God's wrath. In this scheme, Jesus is little more than a helpless victim, dragged to the altar as Isaac was by Abraham generations before. Jesus' birth, ministry, teachings, and miracles all become secondary to the essential fact of his death. Even Jesus' resurrection isn't necessary, being merely the cherry on top of the accomplishment of the crucifixion, proving the efficacy of his death. The potency of Jesus' life is exclusively in his death. Needless to say, this does not seem to accord with how the Gospels portray the importance of Jesus' life and teachings or how central the resurrection is to the New Testament.

What does the Payment model say about the relationship between God and Jesus?

The Payment view relies on a hierarchical parent–child relationship similar to that of Abraham and Isaac. While many who hold this view contend that Jesus went to the cross willingly, if this sacrifice of the perfect victim was the one and only way to pay the penalty, then it seems that Jesus really had no choice at all. Even the Son couldn't go against God Almighty. Jesus is subservient to the Father's will, a mere cog in the machine built by God to satisfy God. If Jesus represents love, then he stands in contrast to God's justice and wrath. Jesus and God are not reflections of each other in this model.

How does it make sense of violence?

Payment—especially when penalty and punishment are added—requires violence. God is violent, and the means by which we're forgiven of our sins is violent, and necessarily so. In this view, violence is the very means of achieving God's holy demands. Because of our sin, we deserve nothing less than an eternity of conscious, painful torment, so the only way for us to escape that is for a sinless person to experience that torment in our place. With so much violence built into this system of salvation, it's no surprise that advocates are also supporters of war, the death penalty, and even torture.[8] Like a rock thrown into the middle of a pond, the ripples of violence emanate out from the cross to every aspect of life.

What does it mean for us spiritually?

In addition to embracing violence as the means of salvation and thereby perpetuating violence, Payment teaches that God's anger burns against you because of your sin (sin that he created you to be susceptible to). That's enough to screw up anyone's relationship with God. As I was told as a youth, when God looks at me, he doesn't even see me—he only sees Jesus standing between us. That means my identity is not "in Christ," as Paul so often wrote, but my identity *is* Christ. And if God were to look around Christ and catch a glimpse of me, it would only rekindle his wrath. "God hates some of you!" the pastor screams. Who wants to pray to a God like that?

Where's the love?

Proponents of this view claim that God's love is only worth anything because it's just and demanding. Love without justice, they say, is cheap love. For years, whenever Billy Graham preached, picketers would stand outside the stadium, holding signs and protesting that Graham preached "easy believism" and "cheap grace." They thought that Graham was making it too easy to be a Christian when he asked people to come forward, recite a simple prayer, and be accepted into eternal life. Christianity is tougher than this, they countered, requiring serious and costly changes in lifestyle.

This has been debated since the early church—even the New Testament holds both opinions: Paul writes that we've been saved by unmerited grace, but James counters that faith without works is dead. The question that each one of us needs to ask is this: *Does love demand a payment?* Core to Payment theory is that God, even in love, demands remuneration for the honor that our sin has stolen from him. Is that how we are to understand love? I hope not.

Evaluating Payment

Key to all of the recent back-and-forth about the Payment/Penalty/Punishment version of the atonement is God's wrath. Those who think that God demands a penalty to be paid as a result of human sin—and not just that he demands a penalty, but that he's *angry* about it—feel comfortable with nothing less than Payment and Payment alone.

The problems with this focus on God's wrath are several. First and foremost, it contradicts the experience that most of us have with God. Our experience of God is not of wrath, but of love. In fact, that's how most people experience God even before they accept the idea that Christ stands between us and God. The Bible goes so far as to say, "God is love." So it seems odd to first have to convince people that God's wrath burns against them, then to convince them that Jesus willingly took on that wrath.

Second, this model paints a dysfunctional image of God. God is really, really mad about human sin (even though he knew from the beginning of creation that we would sin). So God looks around for someone to punish for that sin. God sends laws and patriarchs and prophets, and people still don't get it. They sin, worship false idols, and fail to sacrifice correctly. So God sends tornadoes and earthquakes and cancer as punishment, but God's anger still isn't sated.[9]

Finally he finds an innocent victim—who happens to be his own son—and only after killing his son does God's anger finally abate.[10]

And consider this. If the whole point of Jesus was that a perfect God-man be sacrificed to pay a debt, why did Jesus live for thirty-three years before being executed? Sure, Jesus' teachings and miracles were great, and he was able to pick some disciples to tell his story. But if all God needed was an innocent, sinless victim, he may just as well have had the baby's throat slit in the manger (Merry Christmas!). At least then there would be no doubt about the real meaning of Jesus' death.

Finally, and adding to the irony, most people who hold this view, like Augustine and Calvin, believe in *predestination,* the doctrine that before the foundation of the world, God predetermined who would be saved and who would be damned to hell. So what's the point of all of it? The Garden? The law? The kings and prophets? Jesus and the crucifixion? Why go to all that trouble when everyone's eternal destiny has already been decided? As a test, basically, to see how strong our faith really is? That's one answer. The other is the old standby: God's ways are not our ways, so stop asking questions.

These days, the church in America is in decline. That's true of Protestants, both evangelical and mainline, and Catholics. Fewer people go to church every year. Why? Could it be the prevalence of the Payment/Penalty/Punishment view of Jesus' death and the image of a wrathful God it requires? In an earlier age, when people feared God as they feared the weather or the lord on the hill, it made sense to preach a wrathful, vengeful, bloodthirsty God. In the Puritan colonies of New England, a drummer marched through town on Sunday morning, and every villager fell in behind him and trooped to church—missing church was against the law. Once in the meetinghouse, parishioners stood through a service that lasted up to four hours, with a sermon of an hour or more. The message was that God disapproved of just about everything you did or thought. *Thank God for Christ, who took on God's wrath for us!,* they preached. In Jonathan

Edwards's famous sermon, "Sinners in the Hands of an Angry God," he told his congregation,

> That God will execute the fierceness of his anger, implies, that he will inflict wrath without any pity. When God beholds the ineffable extremity of your case, and sees your torment to be so vastly disproportioned to your strength, and sees how your poor soul is crushed, and sinks down, as it were, into an infinite gloom; he will have no compassion upon you, he will not forbear the executions of his wrath, or in the least lighten his hand; there shall be no moderation or mercy, nor will God then at all stay his rough wind; he will have no regard to your welfare, nor be at all careful lest you should suffer too much in any other sense, than only that you shall not suffer beyond what strict justice requires.[11]

We've come a long way since the days of Puritan drummers and scarlet letters and God holding you over the pit of hell as a spider on a thread. We no longer attend church because it's the law, and we no longer think that God created us in such a way that he was bound to be disappointed by and angry at us. Many of the accoutrements of the Puritan faith have been discarded, but the theology of Jesus' death remains. And this has cost us. Lacking the entire worldview on which the Payment view is premised, that theology serves only to remove all incentive to worship and pray. The Payment model of Jesus' death stands alone, a single cut flower in a vase that no longer holds any water. In the past, Christians worshipped and prayed out of fear and obligation and a deep commitment to the institution of the church that taught such things. But is that really the ultimate revelation of love?

Before we move on, we might consider whether the crucifixion can be a Payment, even without God's wrath. That is possible if human sin causes a rupture in the God-human relationship. If that were the case, and if it would be unseemly or even cosmically impossible for God to let that sin go unpunished, then Jesus' payment on our behalf becomes redemptive.

But as theologian Richard Beck points out, the strangeness at the root of the Payment/Penalty/Punishment model is that God has to save us from God. At its root, love often involves suffering for each other and for the sake of each other. Love often accepts suffering and pain intended for others. Love often involves protecting and shielding others, even when those others might be "getting what they deserve." If something bad were going to happen to my children I'd rush to substitute myself. That's what love does. So it's not surprising that God does the same thing.[12]

But where does this suffering come from? Why is it necessary at all? And if God both initiates the suffering and supplies the only means of escape from it, that's self-serving.

In the end, the God behind Payment/Penalty/Punishment is a quid pro quo God. God won't do *this* unless his subjects do *that*. But his subjects are constitutionally incapable of doing what he demands. Instead of realizing that fact and coming up with an alternative solution to his problem, God looks around for someone else who can satiate his thirst for justice, and he settles on his own son.

God swings the barrel of his gun away from us, takes aim at Jesus, and fires.

That's the God of the Payment model. He may be a God to be feared, but he's not a God to be loved.

PART FIVE

Minority Opinions

13

The Victory Model
God Is Your Spiritual Warrior

A S WE'VE SEEN, the death of Jesus on the cross is a solution in search of a problem. The Payment view may be the most popular view, but it's far from the only one. Happily, there are other theories for us to consider.

Think of it like penicillin. When Alexander Fleming showed in 1928 that the *Penicillium rubens* mold could be grown in such a way that it would have antibiotic properties, it was a cure in search of a disease. In 1930, after failed attempts to cure other ailments, penicillin successfully cured four infants of a particular kind of eye infection. By 1942, it was used to successfully stave off staph infections among survivors of a horrific fire in Boston, leading the U.S. government to start mass production of the medicine. Now, when I take my kids to the pediatrician, they're prescribed some form of penicillin for everything from ear infections to strep throat to pink eye. When that mold was grown in 1928, Dr. Fleming couldn't possibly have guessed that it was the cure to myriad ailments.

The crucifixion of Jesus has followed a similar path. According to the Bible, Jesus' disciples weren't expecting him to rise from the dead. When he did, it caught them off guard, and it's safe to say that thinking through the theological ramifications of his resurrection was not the first thing on their minds. A couple of decades later, when Paul was traveling around and writing letters, he considered the crucifixion to be the linchpin to pretty much everything. He was fixated on the crucifixion.

After Paul, Christians continued to find the death of Jesus to be the cure to what ailed them. The thing is, different ailments afflicted different generations of Christians. So, journeying through the history of the church provides a fascinating glimpse into what issues confronted people in each era, and how they saw the crucifixion as the cure. We've already looked at the majority opinion these days—that Jesus paid a penalty for sins he didn't commit. Now it's time to consider the other ways that Christians have understood the crucifixion through the centuries.

As I've been writing this book, I've been talking to people about the death of Jesus and what it means to them. One place I've done that regularly is at Solomon's Porch, our church community in Minneapolis. In an occasional, multipart sermon series over a couple of years, I have preached through various understandings of the atonement, biblical views thereof, and my own developing opinion.

At Solomon's Porch, sermons take place in the round and in a dialogic format. One evening, while unpacking my view that the doctrine of original sin isn't particularly biblical, a woman raised her hand and began to speak. "Well, we know why Jesus died," she confidently stated. "It's because we have an enemy, named Satan. And he is currently in control of the world. God had to send Jesus to die to free us from our bondage to Satan."

So matter-of-factly did she make this claim that I sat for a moment considering how best to respond. "Yes," I finally said. "One of the ways that Christians have understood the crucifixion in the past is this: that Satan's reign over the Earth was either defeated or severely weakened by the death of God's son."

She was correct: this is one of the ways that Christians have understood the cross, especially in the first one thousand years of Christianity.

While there has never been one exclusive version of the atonement at any point in church history, various theories have been dominant during various eras. The view that reigned in the first millennium of the church had to do with an epic battle between God and Satan. And this view has come down to us primarily in two subcategories.

Ransom Captive

Remember the climax of *The Lion, the Witch and the Wardrobe* by C. S. Lewis? Young and mischievous Edmund Pevensie, one of the four sibling protagonists, eats some Turkish delight candy and thereby eternally indebts himself to the White Witch. According to the "deep magic from the dawn of time," she has the right to execute Edmund because he has betrayed his siblings—treason is the charge, and forgiveness is not possible. Aslan, the messianic lion, makes a side deal with the White Witch: she lets the boy go and slaughters Aslan on the stone table in Edmund's place. The other three children are grief-stricken disciples, horrified that their brother's sin would mean the murder of their beloved leader.

But the White Witch was tricked! Aslan comes back to life the next morning, more powerful than before. The White Witch seems to have known about some of the deep magic, but not all of it. She didn't know that there was a *deeper* magic from the dawn of time and that resurrection was part of that magic.

This, in sum, is the Ransom Captive theory of the atonement, widely held in the first millennium of the church and the primary target of Anselm in *Cur Deus Homo*. According to the Ransom Captive theory, Adam and Eve bargained away the freedom of the human race to Satan in exchange for the fruit from the tree of the knowledge of good and evil. Humanity was held *captive* by Satan. For thousands of years, Satan held sway over humanity, as recorded in the sins and failings of the Old Testament characters.

But God offered his own son as a *ransom* for the captive human race—in Jesus' own words, "For the Son of Man did not come to be served but to serve, and to give his life a ransom for many."[1] Satan accepted the offer, and Jesus was crucified.

But Satan was duped! Jesus rose on the third day—God got to have his cake (the freedom of the human race) and eat it too (the resurrection of his son). Origen, a church father from the third century, wrote about that quote from Jesus:

> But to whom did He give His soul as a ransom for many? Surely not to God. Could it, then, be to the Evil One? For he had us in his power, until the ransom for us should be given to him, even the life (or soul) of Jesus, since he (the Evil One) had been deceived, and led to suppose that he was capable of mastering that soul, and he did not see that to hold Him involved a trial of strength greater than he was equal to.[2]

Ransom Captive was a powerful and compelling explanation of the crucifixion for a thousand years. And it does have at least one merit over the Payment model: in the Ransom Captive understanding of the atonement, the resurrection of Jesus is central, for the resurrection seals the victory of God over God's evil opponent. What Satan doesn't understand is that death cannot vanquish God. That lack of understanding leads to Satan's downfall and to the ultimate liberation of humanity from Satan's clutches.

God is not wrathful here; he's no monster. God is a warrior, at battle with evil over the fate of the human race.

Christ the Victor

In 1930, an unheralded Swedish bishop revived an understanding of the atonement that had largely been forgotten for a millennium. Gustaf Aulén's book *Christus Victor: An Historical Study of the Three*

Main Types of the Idea of Atonement was translated into English the next year, and it's stayed in print ever since.

The Christus Victor model—Latin for "Christ, the victor"—Aulén argues, was a dominant theory for the first millennium of the church, and it was held by the majority of the church fathers whom we still revere. Anselm came along and changed the game, and Christus Victor was relegated to history's rubbish bin—until Aulén. Today, Christus Victor has had something of a resurgence, made popular by such writers as Greg Boyd, a Minnesota pastor and theological punching bag for many advocates of Payment atonement.

Boyd thinks that a lot happened on the cross and that lots of Bible verses are fulfilled by the crucifixion: God reveals the truth about himself, God forgives sins, God releases the Holy Spirit into the world. "Yet," Boyd writes, "I believe all these facets of Christ's work can be understood as aspects of the most fundamental thing Christ came to accomplish: namely, to defeat the devil and his minions. He came to overcome evil with love."[3]

At first blush, Christus Victor may sound like the Payment model that many of us grew up with. But that's where Aulén and Boyd say we're wrong. The early church did not understand the death of Christ as paying a penalty in some transactional sense that only God's son could pay. The crucifixion is not cosmically *necessary* to reconcile God and humanity.

Instead, Christ's death is God's victory over sin and death. God conquers death by fully entering into it. God conquers Satan using the very means employed by his adversary.

Therefore, the crucifixion is not a sacrifice necessary to appease a wrathful and justice-demanding deity, but an act of divine love to rescue creation from Satan's grip. And it is, according to Boyd, a voluntary act. It's not required by a cosmic framework of justice, nor is it a legal transaction that must be paid. Instead, it's an act of self-sacrificial love in which Jesus throws himself on the powers of evil and destroys them.[4]

God entered fully into the bondage of death, turned it inside out by making it a moment of victory, and liberated humans to live lives of love without the fear of death.

Who Is This Warrior God?

These related views—Ransom Captive and Christus Victor—we'll call the Victory model. In Victory, the crucifixion is a beautiful and powerful thing, and Victory maintains an egalitarian view of the Trinity—one in which the Son and Spirit are not junior partners in the atonement (a major complaint against the Payment model). Plus, the resurrection is of ultimate importance, not an afterthought; it's the defeat of Satan and his minions. In the Victory model, God is bound by something like Narnia's deep magic. But according to Victory, God's in full control—God enters voluntarily into suffering and ultimately defeats Satan.

Victory also accounts for the apocalyptic worldview of the New Testament. In the centuries before Jesus' birth, Judaism had undergone a fairly serious change in focus. We've already learned that during the intertestamental period, the Hebrews had adopted the language of apocalypse: dragons, rivers of blood, angels and demons, and the end of time. New to Judaism, apocalyptic language was fairly common in the religions of Israel's neighbors.

Into this milieu, Jesus was born, and he often appropriated apocalyptic language in his own sermons and diatribes. The question for us is this: when Jesus preached apocalyptically—"And you will hear of wars and rumors of wars; see that you are not alarmed; for this must take place, but the end is not yet. For nation will rise against nation, and kingdom against kingdom, and there will be famines and earthquakes in various places: all this is but the beginning of the birth pangs"[5]—was he speaking literally, or was he using a rhetorical device that his audience would have recognized as such?

Victory atonement is predicated on a framework of unmitigated warfare, enough so that many modern Christians find it unpalatable. Greg Boyd doesn't. He unabashedly writes that the Bible teaches "the understanding that the earth and its inhabitants exist in a *cosmic war zone*."[6] And Boyd preaches that spiritual warfare—an unseen battle between angels and demons—continues today.

If the victory was won on the cross, why does the fighting continue? We might compare this delay to the case of Hiroo Onoda, a Japanese intelligence officer in World War II. He was dropped on a small island in the Philippines in 1944, just months before the United States A-bombed Hiroshima and Nagasaki; Japan surrendered less than a week later. Onoda, however, didn't hear this news and hid in the jungle for twenty-nine years. He was finally coaxed out of hiding in 1974, but only after his long-retired commanding officer flew to the Philippines and convinced him that hostilities had ended.

The Victory model says it's similar with the battle between God and Satan: the war is over, Satan has been defeated by Jesus' death on the cross, but Satan has not yet surrendered so a lot of us are still fighting battles with the forces of evil.

Six Questions for the Victory Model

What does the Victory model say about God?

In the Victory model, we get some mixed signals about God. God's a warrior, a victorious warrior. But in a strange twist, he's already won a war that's still going on. The problem with the world is that it's beset with evil and in the clutches of Satan and other spiritual powers. Did God, the creator of this world, allow this to happen, or did God set the circumstances to make it possible? God is in the odd position of negotiating with Satan, trying to win back humanity by handing over his son as a ransom. This makes sense in a children's novel about a lion and a witch, but it's more problematic to see the Creator of the cosmos having to trick his demonic opponent.

Further, it may not jibe with our modern sensibilities to think of God as a warrior. Isn't this an anachronistic holdover from our tribal forefathers? Perhaps, but it's also possible to construe God as the one who fights on our behalf against all the forces that conspire against us. Many of us experience oppression—from mental illness, addiction, dysfunctional family systems, unjust legal and governmental structures. God's victory over evil doesn't need to be metaphysical, over real demons. It can be metaphorical, over oppression in whatever form that takes. In this way, a God of Victory may be more palatable to a modern person.

What does it say about Jesus?

Jesus is God's soldier, sent into battle by the Father. In his life, Jesus freed people from demons. Some of us today might consider those episodes to be about people suffering from mental illness, but proponents of Victory tend to read those stories literally: demons really inhabit people, and Jesus really sent those demons into pigs and off a cliff. As above, this isn't the only way to read them, however. Jesus' victory can be construed in ways that accord with what we know of the world, modern science, and the like.

Jesus' death, like Aslan's, is a sacrifice required to overcome death, Satan's greatest weapon. And his resurrection holds top billing, for as Christ stands triumphant on Easter morning, he has surmounted humanity's greatest obstacle. Depending on whom you ask, Jesus is either a mighty warrior or a humble warrior, but in either case, he's a warrior. And in the Victory model, his resurrection stands supreme, an emphasis that other models lack.

What does the Victory model say about the relationship between God and Jesus?

Whether Jesus gets a say in this, we really don't know. Victory is a robustly Trinitarian view of Jesus' life, death, and resurrection. It could be seen as the Father sending the Son into battle to do his dirty work, but it's more often emphasized that they are partners in the mission. Jesus confronted the powers of his day—mostly religious powers—with healing and love; in this way, he is the Father's emissary, bringing God's message of victory over evil to the world. Jesus' miracles are episodic victories, and his resurrection the ultimate victory. Victory atonement sees Jesus' death and resurrection as the crowning achievement of that same pattern of confrontation with evil that we see in Jesus' ministry. In the Victory model, Father and Son are united in purpose and share the same aim: to free us from bondage out of love for us. Yes, they have different roles to play, but they are not opposed to one another.

How does it make sense of violence?

In Victory, spiritual warfare is the definitive characteristic of the world into which Jesus appears. The violence that human beings exhibit toward one another simply reflects a larger spiritual reality, that there are evil forces doing battle with God and God's army. Violence, both spiritual and physical, is endemic to the human condition. We still live in the midst of violence, but we know that the forces of evil have been defeated (even if they don't know it yet). In one sense, the Victory model trucks in violence more than any other model.

But in another sense, Victory sees Jesus as the ultimate pacifist. He's a *non*violent warrior, throwing himself into the midst of battle and even suffering a violent death to show the bankruptcy of violence as a solution to our problems. Jesus abjures violence during his life, and he refuses to fight back even when he's arrested, beaten, and executed. It's a strange victory, indeed: not the kind that anyone was expecting, and still hard for many to swallow in a world beset with violence.

What does it mean for us spiritually?

Victory atonement is a boon to prayer when it relies heavily on the activity of spiritual forces. And Christians who believe in angels and demons and spiritual warfare are more likely to pray more often and more fervently than those of us who are skeptical about such things.[7] This view also relies, often, on a literal reading of those Bible passages in which Jesus casts out demons and talks about Satan. That will appeal to some Christians and turn off others. In the end, though, the Victory model threatens to undermine human responsibility, seeing humanity as subject to the influence of larger supernatural forces. How do we become cocreators with God, shepherding God's creation if we are simply the sheep who need rescue? What role do we have in appropriating God's gifts and calling? Some may say that only once we are freed from the bondage of fear and death we can grow into the mature beings God created us to be, but this model has a hard time incorporating all the passages throughout the Bible holding people responsible for their actions and expecting them to live up to God's goals and dreams for them.

Where's the love?

Greg Boyd insists that Victory emphasizes love more than any other view of the atonement, for when it views the life of Jesus, "it becomes apparent that every aspect of his life was an act of warfare, for every aspect of his life reflects Calvary-like love."[8] It is jarring to see a sentence that equates acts of war with acts of love, but that's the odd juxtaposition that Victory affirms. Satan is anti-love—he's literally the *anti*-Christ—and Jesus combats Satan's hate with love. This love comes at a great cost, the greatest cost. We, in turn, are called to fight Satan's ongoing but doomed-to-fail reign as Jesus did, with nonviolent love.

Evaluating Victory

We've got to ask if the worldview on which Victory is predicated squares with our experience of life. Are we, in fact, locked in an epic, cosmic battle between good and evil? In the classical world, when the Earth was presumed to be the center of the universe and humans the crown of God's creation, this made a great deal of sense. Human beings were God's most precious creation and the devil's most coveted prize. But now we know that while we're surely valuable to God, we are on what is the cosmic equivalent of a tiny speck of dust, hurtling around a star that is one of many billions of stars in one of billions of galaxies. Our view of our own grandiosity has been seriously compromised. Victory is based on a metaphysical schema that our civilization left behind long ago, that there are conscious but unseen and immaterial forces battling over our souls and destinies. A more metaphorical reading of Victory is possible, bringing it into alignment with a modern worldview, lacking in angels and demons. The question is whether the Victory model can make the jump to modern times without the premodern worldview on which it's based.

What is most troubling about the Victory model, though, is that it depicts a God who is locked in a battle with a fallen angel of his own making. In the end, this reflects not the monotheism that was Israel's most important contribution to theology and religion, but the religions of Israel's neighbors, in which the cosmos was birthed during a struggle between various good and evil demiurges. A God who's in eternal battle with the devil doesn't accord with the Bible's view of God as the Creator of all things. Since when did Satan become God's equal? The Bible is not a story of a white hat versus a black hat, a good guy versus a bad guy. Satan plays at best a very minor role in the biblical drama.

True, the Bible contains language and metaphor of warfare, and that made sense to a tribal people who were attempting to establish themselves as a military power during the epochs recounted in the Hebrew Bible. And, in the New Testament period, the people of God were groaning under the oppression of the most advanced military empire in the ancient world. War besets our world today, too, much to our shame, but many Christians now see that Jesus himself moved us away from that self-definition. We are to be people of peace, he taught, not warmongers. The storyline of Victory is that both human beings and God are ever at war with evil. But the message of Jesus, while at times reliant upon the rhetoric of battle, was far from the talk of a military general mustering his forces for spiritual war. Paul is more conversant in warfare imagery. He says that Jesus' followers are to battle the wiles of the devil with truth, righteousness, peace, faith, and salvation.[9]

Second, we might ask: if Satan has been defeated, why is there still so much horror? In the Victory model, Jesus' death was God's triumph over Satan, sealed with the resurrection. But if that's the case, why do so many people have the same experience as the woman who spoke up during my sermon, that Satan still rules this world? It's a Pyrrhic victory indeed if the execution of God's own son results in little or no change to the world as we know it. "Justice delayed is justice denied" goes the old saw, leading the American constitution to guarantee every citizen the right to a speedy trial. But Jesus died two thousand years ago, and we're still waiting for God's victory over Satan to be consummated. Why would God defeat Satan at such a great cost yet let Satan continue to vex us?

The Victory model of the atonement relies too much on the language of war and the depiction of a Warrior God for many people. The Roman Empire did not stake a claim to great art, architecture, poetry, or drama—those it stole from Greece and Egypt. No, Rome's brilliance lay in the art of war, and it waged war with savage efficiency. Jesus' people, the Judeans, thrice attempted revolts against Rome after Jesus' lifetime, and each was put down viciously. The first resulted in the razing of the Temple in Jerusalem, changing Judaism forever.

The point is this: Jesus and his people were acquainted with warfare—Roman soldiers in full regalia stood at major intersections in Jerusalem. Scores of miscreants and revolutionaries were crucified on Golgotha before Jesus climbed that hill with his cross. The language of warfare was available to Jesus, yet he rarely used it. He did not primarily paint his ministry as that of a battle, nor did he talk of God as a warrior. Neighboring religions did; the occupying Romans did; the ancient Hebrews did. Jesus didn't. And he most surely did not set himself up as a military general, either celestial or terrestrial, even though that's what his people expected the Messiah to be.

Victory is a major theme in Jesus' death and resurrection. Paul says as much when he writes,

> *When this perishable body puts on imperishability, and this mortal body puts on immortality, then the saying that is written will be fulfilled:*
> *"Death has been swallowed up in victory."*

> "Where, O death, is your victory?
>   Where, O death, is your sting?"
> The sting of death is sin, and the power of sin is the law. But thanks
> be to God, who gives us the victory through our Lord Jesus Christ.[10]

But Jesus' victory is over death, not Satan. Satan, if such a being exists, may be as alive as ever, but he is surely not God's equal.

Anselm, in developing substitutionary atonement, found more than a few holes in the Victory model. For one, he argued, Satan is an outlaw with no bargaining power; God didn't need to cut a deal with Satan to get the human race back. In fact, God had never allowed Satan to be in charge in the first place.

For another, what "deep magic from the dawn of time" binds God to act in a certain way? It seems that if God is the Creator of all that is, then God can act any way that God deems appropriate. It seems rather unlikely that God would set up the cosmos in such a way that Satan could gain the upper hand and force God to negotiate a deal. But in the Victory theory, God does seem to have given up a significant amount of power. In fact, God is reduced to a sparring partner with Satan.[11] We've got to believe that if Satan were the real problem, God could crush him in an instant under his proverbial thumb.

Victory theory redeems the atonement in many ways, releasing God from the legal and judicial commitments to which Payment binds him. It portrays a God who is fighting for us, whether it be against opponents metaphysical or metaphorical. But it's just too reliant on a premodern view of the cosmos, populated by spiritual beings at war, to be very helpful to many modern people. In Victory, God is too small and Satan is too big. And human beings are merely pawns in a spiritual battle over which we have little sway. It's hard to see how a life of following Jesus is a journey of self-discovery and spiritual maturation if the real action is taking place in the clouds. God's love for us is preeminent in the Victory model, but at the cost of human agency, and that's a price too high. Jesus called his disciples to follow him, not into battle, but into fullness of life and into a relationship with God.

14

———

The Magnet Model

God Draws You In

PETER ABELARD IS one of the most fascinating characters in history. Born in 1079 into a noble French family, he excelled at a young age in the study of dialectic, a branch of philosophy that specializes in the resolution of arguments by the contrasting of two ideas. During his late teens, he wandered the French countryside in search of tutors who could challenge his daunting intellect. At the age of twenty-one, he arrived in Paris and joined the prestigious school at Notre Dame Cathedral.

He didn't last long there, as he immediately bested his teachers in debates. So he set up his own school just outside of Paris, and for the next decade students flocked to him, entranced by his lectures on philosophy. Abelard is credited with establishing the method of philosophy called *nominalism*, which would reign throughout the Scholastic period.

By 1110, most agreed that Abelard was the best philosopher in Paris, but his rivals kept him from teaching at Notre Dame. So Abelard moved to Laon in northern France and turned his attention to theology. By 1115, he was back in Paris, appointed a master at Notre Dame and teaching theology to large crowds. He came to think of himself as the only undefeated philosopher in the world. In his autobiography, *The Story of My Misfortunes,* he wrote, "Thus I, who by this time had come to regard myself as the only philosopher remaining in the whole world, and had ceased to fear any further disturbance of my peace, began to loosen the rein on my desires, although hitherto I had always lived in the utmost continence."[1] For that reason, at the height of his popularity, he fell in love.

Abelard's affair with Héloïse d'Argenteuil is one of the most celebrated romances in history. Héloïse was the niece of Fulbert, the canon of Notre Dame, and she was a student of Abelard. For that reason, their love was forbidden. Of their torrid affair, Abelard wrote passionately:

> No degree in love's progress was left untried by our passion, and if love itself could imagine any wonder as yet unknown, we discovered it. And our inexperience of such delights made us all the more ardent in our pursuit of them, so that our thirst for one another was still unquenched.[2]

With love like that, it's no surprise that Héloïse got pregnant. Abelard secretly married her, sent their son to be raised by his family, and dispatched Héloïse to a convent. Fulbert, thinking this was Abelard's way of getting rid of his niece and her child, hired some men to break into Abelard's room one night, and they savagely castrated him.[3] The subsequent letters between Héloïse and Abelard are among the most beautiful and tortured of any epistolary love in history.

Disgraced, Abelard became a monk and tried to confine himself to a cloistered monastery. But his love of teaching theology overwhelmed him, and he gradually returned to lecturing in public. At times, so poor was he that he lived in the woods, and so popular was his teaching that disciples camped out with him so as to hear his lectures.

A dialectical thinker, Abelard put opposing views next to each other, working through their conflict in hopes of a resolution. This is the entire premise of his most controversial book, *Sic et Non (Yes and No),* in which he contrasts passages from the Bible and the church fathers that do not agree with one another. To publish such a book scandalized many of his peers but thrilled the masses who clamored to hear him speak. His theological adversaries, like the famous mystic Bernard of Clairvaux, said that the meaning of any theological proposition is plain, and human reason is of no help in making sense of religion. Abelard countered that since reason and revelation both come directly from God, they must work in concert. Abelard's contemporary, Anselm, had coined the phrase *fides quaerens intellectum* ("faith seeking understanding") to explain the relationship between religion and human reason. While Abelard vehemently disagreed with Anselm's conclusions, their quest was the same: a reasoned faith.

So enraged were Abelard's theological rivals that they brought charges against him. In 1121, he was condemned as a heretic and made to throw his own book, *Theologia Summi Boni (A Theology of the Supreme Good)*, into a fire. Twenty-nine years later, under the continued harassment of Bernard, he was again condemned. Abelard appealed to Pope Innocent II, who responded by excommunicating him. Peter the Venerable, the abbot of the monastery at Cluny, took Abelard in, got the pope to lift the excommunication, and arranged reconciliation between Abelard and Bernard before Abelard died on April 21, 1142.

It is said that Peter Abelard's dying words were "I don't know."

Jesus' Death as Moral Example

Peter Abelard is known today not just as a romantic and a castrato but as the theologian who pioneered an intriguing answer to our guiding question, *Why did Jesus die?* Abelard developed his innovative answer in his commentary on Romans, the very letter of Paul that Penalty proponents say gives a bulletproof defense of their position. In his *Exposition of the Epistle to the Romans*, Abelard makes three intriguing arguments.

First, Abelard interprets everything in Paul's letter through the lens of God's love. God's righteousness? Abelard says it's love. God's justice? Love. In fact, by the grace channeled through Jesus, we are joined to God in an "indissoluble bond of affection," one of Abelard's most beautiful and important ideas.[4] One way to read the difference between Anselm and Abelard is that the former was wired as a lawyer, interested in preserving the uprightness of the law, and the latter as a romantic, a poet, in the vein of medieval tales of courtly love.[5] What concerns Abelard is not God's anger but God's love. His entire argument about the atonement is based on love. And in order to show the power of love to overcome even sin, Abelard points to the incredible power of God's love in Jesus, and even of the power of love in others, like the "sinful woman" in Luke 7 who washed Jesus' feet with her tears and hair and anointed them with expensive oil. To her, Jesus responded, "Many sins are forgiven her because she hath loved much."[6]

It's really an amazing thing, when you think about it: this woman's own love for Jesus was so great that it—her love—washed away her sins. And this is only one of many times in the Gospels that Jesus forgives people their sins. "The Lord was willing to pardon sinful [people] apart from his Passion," Abelard notes. He's saying that the crucifixion could not have been the only means available for God to forgive us; if it were, then Jesus could not have forgiven anyone before his death.[7] If the death of Jesus is the only way to forgive sin, as mentioned earlier, God could have ordered the baby Jesus to be sacrificed in the manger.

Love is this potent, Abelard says. Our love for God can overcome our sin. And he prefigures his own take on the atonement when he writes that God spared not even his own son, "to convince us how much we ought to love him."[8]

Second, Abelard attacks Anselm head-on in a section titled "A Question." It is, in fact, a series of rhetorical and even somewhat snarky questions. But before turning to the Payment model, Abelard objects to the Victory model. He breezily dismisses Victory, reminding us that humans are servants of God, and Satan is likewise a servant of God. Surely one servant can seduce another servant into servitude and then bargain with the master of both. In other words, God wouldn't have to wrest us back from Satan's clutches by sacrificing his own son. He could just take us back, no questions asked.

Then he turns to Payment. Abelard is no fan of original sin, the linchpin of Anselm's atonement. How much more terrible is crucifying God's son than eating a piece of fruit? Abelard asks. The punishment doesn't fit the crime! If God's going to be mad at humans for something, you'd figure the crucifixion might be more irksome to him than the ingestion of a forbidden piece of fruit. "And if that sin of Adam was so great that it could be expiated only by the death of Christ," Abelard asks, "what expiation will avail for that act of murder committed against Christ, and for the many great crimes committed against him or his followers?"[9] He's asking a logical question: how did the death of his son not make God *more* mad at us, instead of less? In his most pointed statement of all, Abelard writes,

> Indeed, how cruel and wicked it seems that anyone should demand the blood of an innocent person as the price for anything, or that it should in any way please him that an innocent man should be slain—still less that he should consider the death of his Son so agreeable that by it he should be reconciled to the world![10]

At which point, Abelard makes his third point, offering his solution to the conundrum: God took on human nature and even bore death in order to more fully bind himself to us. The result should be that, upon grasping what God has done for us, we will be likewise set afire with love for God and desire nothing more than union with him. Jesus' death on the cross arouses us from our slumber, awakens us to the love that God has for us, and drives us to love God and one another more fervently.

Jesus is God's magnet, and the magnetic force is love.

During Jesus' life, God used Jesus to magnetically draw people to himself. Then, when he was crucified, Jesus became an ultra-high-powered electromagnet. The intensity of the love displayed on the cross not only draws us to God but also draws out of us a superhuman love for one another.

Then, like the sinful woman who bathed Jesus' feet with her tears, we are forgiven our sins *by our own love.* Love so overwhelms us—love spurred on by Christ's love for us—that our sins fall away. That's how strong the magnet is. And that's the heart of the Magnet model of the atonement.

It's Jesus' example of humility and sacrificial love to the point of death that catalyzes our own love and activates forgiveness. This has led to some calling Abelard's stance the Moral Exemplar theory of the atonement. But that title doesn't do it justice, since it doesn't really capture the totality of Abelard's thinking. Jesus' death doesn't just point the way to selfless moral living; it actually draws us into a life of love and forgiveness that is the ultimate, overwhelming response to the crucifixion. Jesus' death activates a supernatural love that transcends any earthly love.

So What's the Problem?

Abelard rejected the notion of original sin, arguing that while human beings are guilty and sinful, this is not because we've inherited some depravity from Adam. He also said that whatever sin we inherit from Adam is washed away at baptism, which reveals what a high view of the church's sacrament he held. Ultimately, though, one human cannot be held liable for another person's sin. That's not justice. We are *inclined* toward sin because of Adam, but we are not *guilty* of his sin. And just as one person cannot be held liable for another's sin, neither can a person achieve absolution on another's behalf.

Abelard, a man of the Middle Ages, was not the first to see the atonement this way. The Magnet model of the atonement was the first articulated in the very earliest, post-Apostolic church. You can read about it in some of the first Christian writings, as early as the second century. Here, for example, is Clement of Alexandria (c. 150–c. 215):

> For [Christ] came down, for this he assumed human nature, for this he willingly endured the sufferings of humanity, that being reduced to the measure of our weakness he might raise us to the measure of his power. And just before he poured out his offering, when he gave himself as a ransom, he left us a new testament: "I give you my love." What is the nature and extent of this love? For each of us he laid down his life, the life which was worth the whole universe, and he requires in return that we should do the same for each other.[11]

With this quote, we can see how free will is a core component of the Magnet model: God performs an act of almost incomprehensible love, and it's up to each human being to accept that love or reject it. So it may surprise us to hear that even Augustine, foremost developer of the doctrine of predestination, was himself a proponent of the Magnet atonement.[12]

So, according to Abelard, human beings are not absolved of sin because of Christ's death on the cross. Absolution is achieved only by confession and repentance and our active life of love that follows. Christ's death serves as an example that beckons us to lives of sacrificial love:

> Our redemption through the suffering of Christ is that deeper love within us which not only frees us from slavery to sin but also secures for us the true liberty of the children of God, in order that we might do all things out of love rather than out of fear—love for him who has shown us such grace that no greater can be found.[13]

For the Magnet model, sin is still the problem that the crucifixion solves. But sin neither has us in debt to God nor in the clutches of Satan. Instead, sin keeps us from God and keeps us from being godly. Ultimately, sin keeps us from being who we're supposed to be—namely, loving and free people.

Socinus and Us

Abelard's theory didn't gain near the following of Anselm's. In fact, it pretty much fell off the radar. Five hundred years after Abelard, the Magnet model briefly reemerged during the Reformation in the writing and teaching of Faustus Socinus. Socinus's uncle, Lelio, had left his native Bologna to meet with the Reformers of Northern Europe. In the 1540s, he stayed with Philip Melanchthon in Wittenburg and made the acquaintance of John Calvin in Geneva, both theological rock stars of the era. Lelio, unlike those Reformers, was a Unitarian, having rejected the divinity of Jesus and the concept of the Trinity. He passed this belief on to his nephew, Faustus, who became a Unitarian preacher and traveled across Europe with his message. In his most important theological work, *De Jesu Christo Servatore (The Savior Jesus Christ),* published in 1594, Socinus thoroughly refuted Anselm's Payment model. Among his arguments is this: If grace and mercy are eternal aspects of God's character, then they must also be infinite characteristics, just like God's wrath. So why does Payment assume that the demands of God's wrath must be met, but not the demands of his mercy? Why is wrath a more powerful motivation for God than love?

Faustus Socinus had a small band of followers, but others considered him a heretic, and more than once angry mobs chased him out of town. In 1605, a year after he died, the Racovian Catechism was published, and Socinianism was born. That document captures the beliefs of the Unitarian Polish Brethren Church of the seventeenth century, and it has occasionally been revived by Unitarians since then. In the Racovian Catechism, three reasons are given for Christ's death on the cross:

1. That a hope for remission of sins might be created for sinners;
2. That all sinners might be drawn to Christ by his sacrificial love for them;
3. That God might "in this manner testify his boundless love to the human race, and might wholly reconcile them to himself."[14]

Other than that historical footnote, the Magnet model has been mostly absent from modern conversations about Jesus' death. That's because, as we will see in the next section, it falls short of embracing the full divinity of Jesus, making it primarily attractive to today's Unitarians and Universalists. However, with its heavy emphasis on love, this view does appeal to our commitment to finding God's love at the center of the crucifixion.

Six Questions for the Magnet Model

What does the Magnet model say about God?

In the Magnet model, God is a beautiful, loving Being. God is not coercive. God does not demand. Instead, God invites and beckons. And the cross is the ultimate invitation to each human being to live the life that God wants us to live. The death of Jesus is the world's most powerful magnet, drawing people in by its intense power of love. Why God would choose to activate this supernatural love through an execution is largely unanswered. In other models of the atonement, death and blood and sacrifice are required by some system of justice or some ancient law. In Magnet, no such requirement exists, leaving us to wonder why God could not have chosen a less brutal way to pull us toward him.

Also, the magnet does not seem to work for everyone, for as beautiful and magnetic as the cross is, it is also terrifying and violent and off-putting to many. Paul calls the message of the cross "a stumbling block to Jews and foolishness to Gentiles."[15] That's a far cry from a magnet. And to others still, it's merely ho-hum, like the philosophers who Paul met on the Areopagus.[16] So the power of God seems a bit ambivalent, since not everyone is caught in the magnet's power.

What does it say about Jesus?

Of all the models of the atonement available, the Magnet model most thoroughly embraces all of Jesus' life as an example of love and service. Jesus is sent by God to inaugurate a new way of love in the world. He lives in love, and he dies in love. But Jesus' divinity is unnecessary in this model, which will be deeply unsatisfying to many people. In fact, isn't Jesus' willingness to die in order to inspire us to lives of love more impressive if he is merely human? Does divinity add anything to this story? And if he's not divine, how is his life and death different from those of other noble and virtuous people who have been martyred for their beliefs?

The Magnet model doesn't really confront the need that most of us have for the forgiveness of our sins. Has Jesus' action on the cross really taken care of the problem we feel in our hearts? Abelard says that our love for Jesus wipes out our sin, but this answer is deeply problematic for most of us. Our own, very human love just doesn't seem that pure or that powerful.

What does the Magnet model say about the relationship between God and Jesus?

Jesus comes from God to show love. He's an emissary, he's even God's son, but he's not necessarily divine. In the Magnet model, God is almost as cruel as he is in substitution, for here too God authors the brutal death of his son in order to beckon us to love him and others more completely. Victims of violence and abuse struggle with this version of the atonement as much as others because it makes Jesus, the son, the sacred object of some terrible violence at the hands of his own father.

That's the Unitarian (Socinus) version of the Magnet model, but it's not the Trinitarian (Abelard) view. In the latter, the Father and the Son are united in their commitment to activating love between God and humans. Jesus does not wander the Earth as God's abandoned Son. Instead, he is one with the Father, as he says in the Gospel of John.[17] Their mission is the same: to flip a switch that turns on the power of love in ways previously unknown.

How does it make sense of violence?

Couldn't God have chosen another way—*any* other way—to unlock this love? Indeed, wouldn't a nonviolent example have been far more compelling to us than execution? Abelard was unconcerned with these questions, which is unfortunate, being that he had been a victim of violence himself. And, as we've already noted, the medieval mind was not particularly troubled by violence. We might answer this question now as we did with the Victory model, that Jesus' death was the ultimate display of nonviolence in the face of violence. Jesus isn't an unwitting victim so much as he powerfully throws himself into the mechanism of death and exhibits love in the face of torture.

What does it mean for us spiritually?

A recovery of the Magnet model in modern times holds great promise. So many people teeter on the edge of Christian faith, and the metaphysical answers of the Payment and Victory models of the atonement fall short. People are often not attracted to a theory of a cosmic transaction between God and the law or God and Satan. They want a personal, relational connection to God. And this is just what the Magnet model offers. When the faithful bow or kneel or weep at the foot of a cross or crucifix, they're probably not weighing the merits of different versions of the atonement. More likely, they're drawn to the symbol of the immense and sacrificial love of Christ on the cross.

However, how does Jesus' death confront the problem of sin? Abelard sidestepped this issue by teaching that original sin was washed away at baptism. But most Christians will struggle with that explanation. We'd like the crucifixion, something with so great a cost, to be more than merely an example of sacrificial love. We'd like it to actually *do* something. Abelard says it does do something—it activates a magnetic love. The problem for many of us is that the

Magnet view downplays the forgiveness of sin that Paul finds in the crucifixion. We might ask whether the crucifixion is necessary at all if Jesus is simply an example of a good moral, sacrificial life. How is Jesus any different than, say, Gandhi or the Buddha? However, in spite of its shortcomings regarding the forgiveness of sin, this view's rootedness in love is something that can enhance even the most jaded among us.

Where's the love?

To this question, the Magnet model has the ultimate answer: it's all about the love. There's no transaction here, and no battle with Satan. There is only love, shown by God to all humanity in the life and death of Jesus. An "indissoluble bond of affection" eternally links us to God, and that link was forged in the fire of the crucifixion.

Evaluating the Magnet View

At the Last Supper, Jesus washed his disciples' feet and then told them,

> Do you know what I have done to you? You call me Teacher and Lord—and you are right, for that is what I am. So if I, your Lord and Teacher, have washed your feet, you also ought to wash one another's feet. For I have set you an example, that you also should do as I have done to you. Very truly, I tell you, servants are not greater than their master, nor are messengers greater than the one who sent them. If you know these things, you are blessed if you do them.[18]

Wouldn't this have been enough to provoke us to sacrificial love? If catalyzing love were the only reason for Jesus' life, surely he didn't have to die. This has been the lingering problem for the Magnet model of the atonement. While it redeems the loving and selfless life that Jesus lived, it struggles to explain whether anything truly redemptive happened on the cross. As we've seen, it sells Abelard short to complain that the crucifixion is simply an example of a self-less death. He clearly held a more mystical view of Jesus' death than that, saying that it unlocks a love that is supernaturally attractive. Nevertheless, Jesus' divinity is rendered unnecessary in the Magnet model. God could have chosen just about anything to draw people into his love, and he just happened to choose a first-century Naza-rene craftsman. One could even argue that God also chose Gandhi and Mother Teresa in addition to Jesus, for they, too, have catalyzed great love in many people. There have been many martyrs, sacri-ficing their lives for their beliefs or for the sake of others. Since its earliest centuries, the Christian church has held Jesus' divinity to be of utmost importance, and the relationship between Jesus and God the Father to be a central aspect of the forgiveness that comes by way of the cross. Insofar as the Magnet view of the atonement does not address that, it falls short for Trinitarian Christians.

Much is to be learned from the Magnet model, however, and we would do well to resuscitate it. It appeals to our sense that God is love and that the crucifixion unlocks God's love in a new way and pours that love out on the world. Abelard's contribution has been forgotten for too long. Let's bring it back into the mix.

15

The Divinity Model
God Wants You to Be a God

I N THE FIRST millennium of Christianity, there was basically
one church. When disputes arose, for instance, over the Trinity
or the dual natures of Christ, bishops from around the known
world would gather, discuss, and decide. But divisions grew toward the end of the first millennium. Those in the East (present-
day Greece, Turkey, Romania, Russia, and surrounding countries)
thought that the church should be governed by a pentarchy—that is,
a coalition of leaders from Rome, Constantinople, Alexandria, Antioch, and Jerusalem. But in the West, the leaders in Rome claimed
that their city was the *caput et mater omnium ecclesiarum*—the head and
mother of the entire church.

That wasn't all. In the East, they used bread baked with yeast for
communion; the Western church insisted on unleavened bread. In
the East they spoke and preached and wrote in Greek; in the West,
they preferred Latin. The East emphasized that theological insight
was gained from mystical experiences with God; the West preferred
academic study and intellectual debate.

Then there was the small matter of the *filioque* clause. Sometime
in the middle of that first millennium, some Christians in the West
slipped an extra word into the statement of belief that they recited

during church services, known as a *creed*. Based on a line in the Gospel of John, the creed traditionally professed that the Holy Spirit came from the Father.[1] But some Westerners added the word, *filioque,* which means "and the Son," rendering the creed,

> We believe in the Holy Spirit, the Lord, the giver of life,
> who proceeds from the Father *and the Son,*
> who with the Father and the Son is adored and glorified.

What seems trivial today was of utmost importance to churchmen in the Early Middle Ages. For one thing, Easterners resented the fact that Westerners unilaterally changed the creed. And for another, they thought that adding this word undermined the Father's role as progenitor of the entire Trinity. In the mid-600s, the patriarch in Constantinople wrote to the pope in Rome to object to the *filioque* addition. The pope responded by excommunicating the patriarch. And so it went, with this one word debated at synods and councils in 767, 796, and 809. In 1014, the creed was sung with the disputed word at worship in Rome for the first time, and it's been part of the Latin mass ever since.

But the leaders in the East didn't back down. In 1053, the patriarch closed all Latin-speaking churches in Constantinople. By the next year, matters came to a head. Mutual excommunications ensued, again. The East and the West declared each other anathema. Everyday Christians were largely unaware of the schism at the time, but it turned out to be one of the pivotal events in world history.

The Eastern Church, also known as the Orthodox Church, is unfortunately unknown by most of us as a result of the Great Schism of 1054. After that, the bishops of the East and West went their separate ways and thereafter met only rarely. Prior to a meeting between Pope Paul VI and Ecumenical Patriarch Athenorgas I in 1964, the heads of the two churches hadn't met since 1439. That's a 525-year gap between meetings, and it takes a lot to bridge all those years of animosity.[2]

As a result of this schism, we are mainly unfamiliar with the theology and practice of the East. Among the peculiarities of Orthodoxy is the view that we don't really have theologians, per se, these days. All theology was done in the Bible, by the church fathers, and in the early church councils. Modern writings and sermons simply explicate the theology that was set in stone in those first centuries of Christianity.

As seen in the *filioque* controversy, the Orthodox hold the Trinity very dearly. The connection between Father, Son, and Spirit is sometimes described using the word *perichoresis,* which is best translated "mutual interpenetration." The three persons of the Trinity live in an eternal relationship. This is key to their view of Jesus' death. But even more important to the Orthodox church is Jesus' birth.

It's sometimes said that the three major branches of the Christian family tree can be categorized by three holidays. Catholics emphasize Good Friday, as seen in the crucifixes—a cross with Jesus hanging on it—on their necks and in their churches. Protestants, as witnessed by their empty crosses, most love Easter. And the Orthodox are partial to Christmas, the day that Jesus was born as a God-man. Catholics highlight crucifixion; Protestants, resurrection; and Orthodox, incarnation.

This has everything to do with how Orthodoxy views humanity and the story of Adam and Eve. While Augustine and the other theologians of the West looked at the Genesis accounts of the first humans as historic reports of a moment in time, some of the earliest theologians in the East interpreted the stories as recounting a process by which humanity lost its most sacred possession, its divinity.[3] Human beings were created to share in the immortal divine life, as established by the telling verse, "Then God said, 'Let us make humankind in our image, according to our likeness.'"[4] But the sin of Eve and Adam began a process of distortion by which humanity lost its divinity and immortality. Death is the result of that distortion. That's what the initial sin did. Now we're broken, sick, and distorted because we're not divine as we were meant to be. Although a small spark of divinity still resides within us, we stand in need of repair. And death is the ultimate chasm between us and the immortal God.

Building on their strong affection for the Trinity and their view that we hold the potential for divinity within us, Orthodox Christians regard the birth of Jesus as a monumental act of love by God to overcome the chasm of death. Since we can no longer reach God, God came to us. Possibly the most famous quote in all of Orthodox theology comes from Athanasius (c. 293–373), who in his book, *On the Incarnation,* wrote of Christ, "For he was made man so that we might become God."[5] Some people try to water this down, and they translate it, ". . . so that we might become *like* God." But in the Greek, it literally says, "For he was en-humaned so that God-made we could be."[6]

For Athanasius, the incarnation of God in the person of Jesus of Nazareth rekindles the possibility of our own divinity, our union with God. This theology, called *divinization* or *theosis,* sounds strange to our Western ears. We most often think of God as Other, a being who lives exclusively outside of us and is basically unreachable by us except through Jesus. While the Orthodox don't necessarily reject that notion, they also firmly believe that God lives *inside* of us. We reach God by going *within*. Jesus came to reignite that spark of divinity within us.

The Orthodox take this idea straight from the Bible. In John 10, Jewish leaders take up stones to execute Jesus for blasphemy. He responds by saying,

> Is it not written in your law, "I said, you are gods"? If those to whom the word of God came were called "gods"—and the scripture cannot be annulled—can you say that the one whom the Father has sanctified and sent into the world is blaspheming because I said, "I am God's Son"?[7]

And later in John, in one of the most theologically potent passages in all of scripture, Jesus proclaims that there is a mutual indwelling between him and the Father—"Do you not believe that I am in the Father and the Father is in me?"[8] Jesus goes on to assure his disciples that he offers them a similar relationship, that he is their conduit to the Father. Paul, too, hints at this, telling the Corinthian church that they are being gradually transformed into the same glory as the Lord, and that they are assured of immortality by the resurrection.[9] The Holy Spirit dwells within us, proclaims Paul: "Do you not know that you are God's temple and that God's Spirit dwells in you?"[10] And many other passages in both testaments echo this claim.

Building a Bridge Between Divinity and Humanity

This spark of God within us animates the Orthodox vision of theosis, and it also drives the Orthodox understanding of the crucifixion. As we've seen with other interpretations, the atoning work of Jesus on the cross is always the solution to a problem. For the Orthodox, the problem is that we've lost our access to our divine nature; we've lost our immortality.[11] In other versions of Jesus' death that we've investigated, certain words have been prominent: *satisfaction, substitute,* and *penalty; battle, war,* and *victory.* In the Divinity model, *exchange, participation,* and *sharing* are the operative words. The Son exchanged his divine life for human, indwelling Jesus of Nazareth so that he could participate with humanity. By sharing in mortal, human life, Christ makes it possible for us to again share in the divine life of God.

So first, *Jesus' birth begins to rebuild the bridge between God and humanity.*

Some Western church fathers shied away from the idea that God experienced death on the cross, even suggesting that Jesus' divinity left his body in the moment before he died. The Divinity model has no such hang-up. The union of divine and human in the person of Jesus is essential and indivisible, and it's that union that makes his death powerful. Twentieth-century Russian Orthodox theologian Georges Florovsky wrote, "The death on the Cross was effective, not as a death of an Innocent One, but as the death of the Incarnate Lord."[12] In the fourth century, the Eastern Church father Gregory of

Nyssa made an analogy to fishing. Death swallowed Jesus, the bait, but hidden under Jesus' human flesh was a hook, his divinity:

> The Deity was hidden under the veil of our nature, that so, as with ravenous fish, the hook of the Deity might be gulped down along with the bait of flesh, and thus, life being introduced into the house of death, and light shining in darkness, that which is diametrically opposed to light and life might vanish; for it is not in the nature of darkness to remain when light is present, or of death to exist when life is active.[13]

Second, *Jesus' death keeps building that bridge by entering into death, the ubiquitous human experience and the consequence of sin.*

Since the problem is death, we can see why the solution in the Divinity model focuses as much on the resurrection as on the crucifixion. To the Orthodox, it's not about what we *do,* it's about what we *are.* We are mortal; we are condemned to die. We are hedged in by our mortality and our always impending death. That's what defines us, and that's what separates us from God. The problem is death, not guilt. In the resurrection on Easter morning, God defeats death and gives us the ability to once again claim our divinity. In this scheme, the crucifixion is a means to an end: Jesus can't be resurrected unless he first dies.

And third, *Jesus' resurrection as the Risen Lord completes the bridge by overcoming the one thing that separates God and humanity: death.*

Orthodox theologian John Zizioulas puts it this way: "This victory is achieved in the Resurrection, without which there can be no talk of salvation, because death is the problem of creation."[14] He goes on,

> The West (Catholic and Protestant) has viewed the problem of the world as a moral problem (transgression of a commandment and punishment) and has made of the Cross of Christ the epicentre of faith and worship. However, Orthodoxy continues to insist upon the Resurrection as the centre

of its whole life precisely because it sees that the problem of the created is not moral but ontological; it is the problem of the existence (and not of the beauty) of the world, the problem of death.[15]

Here we see just how differently the Divinity model conceives of both the problem and the solution posed by Jesus' death and resurrection. The difference stems from the very nature of our existence vis-à-vis God's existence: God is eternal, we are mortal; God is uncreated, we are created; God is love, we are far from perfect in our love. Because of our mortality, the gap between God and us is unbridgeable—at least by us. We simply cannot overcome the power of death. And so God sends Jesus Christ to unite with us in death, and thus allows us to overcome what would otherwise subsume us. Because just as Christ shared in our mortality by dying on the cross, we can share in his divinity through his resurrection.

Six Questions for the Divinity Model

What does the Divinity model say about God?

Orthodox Christians operate by a different metaphysic than the one that dominates the Western church. In the West, the early church was virtually consumed by the question of who was God and who was Jesus in relation to God. Ultimately, at the Council of Nicaea in 325, they settled on a definition that was heavily laden with Greek philosophy. They decided that the divinity that dwelled within Jesus was the same essence as God the Father, even though the Father and the Son are different persons.[16] Virtually every Protestant and Catholic seminarian is taught this difference, and they can often explain it to you in intricate detail.

Ironically, though the technicalities of the Nicaean definition of Christ are based on intricacies of Greek philosophy, the Eastern Orthodox are not too concerned with the substance–essence debates of the early church. Their starting and ending point is 1 John 4:8, "God is love." Father James Bernstein, an Orthodox priest in Washington, D.C., writes, "God is love—even before He creates; His love is not just an expression of His will towards creation, or simply an attribute, but rather God loves by nature—because of who He is. Love is intrinsic to His Unknowable Essence."[17]

In other words, God's love is not a *characteristic* of God. God and love are one and the same. If there is love in the world, it is God. If there is love in *you,* that is God. Maybe you've heard someone say, "Sure, God is loving, but his love is balanced with his justice" or "Without justice, love is not possible." These statements speak of God's love as an attribute of God. But, for the Divinity model, God's very nature is love. Love is not an aspect of God's being; *love is God's very being.*

What does it say about Jesus?

The incarnation of God in Jesus is of prime importance in the Divinity model—the incarnation is the ultimate invitation into God's love, and the crucifixion is an extension of this invitation. Again, Father Bernstein: "Orthodox incarnational theology, which is at the core of the original Gospel, teaches that God Himself, the second Person of the Trinity, became incarnate, not in order to pay a debt to the devil or to God the Father, nor to be a substitutionary offering to appease a just God, but in order to rescue us from our fallen condition and transform us, enabling us to become godlike."[18] Jesus is fully God, and there is no hedging on this. And his death is only efficacious at defeating death because he is God.

What does the Divinity model say about the relationship between God and Jesus?

The Trinitarian relationship between Father, Son, and Spirit stands at the center of the Divinity model, and everything that God does in Jesus is bent toward an invitation into that divine union. Everything. God neither abandons Jesus nor vacates his body before the crucifixion. They are together until the end, along with the Holy Spirit. Maybe more than in any other model, Divinity offers a truly robust and spiritual relationship between the Son and the Father. God and Jesus are perfectly united in bringing the potential for divinity back to humanity.

How does it make sense of violence?

Gregory of Nazianzus, a fourth-century bishop and theologian in the East, wrote, "That which is not assumed is not redeemed." In other words, it's only because Christ assumed human flesh that humanity is redeemed. And the same goes for the violence of the crucifixion. Because Christ entered fully into humanity, including a cruel and violent death, the terror of violence is defeated along with death. God avoided nothing in his quest to reunite with humanity and rekindle the divine spark within us. And among the attributes of humanity is violence, so God endured that, too.

What does it mean for us spiritually?

We can safely say that no other model offers us divinity. Only the Divinity model, predicated on the Orthodox doctrine of theosis, presents us with the opportunity to unite with God to the point of becoming God. That's an amazing promise, and one that may be hard to believe. Gregory of Nyssa, a contemporary of Nazianzus, wrote about how a life of prayer and virtue allows our godliness to come out:

> All of you mortals . . . do not despair at never being able to behold the degree of the knowledge of God which you can attain. For when God made you, He at once endowed your nature with this perfection. . . . You must then wash away, by a life of virtue, the dirt that came to cling to your heart like plaster, and then your divine beauty will once again shine forth.[19]

This is a profound spiritual promise, that we might partake in divinity by a life with Christ. What better motivation for prayer and discipleship could a model of the atonement offer?

Where's the love?

God's greatest act of charity was incarnating himself in the person of Jesus of Nazareth. In the life of Jesus, God showed the way of love in service and in healing miracles. And in the death of Jesus, God showed the extent of his love by suffering through and ultimately vanquishing death so that he could be reunited with us. That's how much he loves us. In fact, God loves us so much that he wants to share his divinity with us.

Evaluating the Divinity Model

To sum up the Divinity model of the atonement: (1) God is love; (2) we human beings have latent divinity within us, but we've lost our connection with God because of death, which came as a result of sin; (3) God conquers death and thereby reunites us with himself in the incarnation, death, and resurrection of Jesus.

But it's not quite that simple.

The Divinity model is weak on some aspects of the atonement, like the clearly Pauline view that Jesus' death saves us from our sinfulness, not just from death. This moral component is essential to a biblical understanding of Jesus' death, even if it is too often overplayed by Western theologies.

The Divinity model is also, like every other aspect of Orthodox theology, hemmed in by a worldview that was set in the third and fourth centuries and has not been updated since. While most of us believe that God is revealing new things to us all the time—even about the crucifixion—the stance of the Orthodox church is that we're merely teasing out what the church fathers and the ecumenical councils decided long ago.

Further, Orthodox understandings of atonement are wrapped in a very restrictive understanding of the church. Modern Orthodox theologians make no bones about their belief that salvation comes exclusively through the Orthodox Church. In the words of one Orthodox author, "Only within a church can one receive the sacraments which are essential to deification."[20] A similar sentiment is voiced by Bishop Kallistos Ware: "So far as we on our side are concerned, the appointed means to salvation is always in and through the community of the Church."[21]

This may stop you short, and it should. The idea that God's power to save would be restricted to the church—and to one particular denomination and to that church's administration of the sacraments—simply doesn't accord with common sense. In the end, all Orthodox theology, including the Orthodox view of the atonement, is just too constricted by a premodern cosmology and metaphysic and a view of the church that is too exclusive.

Finally, we've got to ask the same question of Divinity atonement that we've asked about others: If Jesus' resurrection conquered death, why do we still die? As we continue to look for ways that the death of Jesus is actually efficacious in our lives, union with God to the point of personal deification is the best promise we've heard yet! But the struggle we have to experience this union is real. How many of us no longer feel bound by sin? How many of us have escaped the reality of death? And how many of us feel divine?

These concerns notwithstanding, the Divinity model offers us a compelling alternative to the views of the atonement that emphasize a legal transaction or a spiritual war. A closer connection with God is what so many of us desire, and the belief that we've each got a spark of the divine within is both comforting and challenging. It's so foreign to think of ourselves as little gods that we might find it off-putting at first. But if we can get comfortable with the idea that God wants nothing less than for us to join his divine life, then there could be no greater reward for participating in the life, death, and resurrection of Jesus.

16

The Mirror Model
God Is Showing Us What We've Done

WHEN I FIRST visited a doctor about back pain, I was in my midtwenties. After having me perform a couple of movements and describe the pain, he taught me three stretches and told me I would be okay until the pain got so bad that it kept me home from work. That started to happen about fifteen years later. The pain shot down the back of my left leg. Sometimes it was worse, and other times it was better. And while it didn't keep me home from work, it did keep me up at night.

Then I had a couple of episodes that really knocked me flat. One morning about six, I started a sprinkler in the backyard. I turned on the hose and walked over to the sprinkler to adjust where it sprayed. I bent over, and my back seized. I fell to the ground, barely able to move. I definitely could not stand up, so I army-crawled my way toward the house. All the while, the pulsating sprinkler was soaking me. After probably ten minutes, I made it to the back door. It was locked. There I lay, getting doused, waiting for someone in the family to wake up and find me, immobile and in desperate pain. It was time to get help for my back pain.

First I tried massage. It felt great while I was on the table, but as soon as I tried to stand up I could tell that it had done no good.

Then I went to a chiropractor. He attached electrodes to my back and sent electrical stimulation into the muscles. It felt a bit like someone was rubbing sandpaper on my back, but it did nothing for the pain.

Next I went to physical therapy. They strapped me into a medieval torture device also known as a traction machine. The basic premise of these machines is that pulling the upper and lower parts of your torso in different directions will release pressure on the disks between the spinal vertebrae, thus allowing a herniation to retreat. After about six visits and no relief, I decided this was voodoo, too.

Cortisone shots came next. Lying facedown on a table in urgent care, a kindly physician's assistant produced the biggest needle I'd ever seen. "You absolutely cannot move," he told me, "or the consequences could be very, very bad." When he inserted the needle into my back, I felt a sharp pain, followed by warmth, followed by a complete absence of pain. Cortisone is a steroid, and it's used to decrease inflammation and mask the pain of a structural back problem so that the nerves and muscles around the injury will calm down. Because cortisone takes some time to kick in, the syringe also has a bit of Novocain in it, which is what provides the immediate alleviation of pain.

I received three cortisone shots over about a year. The first two times, the relief was immediate. As the third shot was going in and I felt no change in my back, I thought, *Oh crap.* Sure enough, it didn't do anything. I walked out of the clinic in as much pain as ever.

That was the fall of 2008. In January 2009, I flew to Nashville to speak at a gathering of fifteen hundred Methodist teenagers, and I was hurting. I left my hotel room on Friday evening and walked to the convention center where the conference was happening. By the time I arrived, my left leg was numb below the knee, and I could barely breathe. I went ahead and spoke at the conference, but they had to roll me onstage in a wheelchair.

I met with a surgeon the next week and had back surgery the week after that. I had a bulge in one of the disks in my back, and it was rubbing against the sciatic nerve. When I awoke from the anesthesia, the surgeon showed me a photo of the part of my disk that he'd clipped out and told me it was one of the biggest herniations he'd ever seen. He also said that he couldn't tell if the nerve damage was permanent or whether I'd regain feeling in my left foot. It was, and I haven't.

I needed surgery. I needed someone to cut through my skin and remove the herniation, and no procedure less radical would work. Other methods caused temporary relief by masking the pain, but nothing short of surgery could fix the problem.

René Girard has proposed the most profound recent addition to models of the atonement, and it operates by a similar rationale. Here it is in its simplest form: Humanity developed a pattern of violent sacrifice meant to assuage guilt and appease the "gods." It worked, but only temporarily. It took Jesus on the cross to provide the remedy that was really needed. Violence is our back pain; offering sacrifices to deal with our guilt is massage and cortisone shots. But Jesus and his work on the cross, that's the surgery we need to really deal with the problem.

Girard's view of the crucifixion can be understood like this: When we look at Jesus hanging on the cross, we are looking in a mirror. God is reflecting back to us the outcome of our systems of rivalry, sacrifice, and violence. Jesus' death shows conclusively that those systems are bankrupt, that they do not assuage guilt, and that they do not minimize violence. Jesus is the final sacrifice because he reveals the fiction behind the entire enterprise of sacrifice.

The Violence Virus

René Girard is a professor emeritus at Stanford University and one of only forty members, or *immortels,* of the Académie Française. He received this honor—France's highest intellectual honor—as a result of his groundbreaking anthropological work. His career has spanned many decades and is notable for an unfolding series of discoveries. He started by revealing the central aspect of all myths—triangular rivalry. That led him to see scapegoating and sacrifice as the means of dissipating the violence that rivalry engenders. He then realized that the Christian story reveals what all other myths hide—that the sacrificial victim really is innocent—and this led to Girard's own conversion to the Christian faith. Let's unpack this.

Girard is an anthropologist, and he came to his groundbreaking view of the cross not by asking theological questions but by examining the claim that the Jesus story was just one more in a long line of myths involving sacrificial death. But this only came after he had already become famous for his theory of *mimetic rivalry*.

In studying ancient societies and their myths, Girard discovered that human societies are all based on the same thing: triangular rivalry and the means to diffuse the violence that results from that rivalry. Common to all humans is *desire*—for a piece of land, a potential mate, a shiny red bicycle. But, when we live in proximity to other human beings, it's inevitable that someone else wants that thing, too—in fact, when someone else desires something, that causes me to desire it all the more. That's the triangular nature of rivalry: it's between two (or more) people and the object of desire.

Girard came to his understanding of desire and rivalry by studying myths and other literature and looking for structural similarities across genres, cultures, and time periods. What he found was that the better the story, the closer the characters hew to this triangular transaction. This desire, Girard discovered, is the plumb line of all great literature, beginning with the ancient myths.

So, a human being desires what another human being has. This is not necessarily bad. According to Girard, it is a deep, anthropological truth, rooted in our evolutionary history. But it does lead to Girard's second great hypothesis: Because human beings want what others have, violence results. Think Oedipus and his father; think Cain and Abel. Think Joseph and his brothers—they wanted the love of their father, which Joseph alone seemed to have, so they beat him and threw him in a pit and told their father he was dead. We fight for the things we want. And as human societies grew, rivalries also grew; in fact, they snowballed, and more violence ensued. Girard calls the spread of rivalry and violence *contagion,* and it's his version of original sin, the problem that we've got to overcome. Desire is a seed planted within every human; rivalry causes the seed to grow and bloom; and violence then spreads across society like a virus.

The Sacrifice Vaccine

If rivalrous violence is a virus, then sacrifice is the vaccine.

Societies needed a release valve to relieve the pressure of increasing rivalry and violence, so the *scapegoat mechanism* was developed: On the brink of mob violence, a victim is chosen and sacrificed. Somehow, almost magically, when the victim is lynched, the mob's desire for violence dissipates. Then, in an ironic twist, the scapegoat is often made a saint, or even a god.

The scapegoat mechanism is the foundation of all religion, says Girard. The priest or shaman or witch doctor explains the magic, telling the mob that the death of the victim appeased the gods, allowing them to go on with their lives. Girard argues that human society never would have gotten off the ground without the scapegoat because people would have fallen into violent, rivalrous chaos before they could form even a primitive government. Scapegoating and sacrifice make society possible. Like a car tire that's overinflated, rivalrous violence threatens to destroy a society. But the scapegoating mechanism serves to let out some air, to relieve the pressure, so that the society can establish itself.

But this vaccine is not permanent. It's only temporary. After a time, rivalries build, violence threatens, and at some point, another victim must be sacrificed to stop the virus from destroying society. The priestly class in every primitive society eventually regularized the sacrifices, setting holy days on a cycle so that mob violence would never overtake the scapegoat mechanism.

The priests also control the telling of the origin story. The genesis narrative of nearly every human society has a "founding murder":

Cain and Abel, Romulus and Remus, Oedipus and Laius, Marduk and Tiamat. In each, an innocent victim is "sacrificed" at the hands of another person, and society is then built on this pattern of sacrificial violence. Violence is covered, even justified, in the fact that the founders themselves engaged in the same behavior. And Girard is adamant that his fellow anthropologists have mistakenly classified these stories as pure myth, missing the truth that there's a real murder behind the story. The myth shrouds the truth of violence behind a veneer of romanticized story.

The Jesus Cure

Girard considers the Hebrew Bible an exception to this scheme. He says it begins to subvert the pattern in a couple of ways. For example, let's return to the story of Joseph. First, the story makes it clear that Joseph is an innocent victim. In other ancient myths, some stain of impropriety is imputed to the victim, some reason that the sacrifice is justified. But not here.

And even more significantly, when the tables are turned and Joseph becomes powerful as Pharaoh's right-hand man, he does not kill his brothers. Instead, he grants them forgiveness. This is nearly unheard of in ancient myths. The story of Joseph and his brothers has many of the elements of other ancient myths—rivalry, deceit, violence, mistaken identity, false accusation, and role reversal—but it ends in a most unconventional way: the cycle ends because the protagonist chooses familial love over retribution.

This, Girard says, is how the stories of the Hebrews begin to subvert the pattern of all other ancient myths.

The story of Jesus tears away the veil of myth completely, once and for all showing that sacrificial violence is built on a lie. The lie embedded in myths of violence and sacrifice is that the victim deserved it. Because it worked—because the scapegoating mechanism of sacrifice really does mitigate mob violence—people convince themselves that the sacrificial victim must have done something wrong. Why else would it work? The myth provides an explanation about why it worked: because the victim deserved it, because the victim's blood really did appease the gods.

But myths conceal a deeper, more unsettling truth: the victim is actually innocent, and the only reason that a sacrificial system works is because people have convinced themselves that it does. In fact, it's the system of sacrifice that's bankrupt, simply a trade-off of violence against the one victim for the violence of the mob. And the death of Jesus reveals that lie because the Gospels make it clear that Jesus is truly innocent. Instead of shrouding his death in myth, they expose his death as undeserved and unnecessary violence.

Some scholars of myth like James George Frazer and Joseph Campbell have claimed that the Jesus story is simply a bad myth, or at least a mediocre myth that's been badly interpreted, for it lacks the complexity of other archetypal stories. Both Frazer and Campbell classified Jesus as just another hero myth, part of the monomyth.

But it's the very *un*conventional nature of the "sacrifice" of Jesus that caused Girard to convert to Christianity as he studied mythology. Instead of repeating the mythic pattern and establishing a religion based on violence, Jesus' death is a renunciation of violence, and upon the foundation of his death is based a religion of peace. Girard says,

> What I have called "bad sacrifice" is the kind of sacrificial religion that prevailed before Christ. It originates because mimetic rivalry threatens the very survival of a community. But through a spontaneous process that also involves mimesis, the community unites against a victim in an act of spontaneous killing. This act unites rivals and restores peace and leaves a powerful impression that results in the establishment of sacrificial religion.
>
> In this kind of religion, the community is regarded as innocent, and the victim is guilty. Even after the victim has been deified, he is still a criminal in the eyes of the com-

munity (consider the immoral and unethical behavior of the gods in Greek and Roman mythology).[1]

The death of Jesus reverses the scapegoating process. The subversion of scapegoating begins in the Hebrew scriptures and finally culminates with Christ's death, which Girard calls a "non-sacrificial atonement." The trajectory begins in the Hebrew Bible, where the persecuting community (Israel) is pictured as guilty, and the victim (Abel, Isaac, Joseph, Job) is innocent. Then Jesus Christ, the son of God, is the final scapegoat. Precisely because he is the son of God, and since he is innocent, he exposes all the myths of scapegoating. He shows that the victims were innocent all along, and their communities were guilty.

In Christ, God becomes the one who is rejected and expelled. The scapegoat is not one who is sacrificed to appease an angry deity. Instead, the deity himself enters human society, becomes the scapegoat, and thereby eliminates the need for any future scapegoats or sacrifices.

Girard's theory is commonly referred to as the Last Scapegoat theory, but he's repeatedly said that's a misnomer. Instead, he says that sacrifice was efficacious at mitigating rivalry, but only temporarily. And it was based on a fiction, that the victim somehow deserved it. So Jesus' death is not the last in a long series of sacrifices, the ultimate sacrifice, better than any dove or goat or ox or virgin or prisoner of war. Instead, Jesus' death shows that the entire system of sacrifice is bankrupt, that it never pleased God, and it never really solved human problems.

Jesus' death does have some sense of ultimacy, to be sure. Girard writes, "The Cross is the moment when a thousand mimetic conflicts, a thousand scandals that crash violently into one another during the crisis, converge against Jesus alone."[2] Rivalry is an illness that besets humanity. That sickness is meted out upon victims and scapegoats in many societies, but never more so than when it is concentrated on Jesus. As we see Jesus dying of the contagion of violence upon the cross, he's saying to us, *This is what your rivalry and violence have wrought. This is the outcome. Now you know, so you don't have to do it ever again.*

In Jesus' crucifixion, God is holding up a mirror. We look at Jesus on the cross, and we see our own systems of violence and scapegoating reflected back at us.

Six Questions for the Mirror Model

What does the Mirror model say about God?

It's a bit tricky to evaluate God's role in the Mirror model because Girard explicitly avoids imputing activity to God. Because he's an anthropologist and not a theologian, and because he wants his work to be taken seriously by his peers, he consciously avoids relying on his own faith in his writings.[3] That being said, we can surmise some things about God in this theory. For one thing, God has never wanted blood sacrifice. However, because it worked at lessening violence, God accepted the sacrificial system, and God even endorsed it. What God did in the Hebrews was wean the people off of human sacrifice and move them toward animal sacrifice, which was a step in the right direction. God made it clear that the community (Israel) was not innocent in the violent transactions with enemies and with sacrificial victims. But God allowed humanity to evolve from early, primitive human sacrifice, to less primitive animal sacrifice, until we were ready to learn that sacrifice, in fact, does not please God.

What does it say about Jesus?

Similarly, though Girard may personally believe in Jesus' divinity, his version of the crucifixion doesn't rely on that. In the Mirror model, Jesus' life is little more than a precursor to his death. His life is necessary to establish that he is truly innocent, that he does nothing to deserve a lynching. He lived a life of peace and charity, and he is lynched by mob violence. Jesus' story is told by the Gospel writers and interpreted by Paul, and those authors do not hide behind the contrivances of myth. They do not pretend that God required this death or that Jesus deserved it or that the mob is innocent. Instead, they give us an unflinching account of an innocent victim lynched by a mob and a political apparatus. Jesus' own self-awareness of his role is not Girard's concern. Instead, his primary interest is how the Gospels and Paul differ from other, conventional stories in their depiction of this death. Jesus' death is a game changer because it breaks the pattern.

What does the Mirror model say about the relationship between God and Jesus?

Girard writes, "There is nothing in the Gospels to suggest that God causes the mob to come together against Jesus. Violent contagion was enough."[4] God didn't kill Jesus, but God let it happen. Lacking explicit theological answers from Girard, we're left to wonder about the relationship between Jesus and God. Did Jesus consent to be the last scapegoat? Did he embrace his fate? Surely, the Mirror model concurs with the Pauline belief that God works all things together for good,[5] for God took the violent contagion of the masses which put Jesus on a cross and used it to show us that violence is bankrupt.

How does it make sense of violence?

No view of Jesus' death has a better response to the problem of violence than the Mirror model. Violence is endemic and epidemic among humans, rooted in our inevitable rivalries with one another. The sacrificial system allows human societies to exist by both regulating and explaining violence. Violence is regulated by the clergy in the sacrificial system, and it is justified as the method by which sin is expelled and God is satisfied. But over millennia and within one group, God gradually weans people from this understanding of violence. Then in one singular violent act, the entire system of violence is exposed as a farce. If we had really been paying attention, this should have ended violence once and for all.

What does it mean for us spiritually?

The ethics of this view of the death of Jesus are as plain as they are compelling. Once exposed as a farce, we can see how scapegoating permeates human relations. Whether it's one country at war with another or a playground scuffle, we justify our violent tendencies by scapegoating people who are actually innocent victims. The Christian response to this realization is to call out scapegoating when we see it, to advocate on behalf of the victims, to seek forgiveness for past lynchings, and to dismantle systems that promulgate crucifixions. For ourselves, the spiritual discipline is shedding our rivalries, constantly challenging ourselves not to want what another has. If we can evolve past this very human trait, we will weaken the systems of sacrifice and violence that are set up to mitigate our rivalries.

Where's the love?

It's hard to love someone you're trying to lynch. Even nonphysical lynchings do violence to others—verbal abuse, nasty comments on websites, gossip, slander. By revealing the bankruptcy of the system of violence, Jesus opened the way to true charity toward others. His was a loving, sacrificial act in that he gave up something so valuable—his very life—to show us that we were caught in a loop of never-ending violence. We follow his example by doing the same, exchanging rivalry and violence for sacrificial love. When we choose love over violence, we step out of the loop, and we are cured of the contagion.

Evaluating the Mirror Model

Girard writes,

> Medieval and modern theories of redemption all look in the direction of God for the causes of the Crucifixion: God's honor, God's justice, even God's anger, must be satisfied. These theories don't succeed because they don't look seri-

ously in the direction where the answer must lie: sinful humanity, human relations, mimetic contagion. . . . They speak
of original sin, but they fail to make the idea concrete. That
is why they give an impression of being arbitrary and unjust
to human beings, even if they are theologically sound.[6]

We can immediately see why the Mirror model has gained so
much popularity so quickly, especially among more liberal and pro-
gressive Christians. But if Girard accuses other theories of being
arbitrary and even unjust, the same can be said of the God implicit
in his view. God assumes a quite passive stance in the Mirror model,
both accepting the sacrificial system of the Hebrews and allowing
the mob to kill his son. Yes, God uses the crucifixion to reveal the
bankruptcy of scapegoating, but we can still ask, *At what cost?* Was
Jesus a willing victim? And doesn't his victimhood simply add another body to the pile of victims?

In general, Girard is weak on God—a result of his anthropological focus. His theory doesn't even really need God to hold water.
It could have been purely cultural and sociological forces that led
early Christians to identify Jesus of Nazareth as the ultimate or final
scapegoat. God's involvement isn't technically necessary. And, for
that matter, Jesus' divinity isn't necessary either. Jesus could have
simply been the innocent victim that came along at the right place
and time for an ever-expanding group of people to see his sacrifice as redemptive. Maybe by the year 30 CE, humanity had finally
evolved enough to see the bankruptcy of blood sacrifice, and Jesus
opened our eyes to that.

But if we take this model and infuse it with God—if that's *God*
up on the cross—then it really becomes the Mirror model. Then it's
not just another innocent victim, lynched at the hands of a bloodthirsty mob—we've already got plenty of those. Instead, if God is
truly in Christ, then our rivalries, our desire for revenge, our violent
system of choosing and executing scapegoats, is truly condemned.
God takes those into himself and shows them for what they really
are. When we look at Jesus on the cross, we see what our sin has

wrought: the death of God, the one truly innocent victim in all of history.

To the question of whether there could have been another way, the Mirror view says no. Only violence could reveal the failure of violence. We could not have been taught this in theory; it had to happen in reality. Just as the Divinity model says that God needs to enter into death to overcome death, the Mirror model posits that God needed to experience violence to defeat violence.

Two more potential shortcomings need to be addressed. The first is a theology problem. Girard pays almost no attention to a major concern of most Christians, beginning with Paul: how the death of Jesus redeems us from sin. For Girard, the crucifixion is the result of human forces—mimicry and rivalry and violence—and when understood correctly, it should put an end to those forces. But didn't something cosmic also happen on the cross, something spiritual? Paul thought so: "For our sake he made him to be sin who knew no sin, so that in him we might become the righteousness of God."[7] That quote and the many like it in Romans and elsewhere have led most Christians to believe that God was doing something supernatural on the cross. So, to many people the Mirror model will seem too human in its orientation.

The second concern is ethical: If Girard is right about Jesus' death, why are systems of violence and scapegoating still so rampant? And for that matter, why did it take so long for someone to discover this truth? That's not to say that we should be suspicious of this interpretation simply because it's new. But it is fair to ask whether Jesus died for nothing, since nothing really changed when he died. (This is one of the reasons that so many people see the crucifixion more as a supernatural, spiritual event than a human, earthly one.) On the day after Jesus' death, the Roman Empire was just as brutal and violent as it had been the day before. Innocent victims were scapegoated and even crucified—probably some on the very cross that held Jesus. And on and on it goes. Even today, parts of the world are rife with violence in Jesus' name. Warriors with crosses around their necks fire guns at their religious rivals. Sacrificial deaths continue unabated. The contagion is spreading.

This question challenges any view of Jesus' death: why hasn't the world changed more as a result of the crucifixion? But it's especially pertinent for the Mirror model, which rests on the idea that when we see Jesus dying on the cross, we should see that our own rivalries nailed him there.

We can't see it because our rivalries continue to blind us to the truth. We can't see it because we choose violence over peace. We can't see it because our systems of sacrifice and warfare overwhelm us—they give us the dominant narrative by which we live our lives.

But if we look—really look—at Jesus hanging from the cross, maybe we can see those narratives of violence and revenge mirrored back at us. And maybe we can conjure up the courage to see that they're empty, reject them, and instead choose a way of peace.

17

Other Models of What God Did on the Cross

SEVERAL YEARS AGO, I tore up the sod in one corner of my suburban backyard. I built four raised beds, each four feet by twelve feet. I found a guy on Craigslist who would deliver a bunch of black dirt to my address. He dumped it in my front yard, and over the course of two days I made dozens of trips with a wheelbarrow, filling the beds. Finally, I fenced it to keep the bunnies out, and I had myself a vegetable garden.

If I can brag for a minute, my garden is pretty awesome. It gets tons of sun in the afternoon, and I've installed automatic sprinklers so that it gets plenty of water, too. I harvest green beans galore, and I grow squash the size of toddlers. I've taken to pickling and canning since we can't possibly eat everything that the garden produces. My relatives are now used to getting jars of zucchini relish and pickled beets for Christmas.

My neighbor Amy and I meet every February and spread seed catalogs across the dining room table. We take nominations from our family members, but ultimately it's the two of us who choose what to plant since we do all the work. I've got my regulars—beans, lettuce, beets, squash, pumpkins, and various herbs. And every year

I try something new, wondering if it will flourish in my particular garden. Last year, asparagus was a flop. This year I tried cabbage, in hopes of making homemade sauerkraut, and it turned out great. And sometimes a vegetable will sprout that I don't remember planting. Maybe the rogue seed came from a mispacked packet, or maybe from something we composted in our bin and then tilled into the soil, or maybe it was carried in by a songbird. No matter how it got there, I'm always pleasantly surprised to see it appear and happy to let it come to bloom. Unless it turns out to be a weed.

The crucifixion of Jesus is like a very fertile garden bed. Several major models of redemption and salvation thrive in its soil, and we've looked at those. But there's enough fertility to give birth to new theories all the time. In this chapter, we'll survey some of the most recent additions to the garden, and while we won't run each through our gauntlet of six questions, we can see views of God, Jesus, their relationship, violence, spirituality, and love hidden in each. You can judge for yourself how well they answer our questions.

Why consider these? It's a bit like our earlier survey of the New Testament—we'd be cutting corners if we only investigated the Gospels and Paul without also visiting those outlying islands. For one thing, a newcomer today may be the dominant theory five hundred years from now. For another, there are brilliant theologians working today who have great insights into the crucifixion, and we should at least hear their voices before moving on to our own constructive phase. And finally, the models that we've studied thus far were all developed by DWM—dead white men (except for René Girard, who is an old white man). Some of the most creative work being done in theories of the atonement today is by voices who have been marginalized in the church for centuries: women and people of color. Although they deserve more space than they are allotted here, I hope they will spur you to read more about them. They have definitely influenced my thinking, and I'm confident they will challenge you as well.

The Trillion-Dollar Coin

During the debt-ceiling crisis in the United States in 2011, some pundits on the twenty-four-hour cable news channels bantered about the idea of the U.S. federal government minting a platinum coin worth $1 trillion. (Strangely, the federal government is not allowed to print paper money of new denominations, but it is allowed to do so with bullion platinum coins.) The thinking went like this: the coin would be deposited into the Federal Reserve, thus increasing the net worth of the U.S. government and immediately (and magically) giving the Fed much more borrowing power.

While this idea was ultimately deemed silly and even dangerous by economists, it did get some theologians thinking about analogies to Jesus' death and the atonement. In a metaphor that would have been embraced by Anselm, they thought of it like this:

1. Humanity, in sin, has incurred a massive debt to God.
2. Jesus' death is like a coin of infinite value, deposited into the bank of heaven.
3. As sinners, we can draw from this infinite worth to pay for our sins.

This will ring a bell for church history buffs. In the late Middle Ages, the Catholic Church raised funds—and supposedly shaved years off of sinners' sentences in purgatory—by selling *indulgences*. Purgatory, a recently abandoned doctrine of the Catholic Church, was the mythical place that Christians went after death to work off their less serious sins before entering heaven. In the Middle Ages, churchmen traveled Europe, offering indulgences for sale, by which the purchaser could decrease the time that a deceased loved one would spend in this less-than-savory experience. Jonathan Tetzel was the most notorious Pardoner, and he is credited with the saying, "As soon as a coin in the coffer rings, a soul from purgatory springs."

The theological question is this: since the sinner is justly sentenced to a number of years in purgatory, what does the money paid for an indulgence actually buy? The church answered that an indulgence is a withdrawal from the "infinite treasury of merit" accrued by Jesus' death. When Jesus died, a deposit was made into God's heavenly bank, and the deposit slip was for an infinite sum. Only the church could withdraw from that account and apply it to your debt, they claimed.

This practice particularly angered a young German monk named Martin Luther. In fact, he was so irate that he nailed an angry screed against indulgences to the door of the Catholic church in his town, Wittenberg. Luther objected to the Church's claim that it alone, through its priests, had the ability to grant salvation. His protest, on October 31, 1517, birthed the Great Reformation.

Luther's problem was with the church policy and hierarchy, not with the idea that we owe God a debt because of our sin, nor with the "infinite treasury of merit" deposited by Jesus. Whether in its medieval form or the modern metaphor of the trillion-dollar coin, this version of Jesus' death reckons God a soulless banker, sitting behind a counting machine, keeping a record of every time we let him down and demanding a repayment for every insult to his honor. And the life and death of Jesus is the equivalent of a bank deposit. In that way, it does not offer much to our consideration of the atonement.

However, for those who hold the Payment view, the trillion-dollar coin adds an interesting twist. We incur a debt that we can't possibly pay, but Jesus offers us unlimited funds. We can draw on his account as long as we put our trust in him. And even for those of us who do not think that our sin puts us in debt to God, the trillion-dollar coin analogy impresses upon us how rich in beneficence was Jesus' sacrifice on the cross.

The Lynching Tree

James Cone, an African American theologian, made his name with the book *God of the Oppressed*.[1] In that book, he drew on the "black experience" to compose a uniquely African American liberation theology. In the end, he concludes, the gospel is about both liberation and reconciliation.

Recently, he's penned another book, developing a theology of the crucifixion from the same vantage point, entitled *The Cross and the Lynching Tree*.[2] The cross, Cone says, has long been a confounding and paradoxical symbol of both death and new life. But it's not so confusing to African Americans:

> That God could "make a way out of no way" in Jesus' cross was truly absurd to the intellect, yet profoundly real in the souls of black folk. Enslaved blacks who first heard the gospel message seized on the power of the cross. Christ crucified manifested God's loving and liberating presence *in* the contradictions of black life.[3]

You see, white Americans and Romans used the lynching tree and the cross for the same purpose: to rule marginalized minorities with fear. Step out of line, and you'll get lynched, or crucified.

But surprisingly, and even paradoxically, African Americans have appropriated the cross as a symbol of liberation. Cone says that's because they uniquely understand the cross. Racism is "white America's original sin," says Cone, and the cross stands as a judgment of that history. Bringing the cross and the lynching tree together— seeing them as essentially the same thing—has the potential to unite white and black Americans. And by understanding how these two symbols connect, we can all better understand the gospel.

"No human language can fully describe what salvation through the cross means. Salvation through the cross is a mystery," Cone writes. But if we attend to our social location, as American Christians, we will see that,

> theologically speaking, Jesus was the "first lynchee," who foreshadowed all the lynched black bodies on American soil. He was crucified by the same principalities and powers that

lynched black people in America. Because God was present with Jesus on the cross and thereby refused to let Satan
and death have the last word about his meaning, God was
also present at every lynching in the United States. God saw
what whites did to innocent and helpless blacks and claimed
their suffering as God's own. God transformed lynched black
bodies into the recrucified body of Christ. *Every time a white
mob lynched a black person, they lynched Jesus.* The lynching tree
is the cross in America. When American Christians realize
that they can meet Jesus only in the crucified bodies in our
midst, they will encounter the real scandal of the cross.[4]

These are hard words for white American Christians (like me) to
read, but they offer a poignant, existential take on the cross that we
won't find in our more forensic theories. Jesus was a member of a
marginalized race, oppressed by a dominant empire. He got caught
in the machinery of that empire and was, in effect, lynched for not
obeying the rules. His crucifixion was surely meant by Rome and
the Temple leaders to discourage others from preaching along the
same lines. And yet, the cross became a sign of victory. Similarly,
lynchings were meant in the postslavery era to keep blacks "in their
place." So in this telling, white America in the lynching era (1880–
1940) wasn't on the side of Jesus, but on the side of Rome.

If we can heed Cone's words and see a noose every time we see
a cross, we have the potential to avert future atrocities. But it seems
that first we must face the horror of our own past.

Overcoming Disgust

Richard Beck is both a theologian and a psychologist, and he's one
of the freshest thinkers today. His framework for the atonement centers on the Hebrew obsession with purity and what he calls "socio-
moral disgust."[5]

Beck starts with a couple of experiments by psychologists. In one, a cockroach is dropped in a glass of apple juice, then removed. Even after the juice is boiled and the glass is washed, most people won't drink the juice. Similarly, most people will not eat a brownie that is baked into the shape of a dog turd.

Beck asks his readers this: imagine spitting into a Dixie cup and then being asked to drink it. Why is that disgusting? It's *your* saliva! Because, Beck contends, once something is deemed disgusting, emotion overwhelms reason. Beck writes, "In short, disgust is a boundary psychology. Disgust marks objects as exterior and alien. The second the saliva leaves the body and crosses the boundary of selfhood it is foul, it is 'exterior,' it is Other."[6]

The disgust mechanism dictates many human affairs: how we treat the disabled, the disfigured, the "colored," the GLBT, the "slut"—each is deemed *disgusting*. Jesus' own people had enshrined disgust in religiopolitical laws, castigating as "unclean" anyone who was paralyzed, disabled, mentally ill, leprous, or menstruating. Not only were these people disgusting, they were contagious—whatever sin caused them to be unclean could be spread. As a result, they could not worship in the Temple—in fact, they could not even be touched; if they were, the one who had touched them needed to go through a ritual bath to become clean again.

The power of the atonement begins with the incarnation, in which the perfectly "clean" God enters into the "unclean" body of Jesus of Nazareth. Even in this act, a disgust boundary is crossed. Then, in his life, Jesus repeatedly violated those boundaries, touching lepers and blind men and menstruating women. And ultimately, in his death, Jesus *becomes* the object of disgust. Virtually every aspect of Jesus' death on the cross was *disgusting* and in violation of Hebrew purity laws—public nakedness, shedding of blood, broken bones, hanging on a tree, and the onset of the Sabbath.

In Jesus, God stepped over the boundaries; God made the disgusting sacred; God overturned the conventional wisdom of purity and brought those who were "unclean" into the bosom of his love. The wall between clean and unclean fell, and that means all of the walls that separate people also fell. As Paul wrote, "There is no longer Jew or Greek, there is no longer slave or free, there is no longer male and female; for all of you are one in Christ Jesus."[7] God removed the boundary of socio-moral disgust by himself crossing that boundary.

What's interesting about Beck's model is how much it makes sense of both the ancient Hebrew laws that governed Jesus' people and our own visceral reactions to people who have something "wrong" with them. As Christians, we know that we're supposed to treat everyone equally, and we're supposed to reach out to those who are cast off by society. But when we reconceive of the crucifixion as an act that breached the boundaries of disgust—that it even made God *disgusting*—we can use this central act in the life of God as our impetus for a life that truly emulates Jesus.

Violence Against Women

Feminist theologians have long struggled with the death of Jesus, for it is undeniably a story of violence of *men* against a *man,* and it has subsequently been interpreted primarily by male theologians. In one of the most harrowing and widely lauded feminist versions of the cross, theologian Rita Nakashima Brock and pastor Rebecca Parker recount the stories of women who've been terribly abused yet been told that following Jesus requires them to suffer in silence. They conclude, "At the center of western Christianity is the story of the cross, which claims God the Father required the death of his Son to save the world. We believe this theological claim sanctions violence."[8]

Brock and Parker vividly show the shortcomings of primary theologies of atonement from a feminist perspective. They argue that violence does not save and that Jesus' death did nothing to further his life and ministry. It was, they think, a morally repugnant act. They do affirm that they've been saved, but not *by* violence, but *from* violence.

They counter other theories of the atonement by saying that salvation does not come from the one-time event of Jesus dying on the cross. Instead, salvation is a process of healing that happens when we overcome violence, when we grieve the violence that's been done to us and in the world, and when we decide to survive in spite of the world's violence.

Dealing with violence differs from dealing with other forms of trauma, like cancer or a car accident. Violence comes from another person, so it bears that added trauma of intentional harm. Violence is to be resisted, and this is part of our salvation from it. Therefore, Brock and Parker want us to focus not on the suffering of Jesus but on the violence that was perpetrated against him.

They also look at early Christian art, and they conclude that images of the Risen Christ, alive and among the people, are much more common than images of the crucifixion. The latter, they claim, rose to prominence only with the Crusades and the crowning of Charlemagne in the eighth century. But in the early church, the saving power of Jesus came from the idea that his spirit lived on and walked the Earth. If we can focus on this aspect of Jesus, rather than his violent death, they write, "Another Christianity is possible. It begins when we understand that paradise is already present. We have neither to retrieve it nor construct it. We have to perceive it and to bring our lives and our cultures into accord with it."[9]

Listening to the voices of victims has never been a strong characteristic of the church. Thankfully, these days we are learning to hear these voices, and we should let them implicate our views of Jesus' death. Too often, Jesus has been portrayed as a willing victim of a terrible crime, and his crucifixion has been used to silence other victims—he suffered gladly, and you should, too. Brock and Parker and other feminist theologians yank us out of our complacency on this issue, and they force us to come to terms with the real costs of violence in the lives of victims. We may not want to say, with them, that the cross doesn't save, but we at least have to account for just *how* Jesus was a victim and how his victimhood has been used to subjugate women and others.

A New Reality for the Trinity

Another view comes from Andrew Sung Park, a Korean American Methodist theologian.[10] Park argues, first, that Jesus' life and teachings, not just his death, are redemptive. Second, he says that Jesus' death does several things: it exposes the violence and injustice of oppressors, it reflects the sin and wickedness in the world, and it shows the world forgiveness.

But most intriguingly, Park believes that the death of Jesus released the Holy Spirit into the world. Central to Park's theory of "triune atonement" is *han,* a Korean concept of collective oppression that leads to feelings of hopelessness. *Han* likely resides in the Korean psyche because of the vulnerability of the Korean peninsula and the frequent invasions they've endured. Even now, South Koreans live in constant anxiety about a nuclear attack from North Korea. Park writes, "In Korean, *han* is a deep, unhealed wound of a victim that festers in her or him."[11] It's found, he says, in Holocaust survivors, occupied Palestinians, the hungry, the abused, the battered. It's found in all of us, in one sense or another, as we struggle to find hope in our lives.

When Cain killed Abel, God said to Cain, "What have you done? Listen; your brother's blood is crying out to me from the ground!" And Cain replies, "My punishment is greater than I can bear!"[12] This, Park says, is *han.* And when Jesus cries from the cross, "My God, my God, why have you forsaken me?" he is crying the *han* of all victims.[13]

Park writes that in Jesus' resurrection, the Paraclete—that's a name for the Holy Spirit, used in the Gospel of John, meaning "defender of the accused"—pours herself into the world to confront *han* and to guide repentant Christians from hopelessness to hope. He writes, "Jesus never shed his blood because of God's punishment, but he shed his blood to death to challenge sinners to turn away from their sins and to live the life of salvation."[14] Jesus unites with victims on the cross, and the Holy Spirit overcomes the hopelessness of *han* in the resurrection by offering ongoing companionship and new life.

Almost every way that we approach the death of Jesus theologically is guided by Western thought—laws, theories, and philosophies. From a uniquely Eastern source, Park's introduction of *han* as the context of the crucifixion and resurrection sheds new light on that event. To look beyond the shores of Western civilization for insight can only make our quest richer.

Jesus Killed God

Perhaps the most controversial and provocative philosopher on the scene today is Slavoj Žižek, a Slovenian who can be found lecturing in universities and shouting through a bullhorn at public rallies. His work is notoriously dense and difficult to summarize, but here's a try.

Žižek says, "The Big Other doesn't exist"—the "Big Other" being God, or fate, or really any system to which a human being submits.[15] The Big Other is fundamental and necessary to humans, as users of language, but it is oppressive in various ways. God was never materially real; God was real only symbolically, real in the imaginations of the people.

The great insight of Christianity, Žižek argues, is that Jesus isn't simply an emissary of God; he *is* God. The entirety of God is poured into Jesus. And when Jesus cries out from the cross, "My God, my God, why have you forsaken me?" God is experiencing atheism.[16] We can say that *the unreality of God died on the cross*. And born in its place was the spirit of Christ, a collective belief of his followers, which is more materially real than God ever was. This is the age of the Holy Ghost, when the Big Other is rendered virtual by Jesus' death.

Philosopher Peter Rollins has built on Žižek's insights in various ways. Rollins writes that Jesus' cry of forsakenness reveals a "gap within God":

> Christianity draws us into an embrace of the idea that there is a gap operating within the sacred-object itself. Our seeming distance from it is then actually a hint at the very nature

of the thing we think we are distant from. In short, the sacred-object does not offer wholeness, because it is not itself whole.[17]

Meditating on Paul's famous axiom that we currently "see through a glass, darkly; but then face to face,"[18] Rollins says that the darkened glass leads us to believe that there's something on the other side, a Big Other, perhaps. But the crucifixion exposes that there's nothing on the other side of the glass. There's no Big Other to lean on, no God to solve our problems. God experiences the same incompleteness that we experience, and we experience freedom in the crucifixion because the unveiling aspect of that event liberates us from our need for the Big Other to solve our problems.

I know many people who've left Christianity, troubled by the transcendence and metaphysics necessary to hold the Christian worldview together. These people have mostly become materialists: what you see is what you get. That is, there's nothing more than the material elements we can see and measure. This view allows these people to continue seeing the cross as a pivotal event in history, as Žižek and Rollins both do. As with other models we've seen, the crucifixion is a liberating act, but instead of uniting us with God, it liberates us from the need for God.

Clues to a Complicated Puzzle

These are just six of myriad views of the atonement, each displaying a distinct and creative reading of the event of the death of Jesus. Do any of them really grow in the soil of the crucifixion? Do any of them adequately answer our six questions? We now have enough experience under our belts to explore these questions more fully.

So now we turn to constructing our own answers, building on what we've learned but also proposing some new understandings.

PART SIX

What God Experienced on the Cross

18

What Jesus Tells Us
About God

W E'VE TAKEN QUITE a journey so far. We've traveled
through prehistory and history, Hebrew and Christian scripture, and two thousand years in the life of the
church, all the while considering the single most important event in
Christianity. So far we've learned:

- The desire to sacrifice is rooted deep in the human evolutionary psyche.
- Israel's sacrificial system (animal sacrifices) was an improve-
  ment on its neighbors' (human sacrifices).
- Through the prophets, God expressed ambivalence about
  Israel's sacrifices—while God valued the sacrifices, God pre-
  fers simple obedience.
- Jesus did not explicitly condemn the sacrificial system, but
  neither did he endorse it.
- The Gospel writers clearly saw Jesus' death as a Passover
  sacrifice.
- Paul considered the crucifixion the single event through
  which all of faith and life should be understood, and he introduced the idea that Jesus' death atoned for human sin.

- Theologians of the church introduced various ways to explain what God did in the crucifixion, each with his own model of the problem and the solution. Those models are the following:
  - » Human sin took honor from God, and Jesus' death made payment for that sin. Further, our sin incurred a penalty, and Jesus took the punishment that was meant for us.
  - » Our sin made us subjects of Satan, but the crucifixion was God's victory over the devil and evil.
  - » Sin introduced a distance between humanity and God, and the cross is a magnet that draws us back to God.
  - » Sin diminished our intended capacity to be one with God, and Jesus' death restores our divinity.
  - » Blood sacrifice allowed human society to develop by temporarily mitigating rivalries, but it institutionalized violence; on the cross, God held up a mirror, showing us that our sacrificial systems are ultimately bankrupt.
- Various other explanations of the death of Jesus have sprung up as well, each attempting to make sense of the reason that God would save the world through the death of his son.

Now it's our turn to think through the reasons for Jesus' death, both theological and personal. To put it bluntly, if there's no good reason for the crucifixion, then there's no good reason to be Christian. If the crucifixion doesn't bring us closer to God and inspire us to be more loving to one another, then we may as well abandon the faith altogether.

But if Jesus' death somehow brings us closer to God, then on this event everything hinges. If God can bring peace out of a violent act, then we should put our faith in this event—we should even follow Paul and make this event the central aspect of our lives.

If we can figure out how the crucifixion of Jesus is good news, then we can be proud to wear crosses around our necks.

We've seen how others make sense of Jesus' death. Now it's our turn.

Smelling the Cross

Remember the smell test from chapter 3? I've had a couple of real-life examples of that concept lately. Our garden emits more produce than we can eat or give away, so, as I mentioned earlier, I've taken up canning. My grandmother canned like crazy, but the expertise was lost in my parents' generation. So I've had to teach myself, using books and YouTube. I've become quite proficient at pickling, especially cucumbers, beets, and beans. Our garden is bean-friendly, so I harvest bushels per year. And beans are not my family's favorite.

So this year, I decided to branch out from pickling and put up cut green beans. I prepped my jars, lids, and rings. I picked about a bushel of beans, trimmed them, and blanched them in salt water. I put them in jars, poured in hot water, and immersed the sealed jars in boiling water for twenty minutes. After they cooled, I brought them downstairs and shelved them with all the pickled items.

A couple of weeks later, I was putting up some more pickles when I whiffed a rancid smell. I looked at all my jars and noticed one of the green bean jars had a bit of a gray tinge to the water. Then I had the experience that every canner dreads: I pushed down on the top of the lid, and I felt and heard a pop. That meant the seal had broken, and the beans were now exposed to the elements. When I checked the other jars, I heard pop after pop. Every jar of beans had gone bad, a dozen in all. I carried the jars upstairs, opened them, and poured them in the sink. The odor was overwhelming as I jammed the rotten beans down the disposal with a dish brush. I could still smell the stink on my hands two days later.

But that pales in comparison to what happened a few years ago. I had an old freezer in the basement, and it was full of ducks, pheasants, and grouse that I'd hunted and cleaned. While I was on vacation, the freezer died. In August. Never have I experienced a smell so vile. I vomited a couple of times while cleaning the rotten blood that had pooled at the bottom of the freezer. Finally, I gave up on cleaning it. I enlisted a couple of buddies, hauled the unredeemable freezer upstairs, and took it to the dump.

Our theological smell test will operate on a similar calculus. We're going to establish what we know of God, Jesus, and their relationship from our investigation of the crucifixion. Along the way, we're going to sniff and see if what we're growing smells sweet or pungent.

And we'll start with the simplest axiom in all the Bible: *God is love.*

This most famous line in the Bible comes from 1 John, a book we considered in chapter 9. Coming out of the same school of thought—if not by the same hand—as the Gospel of John, this letter is more of an essay or homily. Written around 100 CE, it's among the latest and the most theologically sophisticated books in the Bible. It seems that a group of believers had strayed from the essential teachings about Jesus and left the church, and 1 John was written to remind the rest of the church to stick with the faith.

The simple and profound phrase *God is love* is repeated twice in the fourth chapter of 1 John. Loving one another is the thrust of the chapter, and love for fellow human beings is reinforced with the reminder that God is love. Consequently, there can be no love of God without love of others. So strong is this love, the author continues, that when perfected it will cast out all fear. Love conquers all.

Noteworthy for our purposes is that between the two instances of "God is love," comes the phrase, "In this is love, not that we loved God but that he loved us and sent his Son to be the atoning sacrifice for our sins. Beloved, since God loved us so much, we also ought to love one another."[1] You may recall from chapter 9 that this is one of only two times that this word for *atonement* shows up in the Bible. In the very early church, the love of God, Jesus' death on the cross, and love for our fellow humans are inextricable from one another. They cannot be separated.

So this must be our first commitment: the crucifixion must show the love of God, and it must provoke us to greater love for one another.

This, the sweet smell of love, will be our test.

How God Shows Love

Of the various biblical metaphors for God, among the most prominent is that of a parent. In the Hebrew Bible, God is compared to a nursing mother and a mother who comforts her child.[2] Jesus alludes to God as a hen who "gathers her brood under her wings," and he regularly refers to God as his father.[3] And in related analogies, God is compared to a bridegroom, a lover, and a spouse.[4]

In either the parent-child or the spousal relationship, one thing we know: the relationship will only flourish if each individual is given room to grow. There's no better way to destroy a romance or drive away a teenage child than to smother. The latest term for this is the "helicopter parent"—someone who hovers over his or her child at every moment.

When human children are born, they rely completely on their parents. In fact, human children depend on their parents for survival much longer than other species do. Nevertheless, as children grow, their parents must pull back. Only through self-limitation do parents give their children the space—physical, intellectual, emotional, spiritual—that they need to grow.

It's not much different in a romantic relationship. At first, young lovers smother one another in love and affection, and they likely have a great deal of understanding with one another about this. But as time passes, an equilibrium develops: the public displays of affection decrease so that friends and family no longer roll their eyes; the couple doesn't feel as if they have to spend every waking moment together; and the two become comfortable enough in their love that they don't have to constantly profess it. However, if one partner keeps pressing, keeps smothering, the tolerance of the other partner is likely to run out.

Whether it's parent-child or lover-beloved, boundaries and self-limitation are essential for relationships. Without them, relationships suffer and die. With them, they thrive.

As the biblical metaphors of parent and lover indicate, God's story is a story of humility, of self-limitation. Before the creation of the cosmos, God was all there was. For there to even be anything other than God, God had to withdraw, to retreat. That is to say, God had to make room for something that was other-than-God. You and I and everything else that's not God exist because God withdrew enough to make room for us. God began creating with an act of self-limitation.[5] And that act set the course for God's activity up to the present day.

This does not in any way compromise God's freedom. In fact, core to the very notion of God is the idea that God must be a totally free and independent being. God can't be contingent. For years, a billboard stood on the northbound side of Interstate 94 in central Minnesota. It read, "Unless You Confess, God Cannot Bless." That theology works on the same pattern as the Payment and Victory theories. In each, some other law or framework precedes God and transcends God. In each, God is subservient to something else, either a law of justice or an epic struggle with Satan or an "if . . . then" conditional statement.

Let's think about that billboard. If God is really unable to bless someone unless they confess their sins, then God is handcuffed by us; God is bound by human action. If the billboard were accurate, Jesus could not have welcomed the thief on the cross next to him into paradise that very day, for that man did not confess his sins. He simply asked that Jesus remember him when he came into his kingdom. The emperor Constantine, the first really famous person to convert to Christianity, waited to be baptized until he was on his deathbed in 337 CE. He didn't want to take a chance that he might sin and tarnish his baptism; he wanted to meet his creator with a clean slate. While this was a somewhat common practice in the early church, it fell out of favor as centuries passed, and with good reason. Baptism isn't some magic act that erases past sins and has no power over future sins. Baptism doesn't work like that, and God doesn't work like that. God cannot be reduced to a mechanistic formula.

God is by nature noncontingent because, as Jesus says, "for God all things are possible."[6] God has complete and utter freedom—in fact, more freedom than we can imagine. As human beings, we are limited by our nature. The frameworks to which we are held captive are obvious upon some reflection: language binds us, as do our bodies, our governments, our allegiances, our emotions, and finally death. Paul calls these frameworks principalities and powers, and philosophers call them structures and superstructures. Try as we might, we cannot free ourselves from their constraints, and we are thereby limited by them.

Not so for God, who by definition moves freely, unlimited by any supervening structure. This freedom set the Israelites' Yahweh apart from their neighbors' gods. The gods and demiurges of Mesopotamia fought with one another until the cosmos was birthed out of their violent conflict, and the gods of Greece and Rome notoriously acted like petulant children, even mating with humans when they felt the urge.

Israel's theological innovation was the belief that there is *one* God, and that God created the cosmos freely, independently, and out of nothing (*creatio ex nihilo*). God was not forced to create out of conflict, as in other creation myths, nor did he spurt us out in a mistake. We do not exist because a Titan created us from clay and then stole fire from the gods, as in the Greek myth of Prometheus. In Israel's telling, our creation was voluntary and deliberate. It was an act of love by God, and love is neither coerced nor required.

Danger stalks us when we anthropomorphize God or God's activity. Nevertheless, let me venture to say that we know something of the nature of love based on our human experience. Love is, by its nature, self-sacrificial. To love another, I must limit myself. Anyone who has loved or been loved knows this to be true. In order to love my spouse, my children, my parents, and my friends, my ego must retreat. That's a constant challenge and a constant necessity. But love doesn't work any other way. Love makes space for the other to thrive. Without that space, my desire to care for another is merely an extension of my ego. Without that space, others don't feel loved; they feel swallowed. Think of a time that you've been at a dinner party, and there's been one guest who, as they say, sucked all the air out of the room. That person's ego was so big that no one else could make a point or start a new conversation. The way that true, healthy conversation happens is when there is a genuine back-and-forth, and that means sometimes biting your tongue, pulling back, and letting someone else have the floor. When we engage in this kind of self-limitation, we allow those around us to flourish.

So it's not such a stretch to claim that God, in the act of creation, began with an act of self-limitation. God withdrew his essence so that something other than God—something with which God could enter into relationship—could be born. While we can only guess as to God's *motivation* for creating us,[7] we can conclude that God's act of creation was an act of self-limiting love.

God's very first act was an act of humble love, an act in which God retreated and gave us room to live. In complete freedom, God gave up an aspect of noncontingency. From that day forward, God was bound to creation. Again, this was a free act by the sovereign God. But the Hebrew Bible is clear that God is in an interactive relationship with Israel. There's a back-and-forth between them. The God of the Hebrew Bible is not the immaterial Mind of the Greek philosophers, hovering above the ether. No, Israel's God is *involved* in the world, *engaging* with the people, *responding* to their cries. God is now somehow contingent, for when Abraham and Moses (and you and I) deeply engage with God, God responds. In the language of the Hebrew Bible, "God changes his mind."[8]

God shows us love by giving us freedom. God even shows us love by allowing us to influence him.

The Freedom of God, the Freedom of Jesus

Could there have been another way for God to save us, or did he have to kill his son?

The question comes in different forms and at different times, but every youth pastor knows it. In my fifteen years as a youth pastor, I heard it often. Teenagers are renowned for their ability to cut to the heart of the matter, to ask questions that adults find impolitic. No matter when the question came, or in what form, I found it challenging to answer. Behind that question lies all sorts of presumptions about God's freedom to do whatever God wants, God's relationship to time, God's plans for the world, and the relationship between the first and second persons in the Trinity (Father and Son). And any answer to the question is similarly laden with assumptions. To answer this question is to begin peeling away the layers of an onion: there's always another layer beneath.

If, on the one hand, God could have chosen any way he wanted to save the world, it's discomfiting to think that he chose his son's death as the way. Wouldn't a loving God choose a nonviolent way to redeem us?

If, on the other hand, God had no other choice but to save the world through the death of his son, we're left to wonder how powerful he can really be. Is the God of the universe so helpless that he's limited to one option?

And then there's the altogether complex set of questions around the relationship between Jesus and God. As I was asked by numerous teens over the years, "Wait, you said that Jesus is God's son, and you also said that Jesus is God. How does that work?" Through our six questions in previous chapters, we've already concluded that God and Jesus must be united in their work on the cross. But we'll also have to consider just how this relationship works in order to determine what happened between them when Jesus died.

The adolescents in my youth group saw this dilemma, and they didn't want to be stuck on its horns. They wanted an answer, and I thought they deserved one. But I struggled to give them a response that was satisfying, because I wasn't satisfied with the answers I'd heard. Some Christians are not bothered by this conundrum, but I was (which led ultimately to this book).

My friend, Ron, asked me about my progress on the book the other day, and that got us talking about Jesus' death. He asked how people have traditionally interpreted the crucifixion, and I replied that they often say that God had no choice; that the only way to atone for human sin was the death of a perfect, sinless God-man.

"That's ridiculous!" Ron exclaimed. "God set up the whole deal, so God could just change the rules. It makes no sense to say that God had no other choice. Isn't the whole definition of God that God can do whatever God wants?"

Ron's rhetorical question puts a fine point on it. Our definitions of God hinge on God's power and freedom. But part of freedom is the freedom to give up that freedom. That's what God started in creation, and that's what God did most poignantly in the birth of Jesus. Let's return to a passage we've already encountered twice, in which Paul writes poetically about God's humility in becoming human in Jesus of Nazareth:

> Let the same mind be in you that was in Christ Jesus,
>   who, though he was in the form of God,
>   did not regard equality with God
>   as something to be exploited,
>   but emptied himself,
>   taking the form of a slave,
>   being born in human likeness.
>   And being found in human form,
>   he humbled himself
>   and became obedient to the point of death—
>   even death on a cross.[9]

Sorting out the relationship between God and Jesus is one of the trickiest adventures in all of faith. Traditionally, Christians have believed that God was fully in Jesus yet still retained some sense of independence from Jesus—that's why and how Jesus prayed to God. This conundrum is solved with the doctrine of the Trinity, which states that God has always existed in three parts, or *persons,* and it was only one of these three persons—called the *logos* or the Word or the Son—who inhabited Jesus.

If we can hold this concept of the Trinity, even tentatively, we can look again at the Gospel accounts of Jesus' life and see that Jesus was granted full autonomy by God to move about in the world as he chose. The Gospel writers often state that Jesus did or said something "in accordance with the scripture" or so "that the scriptures might be fulfilled," but they never give us the impression that Jesus is a puppet and the Father is the puppet master. Jesus wasn't pushed from town to town and eventually to Jerusalem by the invisible hand of God. And Jesus wasn't nailed to the cross by God. That much the Gospels make clear.

But where was God the Father when Jesus died? We might be ready to say that God did not kill Jesus, but if he stood back and allowed Jesus to be executed, isn't that almost as bad?

Let's return to the parenting metaphor so common in scripture. When I was in therapy during my divorce, an issue that brought up lots of emotion for me was my three kids—at the time they were eight, seven, and four. I struggled mightily with the idea that I wouldn't be able to tuck them in every night, attend every swimming lesson and doctor's appointment, and bandage every skinned knee. I worried about the rules and environment in their mom's house. I wept from missing them so much. Through it all, my therapist coached me toward my new reality, that I *wouldn't* be as involved in their lives as I had been. I had no control over the other house they lived in, only in my own house and the time they spent with me. Like all divorced parents, I had to give up some of my control over my kids' lives well before they went off to college. Circumstances demanded it.

I don't want to make a one-to-one correlation between human parents and God, but the Bible gives us enough backing to claim, at least cautiously, this kind of parental relationship: that God the Father withdrew enough to let Jesus follow his own fate. We so often experience this in our own lives—we wish that God would intervene and help us on a test or cure our friend of cancer. But God doesn't, and we fail the test or the cancer follows its terrible course. Likewise, Jesus experienced the vicissitudes of human life, with all of its joys and its sorrows. In the desert at the beginning of his ministry, Jesus refused the devil's temptation that he throw himself from a cliff and rely on his heavenly Father to send angels to rescue him. And at the end of Jesus' ministry, God resisted the temptation to intervene and save his son from a terrible fate.

Here is what I have learned. God is love, and love means freedom. It means autonomy. And it means that Jesus was beholden to the exigencies of this world just as much as you and I are. God did not show a lack of love by refusing to intervene and stop Jesus' execution. Instead, God showed an extraordinary measure of humble love by allowing Jesus to be fully immersed in the human experience, holding nothing back and encountering nothing less than torture and death.

The Bible is silent about how God the Father experienced the death of Jesus, but we can guess from all the parental language between the two that God the Father surely grieved as he watched his son being hung on a cross—just as God grieves now whenever one of his children is hung, lynched, tortured, or otherwise sacrificed.

And if you believe, as I do, that God was actually *in* Jesus, then we can go one step further and say that God actually experienced all these things, too.

19

The Cry That Changed Everything

TODAY, MOST CHRISTIANS accept the belief that Jesus was both human and divine. We may not understand it, we may chalk it up as a great mystery, but it's not something that keeps us awake at night. And it's pretty much been that way for fifteen hundred years. But that wasn't the case in the first five hundred years of Christianity. During those early centuries, this was the biggest riddle for the young church: how is it that the person we know as Jesus of Nazareth was both a human being and also God? Many theological battles—and some fisticuffs—were fought over this question, and many otherwise thoughtful and faithful believers were excommunicated and banished because they didn't have the "correct" answer.

Take Nestorius, for example, who was born in 386 in modern-day Turkey. Little is known of his early life. Bishop Theodore of Mopsuestia trained Nestorius in Antioch, and Nestorius was subsequently elected Archbishop of Constantinople at age forty-two. But his tenure lasted just three years.

What got Nestorius in hot water was his sincere and heartfelt desire to solve the riddle of Jesus' humanity and divinity. He first got crossways with his fellow bishops when he told them to stop calling the Virgin Mary the "God-Bearer" (*theotokos*). God existed before everything, Nestorius scolded them; therefore God cannot be born. Better to call Mary the *"Christ*-bearer," he said. His suggestion was roundly rejected.

But Nestorius really irked his colleagues when he started talking about Jesus. He preached that within the person of Jesus of Nazareth were two distinct entities—one human and one divine. Because the victors write the history, we don't know exactly what Nestorius taught—most of his writings were burned—but his opponents accused him of separating Jesus' humanity and divinity: as though Jesus of Nazareth were a container, and inside that container were two other containers, one full of humanity and the other full of divinity.

Nestorius was trying to protect God, trying to say that God's holiness was not tainted by Jesus' humanity. He was trying to vacuum-seal the divinity so it wouldn't spoil from the bacteria of humanness. God cannot be born since God is eternal, he said, so only Jesus' *humanity* was born. And it goes without saying that God cannot die, he continued, so only Jesus' humanity died. But Nestorius held a minority opinion; others responded that humanity and divinity mixed within Jesus and that God was not compromised as a result.

What seems trivial to us was front page news in the fifth century. A council was convened at Ephesus in 431, Nestorius was condemned as a heretic, and he was dethroned by Emperor Theodosius II shortly thereafter. He lived the balance of his days in exile, at a remote monastery in the northern Sahara Desert.

Twenty years later, Emperor Marcian convened about 370 churchmen in Chalcedon, close enough to Constantinople that he could keep tabs on them. After meeting for three weeks, the assembly released their report, the "Definition of the Faith," which explicated the nature of Jesus Christ and completely repudiated those still loyal to Nestorius. Jesus Christ was fully and completely human and fully and completely divine, said the council. Here's how they formulated it in the "Definition":

> One and the same Christ, Son, Lord, only begotten, to be
> acknowledged in two natures, inconfusedly, unchangeably,
> indivisibly, inseparably. The distinction of natures is by no
> means taken away by the union, but rather the property of
> each nature is preserved, and concurring in one Person and
> one Subsistence, not parted or divided into two persons, but
> one and the same Son, and only begotten God, the Word,
> the Lord Jesus Christ.[1]

Except in small pockets of the Eastern Church—still referred to as "Nestorians"—the church has held firmly to this statement from Chalcedon. Although it trucks in categories of Greek philosophy foreign to us now, it is nevertheless recited in countless churches every week. To be an *orthodox* Christian, broadly conceived, has always meant just a few things: that you believe there is only one God, that you affirm the Trinitarian nature of that God, and that you affirm the full humanity and divinity of Jesus of Nazareth.

For centuries, the church had proclaimed that Jesus was the long-promised Messiah, and in him—specifically, in his *death*—the world was saved. But the church had never been clear on exactly *how* that worked. By the year 500, they had their answer: they had solved the riddle of how divinity and humanity could coexist in Jesus of Nazareth.

And it's that divine-human connection that makes Jesus' death unique.

The Significance of a God-Man

Human beings of divine parentage were not unknown in the ancient world. Greek and Roman myths are replete with stories of horny gods who had dalliances with handsome humans, resulting in half-divine progeny. Achilles was said to be a demigod, the offspring of a human king and a nymph. Other famous demigods included Dionysus, Helen of Troy, and Hercules.

Four decades before Jesus was born, the Roman consul Julius Caesar was assassinated on the Ides of March in 44 BCE, and two years later the Roman Senate declared him divine. Shortly thereafter, his adopted son, Octavian, claimed to be a son of a god and therefore a god himself. Octavian is better known to us as Augustus, the first Roman emperor, and every subsequent emperor followed Augustus's lead and claimed divinity as well.

What was another god to the Romans? No big deal, really, since they already had a whole pantheon. Mount Olympus was as crowded as a Walmart on Black Friday, with just as much melodrama. The mantel above the fireplace of an average Roman home was populous, too, filled with small idols of family life. Hearth gods protected the home; Jupiter and Venus protected the empire; and lots of other gods protected the in-between spaces.

Judaism, however, operated by a different system altogether. In fact, one of the Hebrews' most significant theological contributions to the ancient world was its fierce monotheism. The very earliest followers of Yahweh probably believed in other gods, but even proto-Judaism taught that "the Lord your God is one," and "You shall have no other gods before me."[2] The Jews' monotheism set them apart from their neighbors, and it caused some real friction with their Roman overlords in the first century.

But no matter how close God came to humanity in the Hebrew Bible—walking with Adam in the cool of the day, leading the people through the wilderness as a pillar of fire and cloud, showing his backside to Moses, wrestling with Jacob, whispering in the ears of prophets—there nevertheless remained an unbridgeable distance between the Creator and the creation. For example, no matter how intimate either party hoped the relationship would be, humans were not even allowed to utter the name of God for fear of breaking a commandment. And how close can two beings be if one cannot address the other by name?

There are different ways of telling the story. One is that God, having tried many methods of rapprochement, withdrew, retreated in the years prior to Jesus' birth. No one had heard from the Lord in centuries. The writings of this era—Daniel and the Apocrypha and the Essene writings of the Dead Sea Scrolls—record not straightforward communiqués from the divine, but apocryphal and apocalyptic tales about dragons and demons. God is silent, and the people are grasping at straws.

Another version is that God never stopped trying to get through to humanity, but we grew more and more obstinate and hardhearted as civilization evolved. By the time of Jesus, the Hebrews were just as incapable of hearing God's voice as their pagan Roman overlords.

Then, out of nowhere, God did the unthinkable. God poured himself into a human being. In Jesus, Yahweh returns to Zion, but in the unlikely form of a Galilean craftsman-rabbi. This is unthinkable to the Jews because Yahweh is the One True Inscrutable Being: the Creator, not the created. And it's unthinkable to the Greco-Roman philosopher because God is pure spirit and must be eternally immaterial.

Yet the early Christians held tenaciously to this belief. God was totally and perfectly present in Jesus, they preached. And, as such, God experienced love, joy, grief, tears, laughter, pain, and anguish.

In the last chapter, we saw that God's story is a story of self-limitation from the moment that God retreated enough to make room for creation. God became less so that we could be, and God continued to hold back so that we could experience freedom and fate. God gave up power so that we might have power, even power over our own destinies. God became bound to time, even though God is by nature timeless. God allowed the creation freedom, which inaugurated pain, chaos, and death. In spite of God's various incursions and appearances, the distance between God and us endured, even widened. Between God and humanity, misunderstanding festered.

But then God did the unimaginable and bridged the gap— something that only the Creator could do; the creation could not.

God's Death

In the first centuries of Christianity, it was hard enough for the faithful to understand how divinity and humanity could coexist within one person. But conceiving of the Creator of the universe experiencing death on a cross was just too much to handle. God becoming human was enough of a stretch. God dying? That was a bridge too far.

God, the one immortal and immaterial being in the cosmos, surely couldn't *die,* they thought. So they conceived of inventive ways to protect God from that fate. One group said that just seconds before Jesus' death, the God part of him was whisked away. The divinity was sucked back up into heaven as if through some super-natural vacuum cleaner, and only the humanity of Jesus died.

Another group taught that Jesus only *appeared* to be human and only *appeared* to die on a cross. But in fact, they said, Jesus of Nazareth was an apparition, a spirit, a ghost—God play-acting as a human. In their scheme, God didn't really die on the cross but only pretended to die in order to teach us a lesson.

Both of these groups were condemned as heretics, as were others who tried to get God off the cross. You can understand their desire—they wanted to safeguard God from the terror of execution, from the ignominy of hanging on a cross, naked and dying at the hands of an earthly government. But their versions did not accord with the biblical versions, with the grand narrative of the life, death, and resurrection of Jesus.

From the biblical account, it's nearly impossible to tell if Jesus of Nazareth knew that he was God. In the three synoptic Gospels, written decades before John, Jesus has messianic aspirations but not necessarily divine ones. By the time of John, at the end of the first century, the church had decided conclusively that Jesus was uniquely divine. Yes, he was the long-awaited Messiah, but he was more. By 95 CE, the approximate time of John's writing, the titles Son of God and Son of Man had transcended their Old Testament meanings—

"specially anointed one" and "favored by God"—and had come to imply that Jesus was the progeny of the Almighty. In fact, according to the New Testament's oft-quoted verse John 3:16, Jesus was God's *only* offspring.

Looking back on the event of Jesus' crucifixion, Paul considered it the ultimate saving act. But Jesus himself didn't need the cross to save. He healed and cured one paralytic because he saw the man's faith, and another he healed and forgave because he saw the faith of the man's friends. Even the thief hanging on the cross next to Jesus was welcomed into paradise, though Jesus had not yet died. During Jesus' life, in all four of the Gospels, he did things that only God can do—namely, forgive sins and grant people eternal salvation. These pronouncements of forgiveness, far more than the miracles that he performed, were what got Jesus in trouble with the scribes and Pharisees.

All this—and all of the Gospels—record the activities of Jesus from the human perspective, but what was happening in the life of God during Jesus' life? Here we enter into more speculative territory, but we can draw some tentative conclusions. We can say that in Jesus, God was *experiencing* something that God had not experienced before. To take it one step further, we can surmise that in Jesus, God was *learning*. In Jesus, God crossed the line from *sympathy* with the human condition to *empathy* with humans[3]—that is, God went from pitying us to truly understanding us by actually becoming one of us.

But on the cross, something else happened altogether, possibly something that even God did not expect.

Theologian Friedrich Schleiermacher famously said that the universal human experience is the "feeling of utter dependence"—that sense that we are not alone in the cosmos. That feeling is the beginning of faith and the beginning of religion.

Philosopher Søren Kierkegaard put his finger on another universal human trait: the feeling that God is absent, which leads to despair. Despair, he wrote, is what sets humans apart from the beasts, for it's something that every person experiences—the despair of being very far from God or even without God. It's the acknowledgment of this despair that sets the Christian apart from the non-Christian.[4]

Ever since Eve and Adam were expelled from the Garden, writers both ancient and modern have struggled to convey the existential terror that comes when we wonder if we might, indeed, be alone. The psalmist cried out to God, both thanking God for presence and questioning God's absence. In the extended proverb called the Book of Job, the protagonist and his friends debate at length why God's providential hand has been withdrawn and why God's voice has gone silent. The Hebrew prophets communicated God's wishes, but even they struggled to hear from God as time went by.

Jesus didn't question God's ways until the end, in the Garden of Gethsemane. So stressed that his sweat came as blood, he begged his Father to alter his fate. But Jesus is met with silence.

Hours later, hanging on the cross, he cries out four words in Aramaic, four words that changed the course of cosmic history.

"Eloi, Eloi Lema Sabachthani?"

All of Jesus' words recorded in the Gospels need to be run through the scrim of historical and critical thought. Did Jesus really say that? Or was it put in his mouth decades later by a Gospel writer with a theological agenda? For example, some scholars doubt that Jesus said, "Mother, behold your son; son, behold your mother," from the cross, simply because it would have been impossible for a suffocating victim to utter such a long sentence. Also, this quote comes from the Gospel of John, universally acknowledged to be the latest and most theologically advanced of the Gospels. And it's a quote that directly benefits the public image of the Apostle John, for he's the son in the episode. In other words, these scholars say, this line may have been put in Jesus' mouth by the author of John's Gospel, many years later.

Another criterion—a smell test, if you will—that Bible scholars use in judging the veracity of a Jesus quote is how Jesusy it sounds. If it tries to make Jesus look good and holy and godly, they surmise, it might have been added later to establish the goodness and holiness and godliness of Jesus. If, however, it's less in keeping with a holy image of Jesus—for example, "Let the dead bury their own dead!" or "If anyone comes to me and does not hate his own father and mother and wife and children and brothers and sisters, yes, and even his own life, he cannot be my disciple"[5]—then it's considered more likely to have authentically sprung from Jesus' lips.

By any of these criteria, Jesus' cry of despair on the cross is authentic. "Eloi, Eloi lema sabachthani?" he cries. "My God, my God, why have you forsaken me?"[6] It comes in Mark, the earliest Gospel, and also in Matthew. It surely does not accord with a sanitized, Sunday-school version of Jesus. Bible scholars and theologians call it the "Cry of Dereliction." Even the most skeptical scholars concur that these words of the dying rabbi are genuine.

More importantly, they are wrenching.

Jesus is quoting the opening lines of Psalm 22, a plea for deliverance from suffering and hostility. Here's some more of that psalm:

> *My God, my God, why have you forsaken me?*
>   *Why are you so far from helping me, from the words of my*
>   *groaning?*
> *O my God, I cry by day, but you do not answer;*
>   *and by night, but find no rest.*
>
> *Yet you are holy,*
>   *enthroned on the praises of Israel.*
> *In you our ancestors trusted;*
>   *they trusted, and you delivered them.*
> *To you they cried, and were saved;*
>   *in you they trusted, and were not put to shame.*

The psalm, attributed to King David, is an existential plea for God to arrive. Jesus' quoting of this single line from the Hebrew Bible is nothing short of breathtaking.

"My God, my God, why have you forsaken me?"

God is in Jesus, so God is forsaken by God.

All three later Gospel writers report other words of Jesus from the cross, all more comforting (and godly sounding) than this cry. In Matthew, Jesus welcomes a fellow victim into paradise. In Luke, Jesus says, "Father, into your hands I commend my spirit," which surely is more a prayer of faith than a lament of abandonment. In John, written six decades after the crucifixion, Jesus bequeaths his mother to his beloved disciple, admits he's thirsty, and says, "It is finished."

None of these contradicts or contravenes Mark's account of "Eloi, Eloi lema sabachthani!"[7]

We can imagine that Jesus' cry sent chills up the spines of all within earshot. Mark reports that some misheard it as a call for deliverance from the prophet Elijah. In response, they dipped a sponge in sour wine, put it on a stick, and lifted it up to him. We don't know if Jesus tasted the wine or not. "Then Jesus gave a loud cry and breathed his last."[8]

And that's it, that's how the death of Jesus is recounted in the first Gospel: Jesus cries out twice, first a cry of abandonment, then something inarticulate, and then he dies.

Already in the Garden of Gethsemane, Jesus dreads his fate. According to Mark,

> He threw himself on the ground and prayed that, if it were possible, the hour might pass from him. He said, "Abba, Father, for you all things are possible; remove this cup from me; yet, not what I want, but what you want."[9]

Jesus wants a reprieve. He is not playacting because he knows that God is going to resurrect him on Easter morning. He truly feels fear.

If we think back to an earlier episode in Jesus' life, we can gain a better understanding of how Jesus' humanity and divinity worked within him. After Jesus' baptism, he disappeared into the wilderness for forty days. There, weakened after fasting all that time, he was thrice tempted by Satan. Jesus was *really* tempted. He wasn't faking it. And Christians for centuries have rightly taken comfort in the fact that, even though he was God, Jesus was truly tempted just as we are tempted.

How is it that God could be tempted by the devil? Wouldn't God know without doubt that Satan posed him no threat and offered him nothing of value? Not if Jesus' divinity was somehow *behind* his humanity. One way to conceive of Jesus being God yet also truly experiencing the love, joy, heartbreak, and temptations of humanity is if his divinity took a backseat to his humanity.[10] This does not diminish his divinity; rather, it is evidence of yet another act of humility by God in God's long story of humility and self-limitation.

If this accurately represents the relationship between Jesus' two natures, then it's not unreasonable to believe that Jesus really was in anguish in the Garden and that he truly experienced despair at his abandonment on the cross.

That's because Jesus' humanity took center stage. His humanity was out front, touching and confronting the world. And, in full humanity, he was hoisted on a cross.

Jesus didn't have years to contemplate his execution, as death row inmates do today. He was arrested in the middle of the night and crucified less than twelve hours later. No matter how at peace he might have seemed with his martyrdom, he still must have felt fear, panic, anguish, and despair. By the time he was hanging on the cross, he'd been both physically and verbally assaulted. Jesus was not a superhero—no laser vision or skin made of steel. He was sleep-deprived, scourged, and weak from blood loss by the time he was crucified.

In other words, there's no reason to doubt that he really was in despair, that he really wondered, *Where the hell is God?*

This question must have been all the more acute with his burgeoning sense of messiahship. While it's not perfectly clear from the Gospels just how Jesus understood his own life and calling, it seems that over the course of his three years of public ministry he had an increasing awareness that he was special, that he had a unique relationship with God, even that he was the long-awaited Messiah.

And this knowledge must have made his anguish all the deeper as he hung on the cross. God had empowered him to heal the sick and insane, to command the weather and walk on water, and to preach to thousands. But now, faced with the powerful foe of the Roman government and the Temple leaders, he was powerless.

On Good Friday, at the very moment that Jesus' fate hit its nadir, God's humility reached its zenith. But Jesus didn't know that. Like so many others before him and since, at the very moment that Jesus was most in need, all he heard was silence.

The Crucifixion Changed God

It's an important tenet of Christianity that God is everywhere; there's nowhere that God isn't. But our experience of God doesn't always accord with this belief. Famously, Mother Teresa preached the presence and love of God to kings and lepers her whole life, but letters published after her death told a different story: she had not sensed God's presence for decades.[11]

This is a central paradox of human existence: We attest to God's reality, but we struggle to experience God's actual presence.

The experience that others had of God, firsthand, was overwhelming as well. For example, when Moses emerged from his encounters with the Lord on Mount Sinai or in the tent of meeting, his face shown with an otherworldly radiance.[12] However, as often as the Israelites experienced God's presence, they also experienced God's hiddenness. Psalm 22 isn't the only song of lament over God's absence in the Hebrew Bible. It's one in a chorus of texts that cry out for God, long for God, and wonder aloud how long God will stay silent.

All the while, we get the sense in the narrative of the Israelites that God and the people have a hard time understanding one another. God initiates a covenant, and the people struggle to keep their end of the bargain. The people beg for God to deliver them from their enemies, yet they keep getting conquered. God gives the people rafts of laws that are virtually impossible to keep, and the people debate and negotiate and legislate in their efforts to keep the laws. By a couple hundred years before Jesus, the relationship has totally broken down. God is silent, and the people are suffering under one foreign dictator or another.

And then, seemingly out of nowhere and surely at a time and place that no one would have predicted, God poured himself into a human being. As opposed to covenants and laws coming from on high, God recast the relationship. God came in weakness, demanding nothing, with no preconditions. The Yahweh of the Hebrew Bible demanded unswerving obedience to hundreds of laws, but God in Jesus didn't even require everyone who heard him preach to convert. He didn't enjoin those he'd healed to pledge him fealty. He put no preconditions on his disciples. Jesus did not build himself a castle nor sit on a throne. Instead, he said, "Foxes have holes, and birds of the air have nests; but the Son of Man has nowhere to lay his head."[13]

So in Jesus, God came to Earth in the posture of humility. That we know. And we also know that in Jesus, God communicated something. We learned that the meek are blessed and that the law was made for us, not vice versa. We learned that we should reach out to those on the margins, and we heard that in God's heavenly mansion, there are many rooms. This all came in the direction from God to us.

But what if we reverse directions? (Here's where I'm going to suggest something a bit novel.) In Jesus, things were happening in the other direction as well, *from us to God*. In Jesus, God was learning what it is really like to be human. In Jesus, God moved from sympathy with the human condition to empathy. And God changed as a result.

The Hebrew Bible contains various episodes testifying to God changing. The Lord "changes his mind" about destroying the people in the face of Moses' pleas.[14] God "regrets" that he made Saul king.[15] And God "changed his mind" about destroying Ninevah after the Ninevites made a public proclamation asking God to reconsider his pronouncement against them.[16] The texts of the Bible, it must be conceded, equivocate on this matter, for other verses seem to indicate that God does not change.[17] But even with those particular verses noted, the overarching narrative of scripture tells a story of a God who is deeply involved with and affected by his creation.

In Jesus, God dove into the deep end of the pool. God became immersed in the human condition, and through the same five senses that you and I have, God took in the experience of being fully human. That means the joys, sorrows, stubbed toes, and sleepless nights that you feel, God felt. God had hangnails and smelly armpits. God felt hungry, and God overate. God caught a cold. God was bitten by mosquitoes.

While I'm not necessarily saying that God did not *understand* what it felt like to get bitten by a mosquito before Jesus, I am saying that in Jesus, God fully *experienced* it. God went from sympathy to empathy with the human condition. *And that changed God,* for in that experience God became passionately connected with humankind in a way that God previously was not.

God, deeply embedded in Jesus of Nazareth, experienced everything that Jesus experienced. And that includes the crucifixion.

And when Jesus cried out from the cross in despair and anguish, God experienced something that God had never before experienced: *God experienced the absence of God.*

God experienced atheism.

And at that moment, God had an epiphany. God understood what it's like to feel godforsaken.

20

How the Crucifixion Changed
God's Relationship with Us

A COUPLE OF harrowing episodes of father-child sacrifice stand out in the Hebrew Bible. One, which we've already considered, is archetypal for the death of Jesus: Abraham takes Isaac to a mountaintop and, just as he's about to plunge a dagger into his son's chest, he's thwarted by an angel who provides a ram in exchange. Everyone from Paul to Kierkegaard has compared Isaac to Jesus.

But the other story is far more terrifying.

In Judges 11 we're told that Jephthah was the son of Gilead. Because his mother was a prostitute, Jephthah was driven out of the family compound as a teenager, and he became a renowned outlaw. But when times got tough for Israel in their running battle against the Ammonites, they reconciled with Jephthah and made him commander of their army. Jephthah's negotiations with the Ammonites came to naught, so he decided to take his men into battle. But before he left for war, he vowed an oath that if the Lord granted him military victory, "Whoever comes out of the doors of my house to meet me, when I return victorious from the Ammonites, shall be the LORD's, to be offered up by me as a burnt offering."[1] His forces were victorious, and upon his return Jephthah was devastated to see his

daughter, his only child, emerge from his home, dancing and singing at her father's return. He explained his vow to her, and she asked
that she might have two months to wander in the wilderness and
mourn the fact that she would die a virgin. Jephthah granted her re-
quest. Two months later he killed and burned his beloved daughter.

Commentators often try to find a moral in the story of Jephthah
and his daughter. "Don't make egotistical promises to the Lord!"
they preach, "Don't bargain with God!" But in the text, there is
no moral. There is only anguish, including an exhortation that the
daughters of Israel spend four days every year, wandering and griev-
ing for Jephthah's unnamed daughter. The story of Jephthah and his
daughter does not elicit a moral; the only appropriate response is
grief and mourning.

Filicide—the killing of one's own child—is among the most horrific of all crimes, an abomination against God and nature. We can
sense that horror in the biblical stories of Abraham and Jephthah.

So it's not without context when we read of Jesus crying out to
his Father, *Abba,* in the Garden of Gethsemane and then wondering
aloud why his God has forsaken him as he hangs dying on the cross.

Did God kill Jesus? We've come far enough now to answer that
question.

No, God did not kill Jesus.

This is not filicide. This is closer to deicide, the killing of a god—
the killing of God.

Where Was God When Jesus Died?

God infuses all that is; God is everywhere. This is indisputably part
of Jesus' message about God. And because of the mystery of the
Trinity, we can also say that God was both within Jesus on the cross
and witnessing his death from another vantage point.

Many people want there to be a nonviolent atonement. They want
God to be off the hook for Jesus' death. They usually want the Jewish Temple leaders off the hook as well. Rome alone is responsible

for the crucifixion in this view—Jesus was lynched by an imperial power, and God used that lynching to show the ultimate weakness of all imperial and colonizing powers. Jesus' death was unnecessary for our reunification with God, they argue, but God brought good out of it anyway.

We can agree with these critics insofar as we have seen that God definitely did not require the blood sacrifice of an innocent victim in order to atone for human sin. But even though God didn't require it, God *was* present as Jesus died. God chose not to stop the execution, as we have seen, because God's chosen deportment is one of self-limitation and humility. That's God's posture throughout the ages with Israel, and it didn't change on Good Friday. In fact, it reached its apogee on that day.

God's power had been evident many times during Jesus' life. One of the most frequent phrases in the Gospels of Mark, Matthew, and Luke comes after a sermon or a healing or a nature miracle by Jesus, when the people around him are described as being "amazed with his power and authority."[2] And in an episode that is repeated in each of those Gospels, Jesus is confronted by the Sadducees with a legalistic question about marriage in the afterlife. His response to them is that they understand neither the scriptures nor the power of God. In the afterlife, Jesus says, God's power to resurrect will obliterate all of the categories of this world. And it's in God's power to resurrect that Jesus places his trust.

But Jesus' trust in God's resurrection power was tested during Holy Week, and his faith flagged. At the climax of the passion—beginning in the garden and ending on the cross—Jesus wondered aloud whether God would rescue him and, finally, why God had abandoned him. These verses are not like Jesus' other utterances—they're not parables or sermons or pithy exhortations. These are existential pleas, cries to God, not unlike the prayers and cries of dereliction that you and I have let fly into the unknown, hoping for an answer.

God stood aside and allowed Jesus to be crucified. God laid down the power to intervene, and that opens God to the charge of being an accessory to the crime. This isn't unique to the crucifixion. Any time a horrific act of violence happens, we ask, *Where was God? Why didn't God stop this?*

In the film, *God on Trial*, a group of condemned prisoners at Auschwitz convene a judicial court asking just these questions—judging whether God is culpable for the Holocaust. One prisoner mocks another for praying, asking if he's helping God to make up his mind about who will die. Another prisoner tells him to stop, saying that questioning God is blasphemy: "The Lord our God can hear you, even here."

"He hears me, and he does nothing about it," the mocking prisoner responds. "He's a bigger bastard than I thought. He hears me; he does nothing about it. *He* should be here, not us. He's an evil bastard. We should put him on trial." And they do, convening a rabbinical court with three judges and a rabbi acting as a living Torah. The trial commences, and the court hears testimony from both sides.

God is charged with breach of contract for breaking his covenant with the people of Israel. The petitioners to the court do not question God's existence, but they do question God's character, God's motives. One claims that the ways of God are inscrutable and should not be questioned, similar to the arguments of Job's friends. Another argues that God is using Hitler to cleanse the Jewish people, the same way that God used Nebuchadnezzar. A physicist claims that it's irrational to believe that God has singled out one small group of people on one small planet to be favored above all others in the cosmos.

Finally the rabbi, the "living Torah," stops his praying and interjects. He tells of the Egyptians and the Moabites and the Amalekites, all of whom were brutally murdered by the Israelites at God's command. "We are becoming the Moabites," he says. "We are learning how it was for the Amalekites. . . . God is *not* good. He was *never* good. He was only on our side."

Then the rabbi says of God, "When he asked Abraham to sacrifice his son, Abraham should have said no. We should have taught God the justice that was in our hearts. We should have stood up to him."[3]

The beauty of *God on Trial* is that it opens the door to question God. And, in the rabbi's closing words, it even opens the door to Judaism's millennia-old assumption that God is on their side. The film is based on a fictional account from a play written by Holocaust survivor Elie Wiesel. Wiesel, however, has a very different answer than the rabbi about the presence of God in moments of horror. In his Holocaust memoir, *Night,* Wiesel recounts another story about God's presence. Standing in a crowd being forced to watch the hanging of an angel-faced child at Auschwitz, Wiesel heard someone ask, " 'For God's sake, where is God?' And from within me, I heard a voice answer, 'Where is He? This is where—hanging here from this gallows.' "[4]

God is here. That's Wiesel's answer. God is present, on the gallows, in the gas chambers. To the cry of godforsakenness—Where is God?—the response is quiet presence. Our God is not Zeus, throwing lightning bolts from on high. It's not even the God of Exodus, plaguing Egypt until the Pharaoh releases his slaves. This is the God who meets Elijah in a still, small voice. This is the God with whom Jesus seeks quiet communion when he steals away from the disciples for moments of prayer.

God's power is presence, quiet presence.

We so easily forget this. We lose track of God's presence, especially during moments of anguish and terror. Jesus is no different. In the Garden and on the cross, he sought assurance from God. He asked. But God's answer wasn't lightning bolts. It was presence.

"Only the Suffering God Can Help"

At one point during *God on Trial,* a prisoner asks, "Who needs a God who suffers?" This question may as well have been asked by a first-century Jew, wondering about the Apostle Paul's claim that the long-awaited Messiah had come not in power but in suffering.

Holocaust-era Christian theologian Dietrich Bonhoeffer struggled against the forces of evil and was ultimately lynched by the

Nazis for his part in a plot to assassinate Hitler. Few theologians have had so poignant an experience of suffering as Bonhoeffer. While imprisoned he wrote many letters, including the letter of July 16, 1944, in which he told his friend Eberhard Bethge that we should live in the world as if God did not exist. This is what God wants us to do, Bonhoeffer writes: "God would have us know that we must live as men who manage our lives without him. The God who is with us is the God who forsakes us." This, for Bonhoeffer, is the first step in leaving behind religion and truly following Christ. "Before God and with God we live without God," he writes. "God lets himself be pushed out of the world onto the cross."[5]

Human beings are inherently religious, Bonhoeffer continues. We want to find ways that God's power manifests itself in the world. We want God to intervene. We want *deus ex machina*—God in the machine. But that's not only a mistake, it is unbiblical: "The Bible directs man to God's powerlessness and suffering; only the suffering God can help."[6]

That's a beautiful line, but we're still left to figure out *how* the suffering God helps us.

In days past, and even today, what *homo religiosis* wants from God is power. Be it a warrior general on an ancient battlefield, sacrificing animals and asking for the gift of victory, or a present-day TV preacher promising the masses that he'll channel God's power and heal all illnesses in exchange for a love gift (cash, check, or credit cards accepted), we go to God in hopes of obtaining a bit of the power that created the universe. In the past, people felt powerless in the face of the weather, the empire, disease, or the tyrannical lord who lived on the nearest hill. Today many of us have gained mastery over some of those things, but we still struggle with feelings of powerlessness—we feel trapped in governmental bureaucracy that we can't escape, climate change that we cannot seem to stop, wars that never end, and relationships torn by brokenness that we cannot heal—divorce, mental illness, addiction. For all of the advances we've made, we still often feel helpless and vulnerable.

But Jesus' life and death challenge our understanding of God.

No longer is God a distant fellow with massive amounts of power, waiting to mete out that power to whomever says the right prayer or offers the appropriate sacrifice. Now God is one of us, among us, suffering alongside of us, experiencing our feelings of powerlessness.

The crucifixion decisively shows that omnipotence, the characteristic that seems invaluable to God, is in fact not definitive of God. Whether omnipotence is an underlying aspect of God, or one that God gave up for a time, is pure conjecture by us. What we *know* is that God is one with the powerless, one with the hopeless, one with the broken. And we know this because of Jesus. Jesus is the most fully realized revelation of God that we've got, and what we can see of God in the life of Jesus is the perfect example of self-limitation and humility.

Many of us were raised being taught that God is a bundle of omnis—omnipotent, omniscient, omnipresent. But the God we find in Jesus is unconcerned with the power that comes in these omnis. Instead we have a God who comes to us in presence and humility.

Now we've got a whole new way of life, made known in the way of Jesus' life and death, which is defined by humility and even suffering. Some have criticized this perspective, saying that it romanticizes victimhood and offers no hope to those who are victimized and abused: is a God who laid aside power and allowed himself to be tortured really bringing good news to a woman who is abused by her husband or a young boy who is sold into sex slavery? Only from a position of power and privilege is victimhood somehow considered noble. This corrective must be noted, and this danger avoided. But the amazing thing about the cross is that both the victim and the victimizer, both the oppressed and the oppressor, are liberated. God plays both of those roles in the event of the crucifixion. In Jesus, God is the victim; in God the Father, God is at least allowing the oppression. In God and in this event are wrapped up everything it means to be human. So the crucifixion does not valorize victimhood, it redeems the victim. And in an unexpected twist, it also redeems the victimizer.

What Jesus did that is different from other forms of victimization is that Jesus suffered *on behalf of others,* which is entirely different than unnecessary and unwarranted suffering. Or take another word applied to Jesus' death: *sacrifice.* If we think of a virgin thrown into a volcano as a sacrifice to appease the angry gods, we know that's a barbaric and terrible act. Yet if we see someone perform a virtuous act on behalf of another, we commend that person for being "self-sacrificial." A sacrifice, voluntarily given, is a beautiful thing; it's a gift that costs the giver something. We value these acts as virtuous, and rightly so.

During Jesus' final week of life, Luke recounts, he saw a sacrificial gift made, and he pointed it out to his disciples:

> He looked up and saw rich people putting their gifts into the treasury; he also saw a poor widow put in two small copper coins. He said, "Truly I tell you, this poor widow has put in more than all of them; for all of them have contributed out of their abundance, but she out of her poverty has put in all she had to live on."[7]

God took a similar course, giving up almost everything that is distinctive about God—the omnis—in order to find common ground with human beings. This was already humble, but ultimately, as Bonhoeffer says, God was even "pushed out of the world onto the cross." According to Paul, this total humiliation of the divine is "a stumbling block to Jews and foolishness to Gentiles."[8] But it's a road map for life to the Christian. The way of Jesus is one of self-limitation and self-sacrifice—always freely and voluntarily entered into, never coerced or forced. Remember the passage cited in chapter 14 about Jesus' last supper with his disciples? On Jesus' last night, he washed his disciples' feet and then, joining them at the table said,

> Do you know what I have done to you? You call me Teacher and Lord—and you are right, for that is what I am. So if I, your Lord and Teacher, have washed your feet, you also

ought to wash one another's feet. For I have set you an example, that you also should do as I have done to you. Very
truly, I tell you, servants are not greater than their master,
nor are messengers greater than the one who sent them. If
you know these things, you are blessed if you do them.[9]

Jesus' entire ministry was equality in action: he spoke to a Samaritan woman, healed those who were too "unclean" to enter the
Temple, and ate with sinners and tax collectors. And here, on his last
night, he puts that lifestyle into a conclusive teaching: a servant and
a master are peers, colleagues, equals.

As a result of his life, his teaching, and his death, the distance
between God and humanity has been obliterated. It is no more. The
master has joined the servants. And the appropriate response to that,
right from Jesus' own lips, is that we too humble ourselves, serve one
another, and take up our own crosses of suffering.

God's Solution to Our Problem

We're still left to solve the question of what it means that *Jesus died for
our sins*. Most theologians start with the concept of sin and then work
toward Jesus' death, showing how that act conquered the problem.
But we've gone in the other direction, investigating Jesus' death as
an act of solidarity between God and humanity, and now we've got
to consider how this death dealt with sin. To do that, we've got to
figure out what sin is.

Rabbi Joseph likes to say that the genius of the Apostle Paul was
that he took what was corporate and communal and made it personal. The atonement that Israel sought in ancient times was always
on behalf of the entire people, the entire nation. The sacrifices
on the Day of Atonement put all of Israel back in right standing
with God. Personal forgiveness was not on the menu. At its best,
this brought a sense of the collective and the communal to people,
something that we are sorely lacking in our individualistic age. But

at its worst, individuals got to hide behind the "sins of the people," avoiding their own personal culpability. As we saw earlier, there was no mechanism in ancient Israel by which an individual was forgiven of sin.

With Paul—that is, with Jesus as interpreted and explained by Paul—that changed. Now it's not about the nation or the people; it's about *God and me.* And this emphasis became even more pronounced in the early church.

The New Testament brims with words for sin—at least half a dozen, each with a different nuance. One means to commit an injustice, another means lawlessness, and another has a more juridical sense. Yet another means to "lose one's way"—literally, to "fall down." But the most common word, used 173 times, is *hamartia,* and it means to miss the mark, to fall short of a goal, to fail.

Before Jesus' arrival, sin was pretty clear-cut. If you disobeyed the laws of the Torah—which everyone inevitably did—your sins were put in the big pot of Israel's sins. On the Day of Atonement, everyone took care of that, collectively. But Jesus introduced a problematic element to this relatively straightforward equation. He changed our relationship to the law: he allowed his disciples to pick grain on the Sabbath, he healed on the Sabbath, and he taught that the law was to be the servant of humanity, not vice versa. The very ones who'd been thought to uphold the law most diligently were said by Jesus to be in conflict with the law. Jesus called them "blind guides," a "brood of vipers," and "whitewashed tombs." He accused them of accentuating the details of the law while neglecting the "weightier matters of the law: justice and mercy and faith."[10]

Suddenly, what was sin was less than clear.

Jay Bakker, pastor and author and famous son of infamous televangelists, is one of my dearest friends. I first met him in 2007, when we spoke at the same conference. Jay had gained some notoriety for changing his mind on whether homosexuality was a sin, and he became one of the first evangelical leaders to publicly affirm gays in the church. I had watched a documentary in which he was featured, and I was excited to meet him.

As we walked down a street from the conference to our hotel, I pelted him with questions about homosexuality and sin. And then, purely by accident, I said something that changed my conception of sin—and maybe his, too.

"It seems that you've got a box called 'Sin,'" I said. "And now you've decided to take homosexuality out of that box. But the problem is, what are you going to take out of that box next? The problem is not with what's in the box or outside of the box. The problem is with the box. You need to get rid of your Sin Box."

As you might guess, we've had a good laugh several times since about that. "Where's your Sin Box?"

"I don't know. I must have left it somewhere."

But there's a more serious underlying issue. As Christians, we often protest the charge that our faith is little more than a list of rights and wrongs, of dos and don'ts. But we persist in thinking that "sin" is a bounded set, a box—some things are inside it, and other things are outside, and the debate between different versions of Christianity is what's in and what's out. Slavery used to be outside the Sin Box, but now it's inside. Gambling used to be in, but now it's out. And homosexuality—well, it depends on whom you ask.

But sin isn't a box. Sin is an ailment. Sin is a chronic disease, and we all live with it. Some of us manage to live with it better, controlling the disease, and others among us struggle against sin but are controlled by it. And some of us it destroys.

Behavior isn't the disease; sin itself is the disease. That is, sin must be thought of as a *condition* rather than an *activity*.

Think of someone who has arthritis or asthma or HIV/AIDS. The sufferer of rheumatoid arthritis could go years with no symptoms or could have a nasty flare-up. But swollen and painful knuckles isn't actually arthritis: it's a symptom of arthritis. The arthritis itself is an autoimmune disease in which your body attacks itself—specifically, antibodies in the blood mistake the cells in the lining in the joints as foreign invaders and attack them. There is no cure; there is only treatment of the symptoms.

Paul wrote that sin came into the world through Adam, "and so death spread to all because all have sinned."[11] Like a plague, sin spread. We have learned that the early church accounted for this sin-disease biologically, spread through semen, from father to child. But we don't need to embrace that mistaken notion to nevertheless affirm that we are each beset with a chronic condition in which we fall short of perfection. We lie, we cheat, we lust, we dehumanize, we marginalize, we fly off the handle. We show the symptoms of the sin-disease that we each carry. It's unavoidable. It is part of the human condition.

For Jesus and his followers, sin and disease were linked. Physical infirmities were seen as resulting from sin—either personal or corporate. When asked about this link regarding a man born blind, Jesus said that neither the man's sins nor his parents' sins were the cause of his blindness.[12] But for his disciples, those were the only two options.

In many other Gospel episodes, Jesus heals those who are sick, and he simultaneously forgives them of their sin. His opponents are scandalized, though they sometimes don't know which is worse: that Jesus touches the unclean, eats with tax collectors, and heals on the Sabbath, or that he claims to be able to forgive sins. Jesus became renowned for his fellowship with sinners, even being called a "friend of sinners"—meant as an insult by his accusers, but clearly a compliment in the eyes of the Gospel writers.[13] What had been a curse was actually a chance to dine with the Messiah.

And in a long stretch of miracle-healing stories in the Gospel of Matthew, we find this paragraph:

> When Jesus entered Peter's house, he saw his mother-in-law lying in bed with a fever; he touched her hand, and the fever left her, and she got up and began to serve him. That evening they brought to him many who were possessed with demons; and he cast out the spirits with a word, and cured all who were sick. This was to fulfill what had been spoken through the prophet Isaiah, "He took our infirmities and bore our diseases."[14]

Matthew takes this quote from the famous "Suffering Servant" section of Isaiah. Prior to Jesus, Jews had not thought this passage was about the Messiah, but the Gospel writers and Paul connected those dots. In Isaiah, physical infirmities and diseases are inseparable from sin, as the very next verse from the prophet makes clear:

> But he was wounded for our transgressions,
>   crushed for our iniquities;
> upon him was the punishment that made us whole,
>   and by his bruises we are healed.[15]

In his life and ultimately in his death, Jesus takes our ailments upon himself—that's a huge part of the humility of God and God's solidarity with humanity that we find in Jesus. Our ailments are both physical and spiritual, and Jesus embraced both. Even before Jesus, Jews considered the coming messianic age to be a time of great healing—no more sin, no more disease. When the first Christians embraced Jesus as the one who inaugurated the messianic age, they found in him the healing that was long promised.

So if we can rejigger our understanding of sin, we can see how Jesus died for our sin. Jesus doesn't just wipe away our sins: he *bears* them; he *carries* them. And on the cross they crush him, just as they so often crush us. But three days later, at the resurrection, Jesus the Christ, the Risen Lord, overcomes the very ailment that crushed him. In his rising, we see that the ailment of sin that is endemic to our human condition is not the end of the story. Sin is not insurmountable. Jesus rises to new life, still bearing the scars of his earthly torture but finally overcoming the consequences of sin. And as Paul makes clear over and over again in his letters, we are promised this same new life. We can live in the midst of the illness of sin with the hope that we, too, can overcome it. The good news of Jesus' death and resurrection is that in Jesus of Nazareth, God entered fully and completely into solidarity with us so that we can find solidarity with God in the Risen Christ.

We'll Never Be Alone Again

What have we learned? From the beginning of time, God has practiced humility and self-limitation. Maybe it's the only way that God could be in an authentic relationship with finite creatures, or maybe it's because God simply thought it best, but in either case God started by retreating enough to create the cosmos. Then God withdrew enough to let Israel chart its own course, for both good and ill. And ultimately God was humbled in a way that neither the Hebrews nor the Hellenists had thought possible, by inhabiting a human being—for that matter, a human being of humble origins. God built a bridge between humanity and divinity, and then God walked over it.

When God fully entered the human experience in Jesus, new vistas of understanding were opened. Joy, pathos, trial, temptation, happiness, grief—God went from observer to participant in the whole gamut of human existence.

And then some things you'd never expect God to experience—existential loneliness, godforsakenness, atheism, death—even that became part of the life of God. In the Garden, Jesus prays for a reprieve, and he receives no answer. And on the cross, just moments before his death, Jesus cries out in anguish and dereliction, "My God, my God, why have you forsaken me?" That is the pivot point of all cosmic history, for in that moment God became fully human. Only when God felt abandoned, alone in the universe, did God gain total empathy with the human condition.

Many have tried to explain just what shifted in the God-human relationship because of Jesus' death. Almost all have assumed that the change took place in us. God never changes, they assumed, so the crucifixion must change us—or it must fulfill some requirement that God had that we can't fulfill on our own. And that's not wrong, for surely the crucifixion changes us, just as it changed Jesus' disciples who witnessed it. But it also changed God.

For two millennia, Christians have found in Jesus a brother, advocate, and friend. Uniquely among the world's religions, the Christian church has preached a *personal* God, a God who wants to be in an intimate relationship with us. God is no longer the abstract, immaterial concept of the Greeks, nor is God the fearsome warrior of the Hebrews. Now God is our *friend*. "Friend of sinners!" was an insult hurled at Jesus, but in fact it's both a compliment and our hope.

The beauty and power of the resurrection is that our friend didn't just die on that cross. He lives on, offering us ongoing friendship. Even death couldn't kill this friendship between God and humanity.

And even more than that, God offers us the ceaseless presence of the Holy Spirit—described in the Bible as the power of God, our Advocate, our Comforter, and our Counselor.

In other words, everything after the crucifixion is meant to ensure that we never again feel forsaken by God. The resurrected Christ is our everlasting friend, and the Holy Spirit is the abiding presence of God. We may at times *feel* alone, but since the crucifixion God has made sure that *we aren't alone.*

PART SEVEN

The Way of the Cross

21

The Way of Peace

I 'VE NEVER BEEN in a fistfight. I did punch my brother once. I was about twelve at the time, which means he was ten. Even though he was younger than me, Andrew was bigger and stronger. He had me pinned on the ground till I shouted, "Uncle!" After he let me up, I sucker punched him in the face, and then I ran like hell. He was stunned enough to give me a head start—he was also faster than me—and I hid behind a neighbor's house until he calmed down.

My mom tells a story from just a few years earlier. I was six, Andrew was four, and she was in the final month of pregnancy with our youngest brother, Ted. Being obstreperous, boisterous, and bossy, I was holding court on the front steps of our home with all the neighbor kids just as she was trying to take a nap. After several unheeded requests to quiet down, she angrily came out the front door, grabbed my arm, and pulled me into the house. But I stumbled and fell, hitting my head on the corner of a slate table. As a lump grew on my forehead, I looked up and said, "Don't worry, Mom, I'll tell the teacher at school that I tripped." We laugh about it now, but my mother still remembers being horrified at the time that she might be considered an abusive mom. I remember these incidents pretty vividly as well.

Violence haunts us. It stalks us. Whether it's a person punching a hole in the drywall after an argument or two nations locked in ongoing military conflict, we are a violent species. It's why, as we've seen, so many Christians are unsettled by the crucifixion as the means of our salvation. Violence-free salvation, they reckon, would be better.

But this is where they are underestimating the good news Jesus came to preach. In a surprising twist, the crucifixion is *the solution* to our violent tendencies. The crucifixion has created the possibility for us to be liberated from violence and enter into a life of peace.

If we do not understand this, then we do not understand the cross at all: the crucifixion of Jesus *must* change how we live. That is the point.

Figuring It Out Ourselves

When Dietrich Bonhoeffer urged his correspondent to live in the world as if there were no God, he was suggesting that Jesus himself lived that way. Bonhoeffer's point was that Jesus didn't look to God to get him out of jams, rescue him from angry mobs, or help him pass his carpentry final. Jesus lived and moved through the world with the confidence of his own convictions and, as the Gospel writers make clear, with the power of the Holy Spirit. And he did so in league with scoundrels and sinners and outcasts and whores.

Bonhoeffer himself surely prayed for the end of the Nazis and the demise of Hitler, but that didn't stop him from taking action.[1] When he wrote that letter to Eberhard Bethge, he did so from prison, there for taking part in the German resistance movement. Among the activities of that resistance were several assassination attempts on Hitler. Though he was a committed pacifist, Bonhoeffer supported these plots, and that ultimately led to his execution on April 9, 1945, just a month before the Allies defeated the Nazis.

In his last book, the uncompleted *Ethics,* Bonhoeffer wrote, "Those who in acting responsibly take on guilt—which is inescapable for any responsible person—place this guilt on themselves . . . ; they stand up for it and take responsibility for it."[2] In other words, human beings are free, and guilt is inevitable. But this isn't an excuse to avoid taking action. Instead, we're compelled to take action, even when the choices are less than ideal. Bonhoeffer called Christians to "participation in the *powerlessness* of God in the world."[3] Others more recently have called it the "weakness of God."[4]

Here is the guiding idea: God has forsaken power in order to give creation freedom. In other words, God's primary posture in the world is that of weakness, not strength. This is a tough pill for many Christians to swallow—we've been taught to claim God's power in our lives, to pray for power, and to trust God's power and perfect plan for our lives. But we've got something to learn from Jesus' cry of forsakenness, and from God's response.

God's power, it turns out, comes in God's willingness to abdicate power. God saves the world through submission to the point of solidarity with human weakness. Jesus' final teaching to his disciples was to wash their feet and then tell them to go and do likewise, to act as servants to the world.

Too often, Christians have done just the opposite. Unfortunately, the symbol of the cross seems to fit perfectly on a military shield, and starting with Constantine, that's where it's often been affixed. Christians have used their faith as a justification for making war on their opponents. It's especially ironic that followers of Jesus have often been the violent persecutors of those they've claimed to be responsible for Jesus' death, the Jews.

Here we might remember the Mirror model of René Girard. What God did in the crucifixion was to show vividly that violent sacrifice gets us nowhere. Violence doesn't mitigate violence. It's a dead end.

One of the differences you may have noticed in churches is that Protestant churches have an empty cross at the front of the sanctuary, while the crosses in Catholic churches—commonly called *crucifixes*—have a likeness of the dead Jesus on them. Growing up

Protestant, I was told this is because we focus on the victory of resurrection, and that the cross will be empty forevermore. (More than
once it was also implied that Catholics are a bit morbid to keep Jesus'
corpse up there on the cross.) But if Girard is right, then there's
something powerful about a Christian worshipper being confronted
by the body of the crucified Savior. If we can fight the tendency
to let it become so familiar that we don't notice it, we can be chal-
lenged every week to remember that God doesn't want our bloody
victories and that sacrifice doesn't really overcome our rivalries. At
least for Christians, that crucifix should be the emblem of the end
of violence. Like a memorial on a Civil War battlefield, the cross
should say to us, "The very last sacrifice happened here, and no religious violence need ever happen again."

Taking Action Against Violence

My friend Shane Claiborne is taking a page right out of Bonhoeffer's playbook. He's not just waiting around for God to solve the
problems of violence in the world; he's using his freedom to act
responsibly. Hebrew prophecy has inspired Shane:

> He shall judge between the nations,
>   and shall arbitrate for many peoples;
> they shall beat their swords into ploughshares,
>   and their spears into pruning hooks;
> nation shall not lift up sword against nation,
>   neither shall they learn war any more.[5]

So he and his friends in North Philadelphia have taken this literally.
On September 11, 2011, a welder among them took a donated AK47
semiautomatic rifle, melted it down, and turned it into a rake and a
shovel. Since then, Shane has taken welding lessons himself, and he's
solicited people to send him weapons, which he promises to turn
into garden tools and mail back. He says,

We refuse to wait any longer. We've prayed for peace, and we will continue to pray for peace. But we've also realized that sometimes we think we're waiting on God, and God may actually be waiting on us. We cannot wait for politicians or governments. The new world that the prophets spoke of begins with us.[6]

Shane's right. We cannot wait to end violence. And it starts with us. When a law passed in Minnesota that allowed registered citizens to carry concealed guns, one Lutheran church stood up. The law allowed guns to be carried in virtually every building except schools without a large sign at every entrance prohibiting guns. Edina Community Lutheran Church sued the state, saying that their religious freedom was being violated, and over five years of hearings, they consistently won. During those years, they had a large sign over their door: "Blessed are the peacemakers. Firearms are prohibited in this place of sanctuary." They won in court, and firearms are now prohibited in places of worship in Minnesota.

Naysayers are quick to point out that the church has often authorized violence. Yes, that's true. But the church's history is also replete with peacemakers. Every generation has them, and some of them are household names: Francis of Assisi, Menno Simons, Martin Luther King Jr. Others should be remembered, like Martin of Tours. Born in 316, only three years after the emperor Constantine legalized Christianity, Martin began attending church at age ten, against his parents' wishes. At fifteen, Martin joined the army, as required by his family's rank, for a twenty-five-year term. According to his biographer, sometime during that tenure, as his unit approached a battle, Martin said, "I am a soldier of Christ. I cannot fight." Jailed for cowardice, he offered to go to the front lines without a weapon, but instead he was released from the military. Another story about Martin tells that he did once use his sword: he cut his cloak in two and gave half to a beggar. Out of the army, Martin joined the priesthood, became the bishop of Tours in 371, and was known among the ruling class as someone who would beg for the forgiveness and release of prisoners.

One of the roles that the church must take up in the twenty-first century is that of standing for peace in the midst of violence. This will be complex, and I'm not unaware of the politics involved. I've admitted that I'm a hunter. I'm also a gun owner—three shotguns, kept in a secured safe with trigger locks. Gun violence is a scourge on the United States, and yet I try to be a responsible gun owner in the face of that.

In a passage that vexes pacifists, Jesus himself showed some ambivalence toward weaponry. On the night of his arrest, Jesus was with his disciples. Luke tells us,

> He said to them, "When I sent you out without a purse, bag, or sandals, did you lack anything?" They said, "No, not a thing." He said to them, "But now, the one who has a purse must take it, and likewise a bag. And the one who has no sword must sell his cloak and buy one. For I tell you, this scripture must be fulfilled in me, 'And he was counted among the lawless'; and indeed what is written about me is being fulfilled." They said, "Lord, look, here are two swords." He replied, "It is enough."[7]

Weapons, it seems, are a part of life. But later that evening, when one of Jesus' disciples used a sword to slice off the ear of the high priest's servant, Jesus rebuked his disciple and healed the slave.

Through the course of that night and into the next morning, Jesus is the victim of violence—lashings and beatings, culminating in his crucifixion. He neither resists arrest nor fights back. Maybe that's because resisting the Roman Empire was futile. But throughout history, Jesus has been seen as a submissive victim. Where does this leave victims of violence? Does Jesus' torturous death mean that we should suffer willingly and without resistance?

You may remember the feminist theologians referenced in chapter 17; they recount harrowing stories of clergymen who've told women to gladly bear the abuse they receive from their husbands, just as Christ bore his suffering. Here is where it's so important to affirm that God was in Jesus and that Jesus was God incarnate. Jesus was not just a victim, one among many. Jesus was God, fully immersed in the human experience. In suffering and death, God found new solidarity with humanity, and especially with those who suffer. God identified with the victims. God stood with them. And God stands with them still.

The church, as the community founded on Jesus' life and death, must now stand with the victims, just as God did in Jesus. We need to be the ones who are in solidarity with the victims of domestic abuse, those sold into sex slavery, and ethnic minorities who face violence simply because of the tribe into which they were born.

If there's a message in the crucifixion for the church, it's that God abdicated power and stood with the powerless. Now the church, formed by the cross, must do the same.

Ceasing Our Inner Violence

I've had my own journey in this area. In my late twenties and early thirties, I was a pastor at a large, suburban church—the same church in which I was reared. Although life seemed good on the outside, I had internal struggles. I was in a troubled marriage that sapped me. And I exhibited a youthful, brash arrogance that served to hide deep insecurities. One day, I blew up in rage at the church's head custodian over a long-since-forgotten slight. In a back hallway, blowing off steam, I slammed a storage room door so hard that the hinge mechanism atop the door burst open, spewing hydraulic fluid across the wall and ceiling.

Sometime later, that same rage flared up at a committee meeting. For whatever reason, I'd felt disrespected, so I let fly invective at a dozen church volunteers. Fortunately, they were all older and wiser than me. They decided to help me rather than fire me. I remember their names—Linda, Doug, and Mark, in particular—and they encouraged me to take an anger-management course, which I did. There I learned to address the fear that underlies anger, the anger that leads to violence. Thank God, my own violent outbursts were confined to slamming doors and shouting, and now I live with much more peace than I did then.

The irony is not lost on me. I worked in a building founded on the crucifixion of Jesus, and my posture was one of aggression instead of peace. Once I gained some control of my inner turmoil, I began to see Jesus' crucifixion as my channel to peace. During those years, I took up a study of ancient spiritual practices. I began earnestly practicing yoga, something I do even more frequently now that my wife, Courtney, is a yoga instructor.

I also simplified my prayers. Rather than barraging God with requests, pleas, and praises, I focused almost exclusively on a prayer formulated by desert monks in the fifth century:

> *Lord Jesus Christ,*
> *Son of God,*
> *have mercy on me,*
> *a sinner.*

To this day, over ten years later, that prayer, said in rhythm with my breath, makes up about 90 percent of my prayer life. I suppose this prayer has brought me so much peace because it's not frantic, not urgent, not frightened.

During that same time, I first studied and then began to acquire icons of the Orthodox Church, my favorite being the icon of the San Damiano cross, which depicts Jesus on the cross and angels, women, and John attending to him. The Eastern Church teaches that icons are not merely paintings, but they are windows into heaven, conduits to God's presence. That icon went from an object of study to an object of veneration for me when I visited Taizé, a monastic community in France. Once a week, on Friday night, at the end of evening prayer, a six-foot-tall version of the San Damiano cross icon is brought to the center of the massive sanctuary and laid on the floor. In a procession that can take over an hour, hundreds of youth crawl to the cross, touch their foreheads to it, and kiss it. Many weep.

The first time I saw it, it took my breath away. But this adoration of the cross also reveals the nexus of the crucifixion and peace, that surprising oxymoron that we're trying to understand. At Taizé, the violence of the crucifixion and the peace of the monastery make perfect sense. But it's not an intellectual sense—it's a mystical sense. In the mysticism of the moment—the singing, the prayers, the crawling, the tears—the humility of God on the cross comes into perfect focus.

This is another challenge for me, as it may be for you. I tend to intellectualize these questions, trying to solve the mystery of how peace can come from such a violent event. But when the intellect can be made submissive to the spirit, something new can be learned. The ancient Desert Fathers and Mothers who came up with my favorite prayer also gave instructions about how to pray it. They said that the pray-er should allow the mind to descend to the place of the heart. They even recommend that you rest your chin on your chest and, with your eyes closed, look toward your heart. They seem to be saying that this prayer will only do what it's supposed to if you can quiet your mind and allow your heart to take the lead.

For some, the cross is a sign of crusade, for others a sign of violence, for still others a sign of victory. For me, the cross has become a symbol of peace, and it has brought me peace. And in this I believe I have finally discovered what God meant all along.

The church still has so much to learn about this cross-inspired, peaceful way of life. In so many of the churches in which I've been involved, nothing is really different because of the cross. We still operate by the same schemes and rhythms of the world around us. Just think of the reaction to Mel Gibson's brutal movie, *The Passion of the Christ*. More than one Christian leader gleefully called it the "greatest evangelistic tool of all time." Instead, we should have watched that movie with René Girard and seen that we are all implicated in the very violence that resulted in Jesus' death.

That movie should have been a mirror reflecting our own violence back at us.

We need to unlearn violence. It's deep in our evolutionary psyches, but in the cross God is calling us to unlearn it and take on new habits—the habits of peace, solidarity, and love. The church should be on the forefront of a movement of peace. And at the front of that procession should be Jesus, on a cross, for that symbol condemns all our violence and cries out, "Never again!"

22

The Way of Solidarity

EVERY YEAR ON Good Friday, many well-meaning churches sponsor a "living crucifixion," in which a willing parishioner—usually one who bears a striking resemblance to popular depictions of Jesus—is hoisted on a cross for all to see. These days, ropes rather than spikes keep "Jesus" up on the cross. A couple of years ago, one image went viral on social media because "Jesus" didn't like the weather, so he was wearing a raincoat as he was "crucified."

In 2014, television station Fox 4 in Fort Myers, Florida, reported that the Lee County Sheriff's Department "ordered 'Jesus' taken down from the cross." This "Jesus" had a Hollywood-level make-up job, including huge, gruesome wounds on his back and sides and blood dripping from his crown of thorns. The problem was that "Jesus" was "crucified" at a busy intersection, causing traffic back-ups and several near accidents. Also, "Jesus" was on public property without a permit. "Jesus" was outraged that the cops told him to move on. While still on the cross, "Jesus" told a reporter, "Easter is not about bunny rabbits and little chicks. This is what our Christ endured for us, for our sins, and to hide that is to not live to the true faith of what he did for us."[1] The news report ended showing the bloody, dejected "Jesus" loading his cross into a trailer.

Well-intentioned though he may have been, "Jesus" was missing the point of Jesus. The real Jesus was not looking to be crucified at a busy intersection, hoping for some media coverage of his plight. Instead, he died as he lived: at the margins and in solidarity with those who dwell at the margins. The way of the cross moves us toward those same places and those same people.

I recently got into a debate with a guy who told me that the biggest problem in America is the marginalization of the church. I told him he's dead wrong. The church is back on the margins, where it's always belonged. Christianity's ascendency to the largest religion in the world probably meant that the marriage of church and state was inevitable. Kings and generals became bedfellows with popes and pastors, and all took on the mantle of Christ for their political and military campaigns. Both good and bad resulted from this marriage. The Christian faith probably made government and even the military more humane. But it didn't help Christianity. As Christian evangelist Tony Campolo is fond of saying, "Mixing religion and politics is like mixing ice cream and dog crap: it doesn't hurt the dog crap, but it sure ruins the ice cream."

The days of Christianity's cultural power are fading. Whether you're in anguish or joy about atheists in Congress and Muslims on the school board, we're not going back to Christian domination. So Christians must decide how to live as we drift from the centers of power.

When we've strayed too far from Jesus' exemplary life, the Christian faith has gotten in some real trouble: the Crusades, the Inquisition, and slavery, to name just a few examples. In other words, the further the church has gotten away from modeling itself after Jesus, the more rotten it smells.

But there have always been those in our midst who have called us back to the life of Jesus, on the margins. In 1205, a young and impassioned man in northern Italy went before the bishop of that town and stripped off the clothes given to him by his wealthy father. Over the next few years, he lived as a beggar and a penitent. When the powerful wouldn't listen to him, Francis of Assisi went to any who would; there are legends of him preaching even to birds and wolves.

Today you can visit small hovels in the woods above Assisi where Francis and his disciples lived. Centuries later, his spirit still infuses the brothers who claim the Franciscan moniker, and now a pope has claimed that name, too. That pope has made worldwide headlines for following the way of the cross: walking unprotected out of the Vatican to have tea with everyday Romans, kissing a man covered in boils, washing the feet of a young female Muslim prisoner.

But we are besieged by the voices of other Christian leaders as well, those who tell us how to vote and whom to hate. They are Christianity's culture warriors, and they think that the fate of the faith rises and falls on its access to power. But the crisis in the church is a crisis of authority, as it is across Western culture. To whom should we listen? The loudest voices? The most educated? The formerly marginalized? The formerly powerful? Those with the most retweets? Those who have traditionally spoken for God are now looked at askance by many people, and with good reason. Too often they've used their Christian platform for political and military gain. They've forgotten that the story of God, exemplified in Jesus, is an abdication of power. It's a story of self-limitation and humility. It's a story lived in solidarity with those at the margins.

To whom should we listen? To Jesus on the cross.

Jesus on the Margins

Many of Jesus' greatest feats were among those on the margins. He met with a Samaritan woman. She was out to fetch water at high noon, presumably because she was an outcast in her town. Jesus gave her hope and sent her home.

He dined with tax collectors and whores and sinners, to the point that the scribes and Pharisees sneered, "He's a friend of sinners."

He touched those who were deemed untouchable: the leprous, the blind, the paralyzed, the menstruating.

He brought peace to those who were demonic, like a man who was chained up outside of town in the cemetery.

And Jesus himself ended his journey, not in the center of Jerusalem, not in the Temple, but outside the city walls on a hill of death. In the ancient world, cemeteries were built outside the city for reasons both sanitary and superstitious. They were literally on the margins. And that's where Jesus died. If we can take a lesson from his life and death, it's that he did not desire to be at the center of power, but instead lived among those who had been marginalized, and he died among the marginalized as well.

In the power scheme of the Roman Empire, Jesus dwelt on the margins. He was a noncitizen, an ethnic minority, and part of an odd religion. He didn't rate.

And in the Jewish power scheme in Jerusalem, the same. Jesus held a position of power in neither the capital nor the clergy hierarchy. He was a wandering mystic and a pebble in the sandal of the Temple leaders.

So they colluded, stripped him naked, beat him bloody, and hung him on a cross outside the city walls. They made him disgusting and unclean, like all those he'd touched over the years. I suppose they hoped this would close the book on Jesus—once his followers saw him like this, untouchable, they'd go back to their lives as law-abiding Jews, subservient to Rome. But his execution had just the opposite effect. Almost immediately, his followers found his crucifixion inspiring—many of them were martyred in similar ways, thereby redoubling the fervency of the young sect. What the ruling powers meant for unclean, Jesus made clean. (Remember what we learned from Richard Beck in chapter 17?) They threw Jesus over the boundary of socio-moral disgust, meaning to silence him. But instead, Jesus pulled everyone over the line with him, redeeming the previously untouchable, revealing that we're all "unclean," and tearing down the wall that religion had erected.

In other words, he was executed outside of actual and metaphorical walls. The Gospels report that when Jesus died, the massive curtain in the Temple was torn in two. The Temple veil was also both actual and metaphorical, separating the Temple courts from the Holy of Holies. When it tore, the divisions between sacred and profane, clean and unclean, so important to first-century Judaism, were symbolically removed.[2]

As in our day, walls and veils and boundaries and barriers were prevalent, both literally and metaphorically, in first-century Judea. Jesus' life and Jesus' death repeatedly breached the boundaries. It's no mistake that a centurion—one of the "unclean"—was the first to proclaim, "Truly this man was the son of God."

And early Christians understood that this was the way to follow Jesus. The Didache, a handbook for Christian converts from late in the first century, has this advice for those new to the faith:

> Be long-suffering and pitiful and guileless and gentle and good, and with trembling, treasure the words you have received. Don't exalt yourself or open your heart to overconfidence. Don't be on intimate terms with mighty people, but with just and lowly ones.[3]

Paul wrote something similar to the Romans: "Live in harmony with one another; do not be haughty, but associate with the lowly."[4]

This was a countercultural message, just as it is today. We're generally encouraged to chase power and to accede to the demands of the mighty. But the earliest Christians turned from this, inspired by Jesus' example, especially his example on the cross. We, too, have imperial desires, and we, too, must suppress them. Today when we see a cross lifted high, it's often at a busy intersection, at the top of a majestic mountain, or in the apse of a soaring cathedral. When our ancestors built cities, a church was central, on the piazza or the town square. So it's easy to forget that the original cross wasn't even inside the city limits.

Cut off from cultural power, Jesus died on the margins, among the marginalized. Surely that's also the place for the church founded in his name.

The way of the cross leads us away from the center of town; it's a road past the city walls, into the places where the lame, the crazy, the broken, and the unclean live. If we're going to follow Jesus on the way of the cross, that's where he's going to lead us.

The Way of Humility

In our study of the crucifixion, we have discovered that the single most revolutionary action taken by God in all of history is the complete solidarity with humankind that God experienced in Jesus' life and death. In many ways, the Greek philosophers were right to think of God as an immaterial Mind, floating in the ether. And in other ways, the Hebrews were also correct to live in fear of the mighty warrior Yahweh. But in Jesus, both of those paradigms collapse, for God became human—God became as immanent as you and me.

God began relinquishing power at the moment of creation. Throughout the history of Israel, God backed off, allowing the people to find their own way, even when it meant sojourns in the wilderness and generations cut off from their promised land. But God wasn't absent. All the while, God supported the people, giving them advice, both stern and gracious, providing them with sustenance, and protecting them from enemies. Then, in Jesus, both humility and love reached a climax. God was humbled beyond all expectation by becoming human. But God also showed extraordinary and proactive care for humanity in the teachings and miracles of Jesus.

Incorporating a spirituality of self-limitation may mean different things to each of us. Of course, providing the necessary space for others to thrive is true for everyone who wants to love another human being. But for someone with a strong sense of self, coming from a place of traditional privilege, self-limitation has a more obvious action step: back off. Make room for others at the table. Use the avenues of power that avail themselves on behalf of others. I find myself in this category, being a child of relative wealth and privilege and the beneficiary of an excellent education. I admit that a spirituality of self-limitation is a challenge for me, especially when I'm often rewarded for *not* holding back. But that is the way of the cross. Retreating so that other voices can be heard is a daily discipline. Humility is required in order to follow Jesus' way of the cross, so I'm called to learn humility. Just before Paul records the poem of God's self-limitation that we've read several times, he exhorts the Philippians, "Do nothing from selfish ambition or conceit, but in humility regard others as better than yourselves."⁵ For me, this verse strikes at the heart of a daily spiritual discipline.

For others, however, life is already so circumscribed that encouraging them to self-limitation may strike them as unfair. Preaching at them to regard others as better than themselves can seem almost cruel, since they're already at the bottom of the ladder. Millions of people struggle with depression, anxiety, and low self-esteem. Others lack the means even to feed themselves and their children. What does it mean for them to follow Jesus' example of crucified humility? The world has already humbled these people—they don't need to work at it. But they can take great comfort in God's humility in Jesus, and they can still follow Paul's advice: "As God's chosen ones, holy and beloved, clothe yourselves with compassion, kindness, humility, meekness, and patience."⁶ Those are characteristics of the way of the cross, no matter one's station in life.

When I look at the life and teachings of Jesus and at the lives of those who best followed his example, I see an intolerance for injustice, the courage to stand up for the marginalized, and an overpowering love that transcends all fear and all barriers. The way of the cross is for everyone. Jesus called it good news and the pathway to true peace and joy. Trusting this is exactly what it means to have faith.

Not Alone

We all know the feeling that we are alone in the universe, the worry that God has abandoned us, that there is no God. Existential loneliness, we might call it. It goes by other names, too, but I suspect that you immediately know what I'm talking about. You can probably close your eyes and be transported to a time and place when you felt totally isolated and in despair. One of those times for me was during my divorce. Over a couple of years, I had a recurring nightmare in which I was screaming at the top of my lungs, but no sound came out of my mouth. Only silence. No one could hear my despair. I felt utterly alone.

I'll be the first to admit that others suffer despair that is both more far-reaching and deeper than mine has ever been. Key for any of us is to recognize that God entered so thoroughly and completely into the human experience that God knows the despair of total loneliness, of abandonment. God's solidarity with all victims—those victimized by external sources and those victimized by internal turmoil—is total. God holds nothing back in the immersion into humanity. And as a result, God's connection to us is complete.

And let us remember that, because of the mystery of the Trinity, in the event of the crucifixion, God is at one with the oppressed and the oppressor, the victim and the victimizer. So those other times, when we're in positions of power and we use that power unwisely, God is ready to redeem us from that. Our sin is condemned, but we are not left alone. Even the oppressor is not out of God's reach.

What this means for us spiritually is a great promise when we meditate on the cross. This may take place in the sanctuary of a church or simply in our mind's eye as we pray. When we concentrate on that iconic image of Jesus dying on the cross, we can allow our souls to be filled with the promise of God's presence. The crucifixion is a bridge between our loneliness and God's reality.

We're not alone. That can be difficult to remember. But the way of the cross is God's solidarity with us, and ours with God. When we look at the cross, we should be reminded that God identified with us. And we, in turn, identify with the dying Jesus. In that two-way identification—God with us and us with God—we are gathered up into the Trinitarian life of God. This is atonement, this two-way identification. This is the good news of Jesus' crucifixion: that you and I can be made one with God. That happens because God identified with our most human frailties in Jesus, and God invites us to identify with Jesus' victory over death in the crucifixion and resurrection.[7]

We're surrounded by people who need to know that they're not alone. You may remember them from the middle school cafeteria, the kids who were at the table reserved for outcasts and loners. But you've also come to realize that even the kids at the cool table were covering anxieties and loneliness and fear. As we age, the cliques that separate us become more subtle, but they're just as real.

For a decade, I served as a volunteer police chaplain in my hometown. My duties included monthly ride-alongs with officers and one week per month on call. During that week, I'd wear a pager. The police in my town get hundreds of calls per day, and occasionally the shift sergeant thought that a situation could use the help of a chaplain. That's when my pager would go off. Oftentimes it was a call to the scene of a suicide or a tragic death, or to notify a resident that a loved one had died. When you enter people's homes under these circumstances, you start to realize how many people live lives of quiet despair. I saw homes that were nearly empty—just a mattress on the floor, makeshift tables of cardboard, and kitchens with no food. Other homes were piled high with the evidence of hoarding, aisles in the rubbish not large enough for a paramedic's stretcher. These were my neighbors, residents of an upper-middle-class Midwestern suburb. But they were alone, ignored by everyone around them. Not until a 9-1-1 call did anyone enter their homes.

The modern world allows for this kind of isolation, even as our world becomes more urban and more "connected." If we follow the example of God in Jesus, we can counter this trend. Remember that in Jesus' last meal with his disciples, he knelt down and touched their feet, washing them, and telling them to go and do the same for others. And the next afternoon, Jesus experienced the deepest loneliness possible—abandonment by God. If our lives are shaped by the crucifixion, then we will follow Jesus' example. We will reach out to those on the margins, and we will find solidarity with those who've been abandoned by our fast-moving society.

The way of the cross demands nothing less than total commitment to solidarity with others, especially those who are lonely and outcast. Again I say, if Jesus' death does not provoke that kind of love in us, then we're not truly understanding the magnitude of the cross.

23

The Way of Love and the Power of Presence

SAINT JEROME LIVED in the fourth century. Among the most celebrated of the early church fathers, he was given the honorific title Doctor of the Church. He is best known for translating the Bible into Latin, known as the Latin Vulgate. In the course of translating the Old Testament from Hebrew and the New Testament from Greek, Jerome had to make thousands of interpretive choices. His Hebrew was admittedly not very strong when he began his project, so he moved for a time to Jerusalem and consulted with native Hebrew speakers. In the years since, while acknowledging the ambitiousness of Jerome's project of translation, many scholars have cast doubts on how well he actually knew Hebrew.

Among the interpretive choices that confronted Jerome was how to translate the names of God in the Hebrew Bible. Jews, forbidden from uttering the name of God in vain in the third commandment, use the word *Jehovah* in place of *Yahweh* when speaking aloud passages from the Hebrew Bible. The Hebrew word *YHWH* is an abbreviation for the name of God delivered to Moses by the burning bush, commonly translated "I am that I am," but more accurately, "I am that which I have yet to become." An enigmatic name, to be sure.

In Latin, Jerome decided that *YHWH* should be translated *Dominus*—that is, Lord. And that's not an insignificant decision, since it occurs 6,519 times in the Hebrew Bible. And the title has stuck. Think of the last time you prayed—you likely addressed your prayer, "Dear Lord . . . ," or some variation thereof. You can thank Jerome for that.

An even older tradition in the Hebrew Bible uses the ancient Canaanite preface *El-* for God. One of the derivatives is *El Shaddai,* used in some form a couple of dozen times. Jerome translated that *Deus Omnipotens,* God Almighty, and to this day, that's how you'll find it in most English Bibles. But in fact, the meaning of *shaddai* is far from certain. Some scholars believe it derives from a word meaning "to devastate"; others say it most likely comes from an ancient Ugaritic word that means "mountain" or "breast."[1] Just consider for a moment if every time you've read "God Almighty" in the Bible you had instead seen "God of the Abundant Breast." Most likely, your concept of God would have been less about God the Fearsome and Powerful and more about God the Nurturing and Motherly.

Jerome was doing the best he could. But it turns out that God as defined by Greek philosophical categories—omnipotent, immutable, impassible—is not the God found in the Hebrew Bible. To the contrary, the Hebrews told of God in a love story in which Israel struggled with her Lover God over the course of centuries.

God's (Feminine) Presence

The rabbis who commented on the scripture in the early centuries CE came up with another Hebrew word that characterized God: *Shekinah,* which means God's presence. In rabbinic Judaism, it was the *shekinah* that the Israelites saw at the Red Sea; it was the *shekinah* that led them through the wilderness in a pillar of cloud by day and fire at night; and it was the *shekinah* that Moses encountered on Mount Sinai and in the Tabernacle. From the root word for "nest" and the verb for "to dwell," *shekinah* was the rabbinic explanation for just how God encountered Israel in the temple. After the fall of the Second Temple, Jews realized that God was not going to come in political or military power. Instead, God was coming in presence. And notably, *shekinah* is a feminine noun.

As it happens, the Hebrew word for God's Spirit, *ruach,* is also feminine in its etymology, though it is used in both masculine and feminine ways in the Old Testament. God's intimate breath, which hovered over the primordial waters in the first creation account and came in the evening breeze in the second, is a personal emanation from God—she speaks, cries, admonishes, sorrows, weeps, rejoices, and comforts.[2] So the concept of the fecund and compassionate Spirit of God was not unfamiliar to Jews when Jesus claimed to be empowered by the Spirit in his teaching and healing. And to those concepts of the Holy Spirit, the Gospel of John adds the idea of *advocate.*[3]

All in all, the Holy Spirit is God's presence. This is abundantly and unequivocally clear in the New Testament: the Spirit that indwelled Jesus is now generously blown out over all the world. The Spirit both constitutes the church and enlivens the individual. We can think back to chapter 17 and Andrew Sung Park's thesis that when Jesus died on the cross, the Trinity was broken open, and the Holy Spirit poured out over all creation. Something changed in the Trinity at the moment of Jesus' death—a grief, yes, but also a new dispensation of God's presence. Or we can look back further, to Peter Abelard in chapter 14. In his model, the Holy Spirit is the power of the magnet, drawing us to Jesus on the cross.

In the very first episode recorded in Acts following the dramatic events of Pentecost, Peter and John and the disciples are going up to the Temple to pray. There, a man lame from birth puts out his hand and asks for alms. Peter tells the paralytic man that they don't have any silver or gold, but they will give him what they have. Then, in an act of supreme faith, Peter reaches out to the man, takes his hand, and says, "In the name of Jesus Christ of Nazareth, rise up and walk." Astonishingly, the man's ankles and legs are made strong before their eyes, he stands up, and runs into the Temple—from which he had

previously been forbidden on account of his infirmity—shouting
and leaping and praising God.[4]

Luke, the author of Acts, makes clear grammatical parallels in
this passage to an account in his Gospel in which some friends lower
a paralyzed man through a roof into a crowded house where Jesus
is teaching.[5] That man, too, is miraculously healed. Luke's point is
clear: the same power that Jesus had to heal is now with the followers of Jesus.

Sadly, the presence of the Holy Spirit is often a contentious issue
today. Some versions of Christianity claim it exclusively in their
signs and wonders, while others preach that the activity of the Spirit
ceased with the death of the last apostle. Most Christians fall somewhere between those two poles.

The presence of the Holy Spirit is the gift of God to the world,
the result of God's experience of godforsakenness on the cross.
When, in solidarity with humanity, God poured himself into Jesus
of Nazareth, God bridged the chasm between the human and the
divine. And when, in Jesus, God died on the cross, that solidarity
was cemented for all time in an event that was both a temporal moment in time and everlasting in its consequence.

But now that God had experienced the loneliness of the human
condition, what was God going to do differently? The answer, according to Jesus, was the advent of the Spirit:

> I have said these things to you while I am still with you. But
> the Advocate, the Holy Spirit, whom the Father will send in
> my name, will teach you everything, and remind you of all
> that I have said to you. Peace I leave with you; my peace I
> give to you. I do not give to you as the world gives. Do not
> let your hearts be troubled, and do not let them be afraid.[6]

The disciples were terribly troubled when, just days later, they saw
their teacher hanging on a cross. But they must have taken some
solace in these words of his.

And for us, these words matter, too. Because God was in Jesus and fully identified with humanity in our forsakenness and death, God is able to be present with us now in a new way. And that presence is the Holy Spirit. That's the promise: that God's Spirit dwells among us as advocate, comforter, teacher, mother. And that Spirit was released to us because of the crucifixion and resurrection.

Practicing Presence

Experiencing this new level of God's presence is the way of the cross, but it does not necessarily come easily. In the seventeenth century, an eighteen-year-old French peasant looked at a dormant tree in the winter. He thought that his own spiritual life was just as barren as that tree, but he also knew that the tree would blossom again in the spring. So the young man joined a monastery. But lacking the education to join the priesthood, he was assigned to the kitchen and given the name Brother Lawrence. For the next fifty years, Lawrence humbly peeled potatoes and washed dishes, all the while attempting to actively experience the presence of God. After his death in 1691, his notebooks were published, along with several interviews he'd given. The book was entitled *The Practice of the Presence of God.*[7]

The message of Brother Lawrence is simple: we are already in God's presence; the challenge is to continually remember that. There is difficulty in that task, Lawrence admitted, but he mastered it, and millions since have read his words and tried to follow his path. Brother Lawrence wrote,

> We do not have to be constantly in church to be with God. We can make our heart a prayer room into which we can retire from time to time to converse with Him gently, humbly and lovingly. Everyone is capable of these familiar conversations with God.[8]

He continued,

> My most normal habit is to simply keep my attention on
> God, and to be generally and lovingly aware of Him. I often
> feel myself attached to God with sweetness and satisfaction
> greater than that experienced by a nursing child. Therefore,
> if I dared to use this term, I would willingly call this state
> being nursed by God, for the inexpressible sweetness which
> I taste and experience there.[9]

Of the mystics in the history of the church, many like Brother
Lawrence spent a great deal of time meditating on the crucifixion. In
the climax of the great twenty-eight-day retreat called the Spiritual
Exercises of Saint Ignatius, the person on retreat meditates on Jesus
being crucified, even having an imaginary conversation with Jesus as
he hangs on the cross. While this may strike our modern sensibilities
as gruesome or strange, now that we've come to see the humility of
God on display in Jesus and the solidarity that God showed to humankind, we can understand how the cross can become a peaceful
meditation, the moment of God's ultimate *presence* with us.

The English mystic Julian of Norwich also meditated on the crucifixion. She dared not look up from the cross, she said, "For I knew
that whilst I looked at the cross I was secure and safe."[10] When she
looked at Jesus on the cross, she experienced God's presence. It is
ironic: looking into the eyes of a man being executed and feeling
peace, safety, security, even tranquillity. But it is possible because the
crucifixion is God's ultimate act of love.

We have something to learn from these old mystics. The crucifixion is a source of peace. It's a magnet that draws us into the
all-encompassing love of God. It's a mirror that shows us the result
of all our violent tendencies. It's a spark that relights the flame of
divinity within us. It's a symbol of God's victory over the forces
that oppress us.

We look into the eyes of the dying savior knowing that in him,
God performed the ultimate act of humility. In the abandonment of

Jesus' cry, God experienced the godforsakenness that every human feels. And a new bond was formed between God and humanity—a bond that is now cemented by God's Holy Spirit.

We, too, can experience the presence of God that Lawrence and Julian and so many others have felt. In some quarters of the church, it is seen as anachronistic or even embarrassing to meditate on the cross—we're too enlightened, too intellectual for that. Well, I'm suggesting that the church needs to make the cross the centerpiece of its practices and rituals; that each of us, no matter how high our station in life, prostrate ourselves at the foot of the cross; that we humble ourselves beneath the Savior who humbled himself, and that we allow the presence of God's Spirit to wash over us.

Resurrection Life

Across the globe every Easter, churches perform their most dramatic liturgy. Ministers and priests don their most colorful vestments, black draping is stripped from altars and pulpits and replaced with linens of brightest white, and trumpets blare as choirs sing, "Hallelujah!" It's a stark contrast from the dark and somber liturgies of Maundy Thursday, Good Friday, and the Easter Vigil. It turns out the story of Jesus makes for good theater.

The resurrection of Jesus is the capstone of the drama that is his life and passion. It's the proof of God's power and, as Paul says, a down payment on the resurrection that each one of us is promised. Without the resurrection, Jesus of Nazareth would have been just another religious martyr. His would have been an inspirational death, but it would have had no cosmic import.

Some today—even Christian theologians—find the resurrection passé. God doesn't break the laws of physics, they say, and God doesn't bring people back from the dead. Not even himself. Even if the disciples did encounter Jesus after his death, what they saw was a spirit, an apparition. His body stayed in the donated tomb, they say, and believers changed the story to make it more dramatic.

But in Jesus we've found that God is extraordinarily interested in what it means to be human. And nothing is more constitutive of our humanness than our bodies. Remember those in the early church who thought that the divinity of Jesus got vacuumed out of him just before he died? They were condemned because that radical bifurcation between the body and spirit of Jesus has long been rejected by the church. It's the same on his resurrection day—we should reject any notion that attempts to divorce Jesus' spirit from his body. Jesus was resurrected in toto, body and spirit, humanity and divinity.

God's commitment to our humanity is complete. It didn't end at the tomb. The true solidarity that united us with God because of Jesus' death becomes glorious and everlasting in his new life on Easter morning. And Jesus' death—all the theories about it, all the questions and debates—only has meaning because of his resurrection.

When he was raised from the dead, Jesus the Christ made several appearances to those who loved him. He spoke with women at the tomb; he appeared among his disciples in the upper room; he explained his life, incognito, to a couple of men walking the road from Jerusalem to Emmaus; he cooked fish on the beach for his disciples. Each appearance was surprisingly mundane. When you read all of the accounts in the Gospels and Acts about Jesus' postresurrection appearances, it's notable how underwhelming they are. Jesus did not come back from death with blaring trumpets and choirs of angels. Instead, he slipped back into his followers' lives in fairly unassuming ways. He was present with them.

When the earliest Christians—including Paul—attempted to make sense of Jesus' resurrection, they first thought it meant that they, too, would be quickly swept into heaven. But as time wore on, they realized there was a bigger plan afoot. "Rejoice in hope, be patient in suffering, persevere in prayer," wrote Paul in one of his later letters.[11] Their hope for a future with God did not diminish, but it did change. The resurrection came to mean not an immediate escape from this life, but initiation of the age of the Holy Spirit.

God identified with our limitations on the cross. In the resurrection, we are invited to identify with God's eternal life. Because of the resurrection, our solidarity with God is not limited to struggle and death on a cross—it's opened to victory over death and everlasting life with God. The crucifixion and resurrection are two moments in the same event, and in them the solidarity between God and humanity is made complete.

The single most important characteristic of any Christian is *hope*. In the face of strife and conflict, we are called to hope. And that hope springs exclusively directly from the crucifixion-resurrection event, God's promise that his commitment to us is not just here and now, but is everlasting. Yes, God dies in ignominy on the cross, sharing our sorrows. But God overcomes death and sin and grief and trouble on Easter morning. And he invites us down the same path with the same promise. The way of the cross leads to resurrection on a beautiful Easter morning.

That is our hope.

ACKNOWLEDGMENTS

I HAVE DEEP gratitude for the many people who journeyed with me on this book. My agent and friend, Kathy Helmers, and I came up with the notion and the title while texting each other from across the room at a conference. She's been invaluable every step of the way. Mickey Maudlin has a well-earned reputation as a tough but fair editor, and I'm glad that I was on the receiving end of both of those attributes. Thanks also to Mark Tauber, Katy Hamilton, Suzanne Wickham, Janelle Agius, and the rest of the Harper-One team.

This book started as a series of blog posts, evolved into a short e-book, and then matured into this full-length book. The readers of my blog have made me an immeasurably better writer and thinker. Thanks to all of you. A graduate seminar at United Theological Seminary of the Twin Cities read an early version of the manuscript, so thanks to Denika Anderson, Kathryn Boyne, Erik Carlson, William Glew, Charmayne Harper, Karen Larson, Catherine Pino, Asafa Rakotojoelinerdrasana, and Karen Swenson.

The closest readers of the manuscript, in whole or in part, are three of my dearest friends: Lauren Winner, Sarah Cunningham, and Joseph Edelheit. Thank you.

My children, Tanner, Lily, and Aidan, are ever supportive. I love you three.

And finally, my spouse, Courtney Perry, to whom this book is dedicated, is quite simply the most loving human being I have ever known. Yes, she twice read the manuscript carefully and gave me notes. But more importantly, she cheered me on, rubbed my shoulders, and warmed up my coffee. I pray that I am even fractionally as supportive of her career as a photographer as she is of mine as a writer.

Many thanks to one and all.

—*Feast of Saint Nicholas, 2014*

NOTES

Chapter 1: "As He Died, He Saw Your Face!"

1. Some Internet research reveals that this story is used by megachurch pastor Max Lucado in his book *The Applause of Heaven* (Nashville: Thomas Nelson, 1990), 93–95. He does not source the story. In Lucado's version, the mother doesn't die. It's retold again in Tim LaHaye, Jerry Jenkins, and Frank M. Martin, *Embracing Eternity: Living Each Day Toward Heaven (The One Year® Book of Left Behind® Devotions)* (Nashville: Tyndale House, 2004), 54. And it is recounted on various preaching websites as a great sermon illustration for sacrifice.

    A little more Internet sleuthing found the original story, filed for the Associated Press in December 1988. According to the story, the mother's doctor made it clear that her blood did not save the child: "'Susanna lost a very little amount of blood,' he said. 'What saved them was that they were together. The mother didn't have time to panic. She had to think of her child.'" John-Thor Dahlburg, "Amid the Rubble, a Mother's Love," *Milwaukee Journal,* December 29, 1988, 4A.

2. Here I must apologize, for I have used a male pronoun for God. In my writing and speaking, I attempt to avoid doing that, but only to the point of awkwardness. After that point, I must submit myself to the limits of the English language, which lacks a personal pronoun that is gender-neutral. So, in this book, I will refer to Jesus as a male, which he was. And I will refer to the Holy Spirit with female pronouns, for that seems in keeping both with the person of the Holy Spirit and the gender of her name in Greek and Hebrew. And I will reluctantly refer to God using the words *he* and *his,* in keeping with the ancient formulations of God as the "Father" of Jesus Christ. In no way do I think that God is gendered. Pronouns in English, however, are.

3. Romans 5:8.

4. In fact, I suggest that we "know" this love is true at a preconscious level. Children must be taught that God feels wrath toward them because in their hearts they know that just the opposite is true.

5. John 15:9.

6. Philippians 2:5–8.

Chapter 2: Why God Matters

1. John 10:30, ASV.

2. Note that *atonement* is the only major theological term with an English origin. Most others come from Greek, Latin, and Hebrew.

3. A feminine noun, *katallagé* occurs in Romans 5:11 and 11:15 and 2 Corinthians 5:18 and 5:19.

4. Interestingly, in the mid-1980s, theologians like Colin Gunton and Colin Grant were bemoaning the lack of interest in the doctrine of the atonement. Grant called it "the abandonment of the atonement." See *The Nature of the Atonement: Four Views,* eds. James Beilby and Paul R. Eddy (Downers Grove, IL: IVP Academic, 2006), 9.

Chapter 3: The Bible and the Smell Test

1. http://www.realclearscience.com/blog/2013/04/belief-in-punitive-god-associated-with-poor-mental-health.html.

2. Matthew 7:15–20.

3. John 13:35.

4. This is not a particularly new idea, to claim that the aesthetics of a theological system are determinative of its truth. The primary articulators of this have been two theologians who otherwise don't agree on much: the eighteenth-century Puritan Jonathan Edwards and the twentieth-century Catholic Hans Urs Von Balthasar.

5. Galatians 5:22–23.

6. William Tuttle, *World Peace Diet: Eating for Spiritual Health and Social Harmony* (New York: Lantern Books, 2005), 210–11.

7. Matthew 21:12–13.

8. Tony Jones, "Subversive Syntax," *The Church and Postmodern Culture: A Conversation,* March 26, 2007 (http://churchandpomo.typepad.com/conversation/2007/03/why_is_the_emer.html).

9. Jerry Falwell, "What's Wrong with the Emerging Church?" preached April 4, 2007, Thomas Road Baptist Church, http://www.sermoncentral.com/sermons/the-emerging-church-jerry-falwell-sermon-on-attitude-general-139173.asp.

Chapter 4: The Mystery of Sacrifice

1. See Walter Burkert, *Greek Religion* (Cambridge: Harvard University Press, 1985).

2. Walter Sperry, "Cast Alive into the Molten Heart of a Volcano," *World Magazine,* May 23, 1926, 9.

3. Hiran Priyankara Jayasinha, "Mervyn Storms Munnesswaram Festival, Stops 'Sacrifice' Ritual," *Sunday Times,* September 18, 2011, http://www.sundaytimes.lk/110918/News/nws_15.html.

4. Pete Pattisson, "Mass Animal Sacrifice at Nepal Festival Goes Ahead Despite Protest," *Guardian,* November 28, 2014, http://www.theguardian.com/world/2014/nov/28/mass-animal-sacrifice-nepal-festival-protests-gadhimai-hindu.

5. James G. Williams in René Girard, *I See Satan Fall Like Lightning* (Maryknoll, NY: Orbis, 2001), xvi.

6. This is taken from 1 Corinthians 5:7–8: "Clean out the old yeast so that you may be a new batch, as you really are unleavened. For our paschal lamb, Christ, has been sacrificed. Therefore, let us celebrate the festival, not with the old yeast, the yeast of malice and evil, but with the unleavened bread of sincerity and truth."

Chapter 5: An Acceptable Sacrifice

1. Babylonian Talmud, Nedarim Tractate, 39b. Also Pesachim 54a.
2. Babylonian Talmud, Nedarim Tractate, 39b. Also Pesachim 54a.
3. Many thanks to Joseph, who has taught me richly and whose friendship is invaluable.
4. Genesis 22:2b.
5. Genesis 22:7b–8a.
6. Genesis 22: 11b–12.
7. Exodus 12:30.
8. Exodus 13:12. (Except donkeys, which are to be replaced with sheep.)
9. Genesis 8:20–21.
10. Exodus 13:16. The meaning of the Hebrew word translated "emblem" is uncertain. It literally means "headband," but modern Jews often consider it to mean phylacteries, small leather boxes containing verses of Torah that are worn by Jewish men during morning prayers.

Chapter 6: Sacred Blood

1. Leviticus 18:21.
2. In one of the most terrifying texts of the Hebrew Bible, Jephthah sacrifices his teenage daughter after the Lord grants him victory in battle (Judges 11:32–40).
3. Leviticus 17:10–16. Italics added.
4. See Numbers 15:31.
5. Leviticus 16:6–10.
6. Shmuel Ahituz, "Azazel," *Encyclopedia Judaica*, ed. Michael Berenbaum and Fred Skolnik, 2nd ed., vol. 2 (Detroit: Macmillan Reference USA, 2007), 763.
7. Talmud, Yoma, 76a–76b.
8. Hosea 6:6.
9. Accounts of Josiah can be found in 2 Kings 22–23 and 2 Chronicles 34–35.
10. This position is called *supersessionism*.
11. We will investigate this perspective more fully in the chapter on René Girard.
12. There is, of course, a nontheistic interpretation as well, in which "God" is made up and used as an excuse for violence.

Chapter 7: History's Most Famous Execution

1. Albert Schweitzer, *The Quest of the Historical Jesus* (London: Adam & Charles Black, 1954), 370–71.
2. Luke 3:22.
3. Luke 4:18–22.
4. Matthew 5:3–9.
5. Mark 13:14–19. See also Luke 17:23ff.
6. For more on these emphases, see Raymond Brown's magisterial, *The Death of the Messiah,* vol. 1 (New York: Anchor, 1994).
7. 1 John 5:4.
8. External sources don't offer much help here: there are no other sources of Jewish

legal procedures from the first century, and the Judean prefecture was a relatively new imperial holding, so Roman sources are also lacking. Scholars tend to think that the Gospels' accounts of Jesus' arrest and trial, ad hoc though they may have been, are reliable.

9. Mark 11:18.
10. Mark 12:38–40.
11. Mark 14:1–2.
12. Matthew 27:3–10.
13. Matthew 27:24.
14. Matthew 27:25.
15. Quoted in Brown, *Death of the Messiah,* 832.
16. Quoted in Brown, *Death of the Messiah,* 384, n. 130.
17. Notably by the reformer Martin Luther, who wrote the treatise *On the Jews and Their Lies* at the end of his career. Four hundred years later, that book was favorably quoted by Hitler.
18. Mark 14:12; compare Matthew 26:17, Luke 22:7. John's dating is off by one day, but the connection with Passover is still explicit.

Chapter 8: Paul's Cross-Centered Life

1. Mark 8:22–26.
2. Acts 9:26b.
3. N. T. Wright, *Paul and the Faithfulness of God* (Minneapolis: Fortress, 2013), 897. This is Wright's own translation. In the NRSV, it reads, "For God has done what the law, weakened by the flesh, could not do: by sending his own Son in the likeness of sinful flesh, and to deal with sin, he condemned sin in the flesh."
4. See Jay Bakker, *Fall to Grace* (Nashville: Faithwords, 2011).
5. Romans 3:20b.
6. See, for example, Deuteronomy 28:45–68.
7. Galatians 3:13.
8. I am borrowing this idea from Robert G. Hamerton-Kelly, *Sacred Violence: Paul's Hermeneutic of the Cross* (Minneapolis: Fortress Press, 1992), 65.
9. Galatians 6:14. See also 1 Corinthians 1:17; Philippians 3:18; Galatians 6:12. See also 1 Corinthians 1:23; 2:2; Galatians 3:1.
10. See Wright, *Paul and the Faithfulness of God,* 836ff.
11. Romans 2:9–11.
12. Romans 3:2.
13. Wright paraphrases this passage: "But now, quite apart from the law (though the law and the prophets bore witness to it), God's faithful covenant justice has been displayed. God's faithful covenant justice comes into operation *through the faithfulness of Jesus the Messiah,* for the benefit of all who have faith." Wright, *Paul and the Faithfulness of God,* 841.
14. Wright, *Paul and the Faithfulness of God,* 839.
15. Romans 3:24–25.

16. Wright, *Paul and the Faithfulness of God*, 896.
17. Wright, *Paul and the Faithfulness of God*, 898–99.
18. See 1 Corinthians 1:23.
19. Philippians 2:5–8.

Chapter 9: Reunited with God

1. The title Hebrews is a misnomer given to the book by early Christian scribes. The best we can guess is that this sermon was prepared for a congregation in or around Rome. The Greek in Hebrews is the most sophisticated of any New Testament book.
2. Genesis 14; Psalm 110. The use of Melchizedek's name in Psalm 110 is disputed. It is clear in the Septuagint, the Greek translation of the Old Testament that the author of Hebrews used, but in the Hebrew version of the psalm it is unclear whether the word is meant as a person's name or as the word's etymological meaning, "rightful king."
3. Hebrew 5:7–10. Italics added.
4. Hebrews 7:26.
5. Hebrews 10:4.
6. 1 Peter 2:23–24.
7. 1 Peter 4:13.
8. 1 John 2:2; 4:10.
9. "John is obviously following the OT. ἱλασμός does not imply the propitiation of God. It refers to the purpose which God Himself has fulfilled by sending the Son. Hence it rests on the fact that God is gracious, i.e., on His love, cf. 4:10. The meaning, then, is the setting aside of sin as guilt against God. This is shown by the combination of ἱλασμός in 2:2 with παράκλητος in 2:1 and with the confession of sin in 1:8, 10. The subjective result of ἱλασμός in man is παρρησία, confidence before the divine judgment, 4:17; 2:28, or victory over the consciousness of sin. As a demonstration of love, 4:9, 10, ἱλασμός begets love (for the brethren), 4:7, 11, 20f. The overcoming of sin as guilt cannot be separated in fact from the overcoming of sin as transgression, which in John is lack of love. In this respect John can even say that he who is born of God cannot sin, 3:9, 6. He deduces this impossibility of sin in the regenerate from the fact that Jesus, who is sinless, is manifested for the putting away of sin (i.e., ἱλασμός), 3:5. If Christians do still sin—and to deny this is to sin against the truth, 1:8, 10—this simply forces them to look again to Him who is the ἱλασμός. The line from 1:8, 10 leads directly to 2:2. John does not say how Jesus accomplished the ἱλασμός. But it is worth noting that neither in 2:2 nor 4:10 does he refer to the death of Christ. He simply speaks of the risen Lord (2:1, πρὸς τὸν πατέρα) and of the total mission of Jesus (4:10). The ἱλασμός is not one-sidedly linked with the single achievement of the death, but with the total person and work of Jesus, of which His death is, of course, an indissoluble part, 5:6; compare 3:16; 1:7. Jesus is our expiation as the One who has fulfilled the purpose of His sending, who has been kept in

perfect love (3:17) and who is perfectly righteous, 2:2. John does not speak of any necessity of expiation. He sees the day of judgment approaching, 4:17, and it is thus unnecessary to establish the necessity of expiation. For John the ἱλασμός is much more than a concept of Christian doctrine; it is the reality by which he lives." Friedrich Büchsel, "ἱλασμός," in *Theological Dictionary of the New Testament,* Gerhard Kittel, ed. (Grand Rapids: Eerdmans, 1965), vol. 3, 316–17.

10. Revelation 1:5b–6.
11. Loren L. Johns, "Atonement and Sacrifice in the Book of Revelation," in *The Work of Jesus Christ in Anabaptist Perspective* (Telford, PA: Cascadia, 2008), 133.
12. Revelation 3:21.
13. Revelation 1:5.
14. Revelation 5:9–10.
15. Revelation 7:14.
16. Johns, "Atonement and Sacrifice," 127–28. See also Richard Baukham, *Climax of Prophecy: Studies in the Book of Revelation* (New York: T&T Clark, 1993), 226–29.

Chapter 10: God Is Very Angry with You

1. In 1982, the Justice Department tried to tally how many federal criminal laws were on the books. After two years and counting over three thousand laws, the practice was abandoned as useless. And in a report on *NBC Nightly News* at the end of 2011, Pete Williams reported that over forty thousand new state laws would go into effect on January 1, 2012. Yes, we live in a society that is preoccupied with "justice" and laws.
2. John Calvin, *Institutes of the Christian Religion,* 2.16.10.
3. Romans 1:18.
4. Galatians 3:10.
5. John Stott, *The Cross of Christ* (Downers Grove, IL: InterVarsity Press, 1986, 2006), 116.
6. Stott, *Cross of Christ,* 120.
7. Stott, *Cross of Christ,* 129.

Chapter 11: The Invention of Original Sin

1. http://valleybiblechurch.org/doctrine. Notice the overtly masculine language.
2. This belief led to the invention of limbo in the Catholic Church, a place where unbaptized babies go when they die, presumably because they're too distasteful to God to be welcomed into heaven. The idea of limbo is still debated by theologians, and it is not doctrinal.
3. Exodus 34:6–7, NIV.
4. Ezekiel 18:19–20, NIV.
5. Romans 5:12–14; 17–19.
6. Tatha Wiley, *Original Sin: Origins, Developments, Contemporary Meanings* (Mahwah, NJ: Paulist Press, 2002), 56.
7. Wiley, *Original Sin,* 58.

8. The Council of Trent, *The Fifth Session: The Canons and Decrees of the Sacred and Occumenical Council of Trent,* trans. J. Waterworth (London: Dolman, 1848), 21–24.

9. John Calvin, *Institutes on the Christian Religion,* II, i, 8.

10. The first question I always ask five-point Calvinists is this: if you believe in total depravity of the human intellect, how can you be so certain that you're right about TULIP?

Chapter 12: Does God Demand a Payment We Can't Afford?

1. See Rita Nakashima Brock, *Journeys of the Heart: A Christology of Erotic Power* (New York: Crossroad, 1992), especially 53–57. This phrase caused a more recent scandal when it was used by British evangelical Steve Chalke (*The Lost Message of Jesus* [Grand Rapids: Zondervan, 2004], 182) and by Brian McLaren (*The Story We Find Ourselves In: Further Adventures of a New Kind of Christian* [San Francisco: Jossey-Bass], 2008), 143).

2. Anselm, *The Major Works*, ed. B. Davies and G. R. Evans (Oxford: Oxford Univ. Press, 1889), 283.

3. Mark Driscoll, "Jesus Sweats Blood," preached October 9, 2011, Mars Hill Church, Seattle, Washington. http://marshill.com/media/luke/jesus-sweats-blood.

4. John Piper, "God's Wrath: 'Vengeance Is Mine, I Will Repay,' Says the Lord," preached February 27, 2005, Bethlehem Baptist Church, Minneapolis, MN. http://www.desiringgod.org/resource-library/sermons/gods-wrath-vengeance -is-mine-i-will-repay-says-the-lord.

5. Mark Dever, "Nothing but the Blood," *Christianity Today*, May 2006, vol. 50, no. 5, 29.

6. Mary Louise Bringle, "Debating Hymns," *Christian Century*, May 2013, vol. 130, no. 10, http://www.christiancentury.org/article/2013–04/debating-hymns.

7. See Augustine, *On the Predestination of the Saints.*

8. White Protestants approve of torture more than any other religious group in America (http://www.pewforum.org/2009/04/29/the-religious-dimensions-of -the-torture-debate/). They are also the most likely to hold the Payment view of the atonement.

9. Like other Reformed spokespersons, John Piper has repeatedly blamed natural disasters on God, saying that God is trying to send us a message about our sinful ways.

10. Although, according to Mark Driscoll and John Piper, God's wrath still burns white-hot today. Piper has notoriously blamed both a tornado and a bridge collapse in Minneapolis on God.

11. Jonathan Edwards, "Sinners in the Hands of an Angry God," *Christian Classics Ethereal Library,* http://www.ccel.org/ccel/edwards/sermons.sinners.html.

12. Richard Beck, "Covenantal Substitutionary Atonement," *Experimental Theology Blog,* http://experimentaltheology.blogspot.com/2012/10/covenantal-substitutionary -atonement.html. Theologian Miroslav Volf argues that punishment is appropriate to deal with midlevel offenses like, say, stealing a car. But the punishment never

equals the crime on major offenses, which is why the family of a murder victim is likely to say, "I'm glad they convicted the killer, but that will never bring my son back." A serious crime is never recompensed by a serious punishment. An eye for an eye simply doesn't work, at least at the level of a life for a life.

God demands justice, Volf claims, because God's very nature *is* moral justice. However, no punishment can pay the penalty for our sin, not even death. God steps in, in the person of Jesus Christ, and forgives us. In Volf's view, Jesus is not an innocent mediator between humanity and a wrathful God. Jesus *is* the forgiving God: "Christ is not a third party inserted between God and humanity. He is the God who was wronged." Volf calls this "inclusive substitution," and it's surely more palatable than Payment/Penalty/Punishment. But it still leans heavily on God's honor being insulted by our sin—sin that we inherited and have no way to avoid, making the whole system rather self-serving for God. Miroslav Volf, *Free of Charge: Giving and Forgiving in a Culture Stripped of Grace* (Grand Rapids, MI: Zondervan, 2005), 145.

Chapter 13: The Victory Model

1. Mark 10:45.
2. Origen, *Commentary on Matthew*, XVI, 8.
3. Greg Boyd, "The 'Christus Victor' View of the Atonement," http://www.greg boyd.org/essays/essays-jesus/the-christus-victor-view-of-the-atonement/.
4. Greg Boyd, "Christus Victor View," in *The Nature of Atonement: Four Views,* eds. Beilby and Eddy (Downers Grove, IL: IVP Academic), 42ff.
5. Matthew 24:6–8.
6. Boyd in Beilby and Eddy, 26. Italics his.
7. See T. M. Luhrmann, *When God Talks Back: Understanding the American Evangelical Relationship with God* (New York: Alfred A. Knopf, 2012), 254ff.
8. Boyd in Beilby and Eddy, 39.
9. See Ephesians 6:10ff.
10. 1 Corinthians 15:54–57.
11. There are obvious parallels here with the Hebrew Bible book of Job, which begins with the Lord and Satan in a debate over the righteousness of Job. As a result of this opening scene, many people read Job as a proverbial fable.

Chapter 14: The Magnet Model

1. Peter Abélard, *Historia Calamitatum,* trans. Henry Adams Bellows (Grand Rapids, MI: Christian Classics Ethereal Library), 22.
2. Abelard, 24.
3. Two of the men, including his own servant who had let them in, were subsequently captured. Their eyes were gouged out and their own genitals cut off. Medieval justice was harsh.
4. Peter Abelard, *Exposition of the Epistle to the Romans,* in *A Scholastic Miscellany: Anselm to Okham,* ed. Eugene R. Fairweather (Philadelphia: Westminster Press, 1961), 279.

5. *The Glory of the Atonement: Biblical, Theological, and Practical Perspectives,* eds. Charles E. Hill, Roger R. Nicole, Frank A James III (Carol Stream, IL. Intervarsity Press, 2004), 246.

6. Abelard in Fairweather, 279. Although the translation of this saying of Jesus is somewhat disputed—what *causes* her sins to be forgiven?—Abelard takes the position that Jesus is claiming the woman's love is what cleanses her sins.

7. Abelard in Fairweather, 282.

8. Abelard in Fairweather, 279.

9. Abelard in Fairweather, 282–83. We'll talk about the word *expiation* in a later chapter.

10. Abelard in Fairweather, 283.

11. Alister McGrath, *Christian Theology: An Introduction* (Hoboken: John Wiley & Sons, 2010), 332. See also *Epistle to Diogentus, Shepherd of Hermas,* and the letters of Clement of Rome, Ignatius of Antioch, Clement of Alexandria, Hippolytus of Rome, and *Martyrdom of Polycarp.*

12. Like many of the church fathers, Augustine was not of one mind on the atonement—he also wrote about the cross freeing us from Satan's reign and about it satisfying God's justice. What Augustine outrightly denied, however, was that God hated us because of our sin. God has loved us all along, according to Augustine. The only enmity in the relationship is from us toward God. J. F. Bethune-Baker, *An Introduction to the Early History of Christian Doctrine to the Time of the Council of Chalcedon* (London: Methuen & Co, 1903), 351.

13. McGrath, 332.

14. *The Racovian Catechism,* trans. Thomas Rees (Longman: London, 1818), 297–98.

15. 1 Corinthians 1:18–25.

16. See Acts 17.

17. John 10:30. See also John 17.

18. John 13: 12b–17.

Chapter 15: The Divinity Model

1. See John 15:26.

2. As I'm making the final edits on this book, Pope Francis of Rome visited the Ecumenical Patriarch Bartholomew in Turkey. The pope bowed his head for a blessing and a kiss from the patriarch, making international headlines. The Great Schism is still news, a thousand years later.

3. For example, Origen and Gregory of Nyssa. See Kallistos Ware, *How Are We Saved? The Understanding of Salvation in the Orthodox Tradition* (Minneapolis: Light and Life Publishing, 1996), 14–15.

4. Genesis 1:26a.

5. Athanasius, *De Incarnatione* or *On the Incarnation in Nicene and Post-Nicene Fathers,* vol. IV: St. Athanasius: Select Works and Letters, 54:3, PG 25:192B.

6. In Greek it reads, Αυτός γαρ ενηνθρώπησεν, ίνα ημείς θεοποιηθώμεν.

7. John 10:34–36. Lest there be any doubt, the word for "God" and "gods" in this passage is the same: *theos.*

8. John 14:10.

9. 2 Corinthians 3:18; 1 Corinthians 15:42ff.

10. 1 Corinthians 3:16.

11. Orthodox writers today do not reject other models of the atonement, but they hold the Divinity model most central.

12. Georges Florovsky, quoted in John Meyendorff, *Byzantine Theology: Historical Trends and Doctrinal Themes* (Fordham, NY: Fordham Univ. Press, 1974), 161. The key theological premise in this claim is the *hypostatic union,* the indivisible connection of Christ's human and divine natures.

13. Gregory of Nyssa, "The Great Catechism," in Phillip Schaff, *Nicene and Post-Nicene Fathers*, series II, vol. 5, http://www.ccel.org/ccel/schaff/npnf205.xi.ii.xxvi.html.

14. John Zizoulas, *Communion and Otherness: Further Studies in Personhood and the Church* (London: Bloomsbury T&T Clark, 2007), 261.

15. Zizoulas, 261.

16. In Greek, the term is *homoousias;* in Latin, *consubstantialis.*

17. http://www.orthodox-christianity.com/2011/11/the-original-christian-gospel/.

18. http://www.orthodox-christianity.com/2011/11/the-original-christian-gospel/.

19. J. Danielou and H. Musurillo, *From Glory to Glory: Texts from St. Gregory of Nyssa's Mystical Writings* (New York: Charles Scribner's Sons, 1961), 98–102. Quoted by Thomas Hopko, *All the Fullness of God* (Crestwood: St. Vladimir's Seminary Press, 1982), 19.

20. James R. Payton, *Light from the Christian East: An Introduction to the Orthodox Tradition* (Downers Grove, IL: Intervarsity Press, 2007), 170.

21. Kallistos Ware, *How Are We Saved? The Understanding of Salvation in the Orthodox Tradition* (Minneapolis: Light and Life Publishing, 1996), 68. Here's the full quote, in context: "Salvation involves the Church. It is ecclesial. We are not to set bounds on God's saving power, and it may be that in His mercy He will grant salvation to many people who in this present life have never been visibly members of any church community. But, so far as we on our side are concerned, the appointed means to salvation is always in and through the community of the Church."

Chapter 16: The Mirror Model

1. Brian McDonald, "Violence and the Lamb Slain: An Interview with René Girard," *Touchstone Journal*, http://www.touchstonemag.com/archives/article.php?id=16-10-040-i

2. René Girard, *I See Satan Fall Like Lightning* (Mary Knoll, NY: Orbis, 2001), 21.

3. Girard writes, "My research is only indirectly theological, moving as it does across the field of a Gospel anthropology unfortunately neglected by theologians. To increase its effectiveness, I have pursued it as long as possible without postulating the reality of the Christian God. No appeal to the supernatural should break the thread of the anthropological analyses." Girard, 191–92.

4. Girard, 21.

5. Romans 8:28.
6. Girard, 150.
7. 2 Corinthians 5:21.

Chapter 17: Other Models of What God Did on the Cross

1. James H. Cone, *God of the Oppressed*, revised ed. (Maryknoll, NY: Orbis Books, 1997).
2. James H. Cone, *The Cross and the Lynching Tree* (Maryknoll, NY: 2011).
3. Cone, *The Cross and the Lynching Tree*, 2.
4. Cone, *The Cross and the Lynching Tree*, 158.
5. Richard Beck, *Unclean: Meditations on Purity, Hospitality, and Mortality* (Eugene, OR: Wipf & Stock, 2011).
6. Beck, 2.
7. Galatians 3:28.
8. Rita Nakashima Brock and Rebecca Ann Parker, *Proverbs of Ashes: Violence, Redemptive Suffering, and the Search for What Saves Us* (Boston: Beacon Press, 2001), 8.
9. Rita Nakashima Brock and Rebecca Ann Parker, *Saving Paradise: How Christianity Traded Love of This World for Crucifixion and Empire* (Boston, MA: Beacon Press, 2008), 418.
10. Andrew Sung Park, *Triune Atonement: Christ's Healing for Sinners, Victims, and the Whole Creation* (Louisville: Westminster John Knox, 2009).
11. Park, 39.
12. Genesis, 4:10–14.
13. Matthew, 27:46.
14. Park, 87.
15. Slavoj Žižek, *The Plague of Fantasies* (London: Verso, 1997), 159. Here Žižek is following Jacques Lacan.
16. Slavoj Žižek, "A Meditation on Michelangelo's *Christ on the Cross*" in *Paul's New Moment: Continental Philosophy and the Future of Christian Theology*, eds. John Milbank, Slavoj Žižek, and Creston Davis (Grand Rapids, MI: Brazos Press, 2010), 174–75.
17. Peter Rollins, *The Divine Magician* (Nashville: Howard, forthcoming).
18. 1 Corinthians 13:12, KJV.

Chapter 18: What Jesus Tells Us About God

1. 1 John 4:10–11.
2. Isaiah 49:15, 66:13.
3. Luke 13:34; Matthew 6:9.
4. Isaiah 62:5, 54:5; Revelation 19:7–8, 21:2; Ephesians 5:25.
5. The Jewish mystical tradition of Kabbalah gives God's withdrawal the name *zimzum*.
6. Matthew 19:26.
7. Actually, maybe we can venture a guess. In the second creation account, the story goes that after creating a man, God said to himself, "It is not good for man

to be alone," and so he made another woman being, woman, and they became companions. In the previous creation story, God says that he will create human beings in his own image. Thus, it might not be so far-fetched to posit that God, too, is a being who desires companionship.

8. See Exodus 32:14; Jeremiah 18:5–10 and 26:3; Joel 2:13–14; Jonah 4:2 and 3:9–10; Amos 7:3, 6.
9. Philippians 2:5–8.

Chapter 19: The Cry That Changed Everything

1. In Greek, the operative phrase is: ἐν δύο φύσεσιν ἀσυγχύτως, ἀτρέπτως, ἀδιαιρέτως, ἀχωρίστως; in Latin: *in duabus naturis inconfuse, immutabiliter, indivise, inseparabiliter.*
2. Deuteronomy 6:4; Exodus 20:3.
3. The definitions of "sympathy" and "empathy" are fraught and argued over. I am using the most common definitions of the two, in which *sympathy* is a feeling of concern for someone else's situation, and *empathy* is the feeling that you can share in another person's situation.
4. "Is despair a merit or a defect? Purely dialectically, it is both. If one were to think of despair only in the abstract, without reference to some particular despairer, one would have to say it is an enormous merit. The possibility of this sickness is man's advantage over the beast, and it is an advantage which characterizes him quite otherwise than the upright posture, for it bespeaks the infinite erectness or loftiness of his being spirit. The possibility of this sickness is man's advantage over the beast; to be aware of this sickness is the Christian's advantage over natural man; to be cured of this sickness is the Christian's blessedness." Soren Kierkegaard, *The Sickness Unto Death* (London: Penguin Books, 1989), 44–45.
5. Luke 9:60; Luke 14:26.
6. Mark 15:34; Matthew 27:46.
7. Some scholars attempt to blunt the force of this cry by letting God off the hook. They say that in quoting the opening lines of Psalm 22, Jesus is invoking the entire psalm, which includes more comforting lines, like,

> *Yet it was you who took me from the womb;*
> *you kept me safe on my mother's breast.*
> *On you I was cast from my birth,*
> *and since my mother bore me you have been my God.* Psalm 22: 9–10.

For this argument, see, for example, William Stacy Johnson, "Jesus' Cry, God's Cry, and Ours," in *Lament: Reclaiming Practices in Pulpit, Pew, and Public Square,* Sally Ann Brown and Patrick D. Millers, eds., (Louisville: Westminster John Knox, 2005), 80–94.

But if Jesus had wanted to preach a sermon of comfort from the cross, surely he would have chosen a line other than this one to cry out. The Hebrew Bible is rife with passages of comfort. But Jesus instead chose a cry of lament—and not just any lament, but one of the most pointed laments in all of the Hebrew Bible, a lament that implies the absence of God.

8. Mark 15:37.
9. Mark 14:35–36.
10. This perspective on Jesus' divinity is called "personal interiority." See Miroslav Volf, *After Our Likeness: The Church as the Image of the Trinity* (Grand Rapids, MI: Eerdmans, 1998), 209f.
11. Mother Teresa, *Mother Teresa: Come Be My Light: The Private Writings of the Saint of Calcutta* (New York: Image, 2009).
12. See Exodus 34.
13. Luke 9:58.
14. Exodus 32:14.
15. 1 Samuel 15:11.
16. Jonah 3:7–10.
17. See Numbers 23:19 and James 1:17, for example.

Chapter 20: How the Crucifixion Changed God's Relationship with Us

1. Judges 11:31.
2. The Greek word that they use for "amazed" is *thaumazo,* and it implies a mixture of amazement and fear. See, for example, Matthew 9:33, Mark 5:20, and Luke 9:43.
3. *God on Trial,* directed by Andy De Emmony (Scotland: Hattrick Productions, 2008).
4. Elie Wiesel, *Night* (New York: Hill and Wang, 2006), 65. Of this passage, Christian theologian Jürgen Moltmann writes: "If that is to be taken seriously, it must also be said that, like the cross of Christ, even Auschwitz is in God himself. Even Auschwitz is taken up into the grief of the Father, the surrender of the Son and the power of the Spirit. . . . As Paul says in I Cor. 15, only with the resurrection of the dead, the murdered and the gassed, only with the healing of those in despair who bear lifelong wounds, only with the abolition of all rule and authority, only with the annihilation of death will the Son hand over the kingdom to the Father. Then God will turn his sorrow into eternal joy. . . . God in Auschwitz and Auschwitz in the crucified God—that is the basis for a real hope which both embraces and overcomes the world, and the ground for a love which is stronger than death and can sustain death." Jürgen Moltmann, *The Crucified God: The Cross of Christ as the Foundation and Criticism of Christian Theology* (Minneapolis, MN.: Fortress, 1993), 278.
5. Dietrich Bonhoeffer, *Letters and Papers from Prison* (New York: Macmillan, 1953), 360.
6. Bonhoeffer, 361. To this point, Slavoj Žižek adds some commentary: "This brings us to the third position above and beyond the first two (the sovereign God, the finite God), that of a *suffering God*: not a triumphalist God who always wins at the end, although 'his ways are mysterious,' since he secretly pulls all the strings; not a God who exerts cold justice, since he is by definition always right; but a

God who—like the suffering Christ on the Cross—is agonized, assumes the burden of suffering, in solidarity with the human misery. It was Schelling who wrote: 'God is a life, not merely a being. But all life has a fate and is subject to suffering and becoming ... *Without the concept of a humanly suffering God ... all of history remains incomprehensible.'* Why? Because God's suffering implies that He is involved in history, affected by it, not just a transcendent Master pulling the strings from above: God's suffering means that human history is not just a theater of shadows but the place of the real struggle, the struggle in which the Absolute itself is involved, and its fate is decided. This is the philosophical background of Dietrich Bonhoeffer's deep insight that, after *shoah*, 'only a suffering God can help us now' [sic]—a proper supplement to Heidegger's 'Only a God can still save us!' from his last interview. We should therefore take the statement that 'the unspeakable suffering of the six million is also the voice of the suffering God' [David Tracy] quite literally: the very excess of this suffering over any 'normal' human measure makes it divine." Slavoj Žižek, *The Parallax View* (Cambridge: MIT Press, 2009), 184.

7. Luke 21:1–4.
8. 1 Corinthians 1:23.
9. John 13:12–17.
10. Matthew 23:16, 23:33, 23:27, and 23:23.
11. Romans 5:12.
12. John 9:1–3. Jesus' response that the man was born blind "so that God's works might be revealed in him" is no less troubling.
13. Matthew 9:10; 11:13.
14. Matthew 8:14–17.
15. Isaiah 53:5.

Chapter 21: The Way of Peace

1. Bonhoeffer's legacy with Nazism is actually quite complicated. He did indeed take part in a plot to assassinate Hitler, but his was a minor and distant role. And in earlier days, he accepted an appointment with German military intelligence, affording freedom to travel—a freedom that many Germans lacked at the time. See Charles Marsh, *Strange Glory: A Life of Dietrich Bonhoeffer* (New York: Alfred A. Knopf, 2014).
2. Dietrich Bonhoeffer, *Ethics* (Minneapolis, MN: Fortress Press, 2005), 282.
3. Bonhoeffer, *Letters and Papers from Prison*, 362. Italics added.
4. John D. Caputo, *The Weakness of God: A Theology of the Event* (Bloomington, IN: Indiana Univ. Press, 2006).
5. Isaiah 2:4. See also Joel 3:10.
6. http://youtu.be/dWH4Ro_–4hg.
7. Luke 22:35–38.

Chapter 22: The Way of Solidarity

1 "Crucifixion Controversy," Fox 4 News, WFTX, Fort Myers, Florida, April 18, 2014, http://www.jrn.com/fox4now/news/Crucifixion-Controversy–255812551.html.

2. See Mark 15:38, Matthew 27:51, and Luke 23:45. These passages also should be read as commentary about the Romans' destruction of the temple in 70 CE. At their rawest level, they can also be seen as God's anger as grief over the death of his son. For this, see Raymond Brown, *The Death of the Messiah* (New York: Anchor, 1994), 1095–1118.

3. Tony Jones, *The Teaching of the Twelve: Believing and Practicing the Primitive Christianity of the Ancient Didache Community* (Brewster, MA: Paraclete Press, 2009), 22.

4. Romans 12:16.

5. Philippians 2:3.

6. Colossians 3:12.

7. For more on this, read any book by Jürgen Moltmann, particularly *The Crucified God: The Cross as the Foundation and Criticism of Christian Theology* (Minneapolis, MN: Fortress Press, 1974, 1991). My own thinking has been profoundly affected by Moltmann.

Chapter 23: The Way of Love and the Power of Presence

1. Gerard van Groningen, "God, Names of," *Baker Encyclopedia of the Bible* (Grand Rapids, MI: Baker Books, 1988), 882.

2. Erik Sjöberg, "*ruach* in Palestinian Judaism," *Theological Dictionary of the New Testament, Volume VI* (Grand Rapids, MI: Eerdmans, 1968), 387.

3. John 14:26. The Greek word is *paraclete*.

4. Acts 3:1–10.

5. See Luke 5:17ff.

6. John 14:25–27.

7. Brother Lawrence, *Practicing the Presence of God: Learning to Live Moment-by-Moment*, Tony Jones, ed., (Brewster, MA: Paraclete Press, 2007).

8. Brother Lawrence, 72.

9. Brother Lawrence, 77.

10. Julian of Norwich, *Showings (Classics of Western Spirituality)* (Mahwah, NJ: Paulist Press, 1977), 144.

11. Romans 12:12.

About the Author

Tony Jones is a writer, theologian, and professor. Currently, he is the theologian-in-residence at Solomon's Porch in Minneapolis, professor in the practice of theology at United Theological Seminary of the Twin Cities, and professor in the Doctor of Ministry program at Fuller Theological Seminary. He edits the Theology for the People series for Fortress Press, he has developed a mobile app, and he runs several conferences each year.

Tony holds degrees from Dartmouth College (A.B.), Fuller Theological Seminary (M.Div.), and Princeton Theological Seminary (Ph.D.). He has written over a dozen books on ministry, prayer, history, and the church. His blog, *Theoblogy,* is widely read, and he speaks regularly at conferences around the world.

Tony lives in Edina, Minnesota, with his spouse, Courtney, and his three children, Tanner, Lily, and Aidan. He's an avid bird hunter, so you can often find him afield with his beloved yellow Lab, Albert.

You can find out more about Tony and read his blog at tonyj.net, and there you can download a free group discussion guide for this book. Tony is also active on Twitter (@jonestony) and Facebook (facebook.com/jonestony).